Violence and the Politics of Research

THE HASTINGS CENTER SERIES IN ETHICS

ETHICS TEACHING IN HIGHER EDUCATION
Edited by Daniel Callahan and Sissela Bok

MENTAL RETARDATION AND STERILIZATION
A Problem of Competency and Paternalism
Edited by Ruth Macklin and Willard Gaylin

THE ROOTS OF ETHICS: Science, Religion, and Values
Edited by Daniel Callahan and H. Tristram Engelhardt, Jr.

ETHICS IN HARD TIMES
Edited by Arthur L. Caplan and Daniel Callahan

VIOLENCE AND THE POLITICS OF RESEARCH
Edited by Willard Gaylin, Ruth Macklin, and Tabitha M. Powledge

WHO SPEAKS FOR THE CHILD: The Problems of Proxy Consent
Edited by Willard Gaylin and Ruth Macklin

A Continuation Order Plan is available for this series. A continuation order will bring delivery of each new volume immediately upon publication. Volumes are billed only upon actual shipment. For further information please contact the publisher.

Violence and the Politics of Research

Edited by

Willard Gaylin

The Hastings Center
Hastings-on-Hudson, New York

Ruth Macklin

Albert Einstein College of Medicine
Bronx, New York

and

Tabitha M. Powledge

Center for Science and Technology Policy
New York University
New York, New York

PLENUM PRESS • NEW YORK AND LONDON

Library of Congress Cataloging in Publication Data

Main entry under title:

Violence and the politics of research.

(The Hastings Center series in ethics)
Bibliography: p.
Includes index.
1. Violence—Research—United States—Addresses, essays, lectures. 2. Aggres-
siveness (Psychology)—Addresses, essays, lectures. 3. Violence—United States—
Case studies—Addresses, essays, lectures. I. Gaylin, Willard. II. Macklin, Ruth,
1938-   . III. Powledge, Tabitha M. IV. Series.
HN90.V5V535   303.6'2   81-15900
ISBN 0-306-40789-2   AACR2

HN
90
.V5
V535

© 1981 The Hastings Center
Institute of Society, Ethics and the Life Sciences
360 Broadway
Hastings-on-Hudson, New York 10706

1981 Plenum Press, New York
A Division of Plenum Publishing Corporation
233 Spring Street, New York, N.Y. 10013

Printed in the United States of America

Contributors

EDITORS

Willard Gaylin, M.D., is clinical professor of psychiatry at Columbia University College of Physicians and Surgeons, as well as cofounder and president since its inception of The Hastings Center, Institute of Society, Ethics and the Life Sciences. He has been involved in questions of jurisprudence over the past twenty years, and has written several books, including *In the Service of Their Country: War Resisters in Prison* (Viking, 1970), *Partial Justice: A Study of Bias in Sentencing* (Alfred A. Knopf, 1974), and (with J. Meister and R. Neville) *Operating on the Mind: The Psychosurgery Conflict* (Basic Books, 1975).

Ruth Macklin, Ph.D., is a philosopher in the Department of Community Health at Albert Einstein College of Medicine. At the time the project from which this book emerged was carried out she was codirector, with Willard Gaylin, of the Behavioral Studies Research Group at The Hastings Center. She has contributed articles to professional journals in philosophy, psychiatry, law, and medical ethics. Her book, *Man,*

Mind, and Morality: The Ethics of Behavior Control, was published by Prentice-Hall in 1981. She is one of the editors of *Moral Problems in Medicine* (Prentice-Hall, 1976), a widely used text in medical ethics.

Tabitha M. Powledge is a writer who is interested in the relationship between biology and politics. She has specialized in genetics and genetic policy, and her book on that subject, *The Last Taboo,* will be published by Houghton-Mifflin in 1982. She currently directs the project on the ethics of genetic engineering at the Center of Science and Technology Policy, New York, New York. At the time this volume was in preparation she was Associate for Biosocial Studies at The Hastings Center and a member of the center's Behavioral Studies Research Group. The author of scores of articles in lay and professional publications, she has taught at Yale, lectured widely to professional and general audiences, and has served as consultant to private groups and government agencies, among them the International Society for Research on Aggression.

OTHER CONTRIBUTORS

Ronald Bayer, Ph.D., is a political scientist and Associate for Policy Studies at The Hastings Center. He has published a number of articles on social policy and heroin use and is the author of *Homosexuality and American Psychiatry: The Politics of Diagnosis* (Basic Books, 1981).

John P. Conrad is a career criminologist, most of whose career was spent in various capacities in the California Department of Corrections, in which he served for twenty years. Since leaving that agency in 1967, Conrad has served in the United States Bureau of Prisons as chief of research, in the Law Enforcement Assistance Administration, and as senior fellow in criminal justice at the Academy for Contemporary Problems.

He is now a senior staff member of the American Justice Institute of Sacramento.

Dorothy Nelkin is a professor in the Program of Science, Technology and Society and the Department of Sociology at Cornell University. She is also a fellow of The Hastings Center. She is the author of several books on controversies over science and technology including *Science Textbook Controversies and the Politics of Equal Time* (MIT Press, 1970), *Controversy: Politics of Technical Decisions* (Sage, 1979), and (with M. Pollak) *The Atom Besieged* (MIT Press, 1980).

T. M. Scanlon, professor of philosophy at Princeton University, is the author of articles on political philosophy, ethical theory, and applied ethics. He is also an associate editor of *Philosophy and Public Affairs.*

Judith P. Swazey, Ph.D., is executive director of Medicine in the Public Interest, Inc. and an adjunct professor of sociomedical sciences at Boston University Schools of Medicine and Public Health. She has been a fellow of The Hastings Center since 1969, and served as its vice-president in 1980. Her major areas of research and writing deal with the history of neuroscience, medical ethics, and social and biomedical aspects of research and therapeutic innovation.

Robin M. Williams, Jr., is Henry Scarborough Professor of Social Science at Cornell University. He has served as president and as secretary of the American Sociological Association. He is a member of the American Academy of Arts and Sciences and is a fellow of The Hastings Center and of the American Association for the Advancement of Science. Among his several books are *American Society: A Sociological Interpretation* (3rd ed., Alfred A. Knopf, 1970), *Strangers Next Door* (Prentice-Hall, 1964), and *Mutual Accommodation: Ethnic Conflict and Cooperation* (University of Minnesota Press, 1977).

Preface

This volume is one outcome of a two-year study conducted by the Behavioral Studies Research Group of The Hastings Center.[1] It is divided into three parts to reflect the several facets of the interdisciplinary project from which it stems. In the opening chapter Willard Gaylin and Ruth Macklin, who directed the study, describe its basic conception and structure, which centered around three programs to conduct research into aspects of violence and aggressive behavior, programs aborted in the early 1970s because they were politically and

[1]This project was supported by the EVIST Program of the National Science Foundation under Grant No. OSS77-17072, and by a joint award by the National Endowment for the Humanities. Any opinions, findings, conclusions, or recommendations expressed herein are those of the authors and do not necessarily reflect the views of the National Science Foundation or the National Endowment for the Humanities. Other published outcomes are the edited transcripts of two of the case-study workshops conducted under this project: "Researching Violence: Science, Politics, and Public Controversy," Special Supplement, *The Hastings Center Report* 9 (April 1979); and "The XYY Controversy: Researching Violence and Genetics," Special Supplement, *The Hastings Center Report* 10 (August 1980). Copies of these transcripts are available for purchase from The Hastings Center, 360 Broadway, Hastings-on-Hudson, NY 10706.

socially controversial. The chapter includes an account of earlier work of the Behavioral Studies Research Group that led to the idea for this inquiry into the ethical, social, and political dimensions of scientific research on aggression. Chapter 1 also contains some reflections by the authors on the difficulties of conducting scientific research on violence and aggression in particular, and on socially sensitive topics more generally.

Chapter 2, "Legitimate and Illegitimate Uses of Violence: A Review of Ideas and Evidence," provides historical and sociological background to enhance our understanding of three controversies that erupted in the early 1970s over scientific attempts to study the causes and possible "cures" of violent behavior. This chapter is based on Robin M. Williams, Jr.'s oral presentation to the project group at its first meeting, a presentation designed to acquaint members of the group with social perspectives on violence. Professor Williams focuses on the ways in which direct physical violence is legitimated, justified, or otherwise rendered socially acceptable or tolerable. Initially he argues that most violence is not deviant behavior or disapproved conduct, "but virtuous action in the service of applauded values." After a brief summary of contemporary and historical data regarding the incidence, prevalence, and cost of violence, Williams isolates four primary types of cross-cultural social definitions that allow for the "domestication" or legitimation of violence. The chapter concludes with a discussion of particular American attitudes toward violence, and how those attitudes contribute to the acceptance of the legitimating definitions described earlier in the chapter.

The second section begins with a detailed account of the three abandoned research projects: an attempt at UCLA to organize a center to study violence, programs to study and expand techniques of behavior modification in federal prisons, and a prospective study of boys with sex chromosome abnormalities in Boston. In her conclusion, Tabitha M. Powledge reflects on some similarities and differences in the sources of controversy over the three cases, and assesses the legitimacy of the critics' complaints. Chapter 3 is based on extensive research Powledge conducted as background to the case studies. She taped interviews with key actors in the controversial episodes, a few by telephone but the majority in person. She also examined newspaper accounts as well as files and correspondence to which she was granted access. Before each of the case-study workshops that were held as part of the project activities, Powledge prepared a detailed chronology of events surrounding each controversy, along with descriptions of the aborted projects and the major parties to the dispute. These were distibuted to the protagonists and also to all participants in the Hastings Center project. It is a comment on her efforts that no participant at any of the workshops questioned the accuracy of a single item. For this volume, Powledge recast those materials into narrative form, adding concluding reflections of her own.

The four chapters that comprise the third part of this book are scholarly reflections on the events and circumstances described in Part II. Written by project participants, each chapter addresses the key issues raised by the project from a somewhat different perspective.

In "Science and Social Control: Controversies over Research on Violence," social scientists Dorothy Nelkin and Judith P. Swazey examine the forces and issues that converge in the social assessment of science through a discussion of the three case studies. According to the authors, the research programs studying violence elicited public controversy because the research and demonstration work in each project raised sensitive questions about some or all of the following: the role of genetically mediated characteristics of human behavior; the morality of modifying behavior by medical or psychological means; the power of social control offered by new biomedical and behavioral technologies; and the power relationships inherent in situations and settings where freedom of choice to participate in research cannot be taken for granted. Underlying each of these projects was a different ideological perspective on the definition of violence and its sources, and on the consequences of the emerging techniques for predicting and manipulating behavior. Nelkin and Swazey claim that none of the actors in any of the controversies—either antagonists or protagonists—could be described as a hero or a villain, but that the researchers' lack of understanding of the ideological underpinnings of their investigations contributed significantly to the controversy.

Picking up on the theme of ideological underpinnings, Ronald Bayer, a political scientist, traces the history of political and social forces that led to the controversies over research on violence. Chapter 5 begins by noting that in the United States, for the greater part of this century, those identified with the reformist political traditions are the ones who most notably aligned themselves with the effort to enhance the role of behavioral scientists in understanding crime, and of psychiatrists in the treatment of offenders. Drawing on scholarly materials in law and the social sciences, Bayer discusses the strong interest in America and Western Europe in merging the law enforcement process with a psychiatric-therapeutic orientation. He explains the affinity between psychiatry and American liberals as deriving not only from the explanatory force of psychodynamic formulations but also from the promise of achieving correctional ends without recourse to punishment. Bayer identifies several factors that contributed to a change in liberal attitudes toward correctional psychiatry by the early 1970s, and concludes by delineating the ways in which those factors led to the political responses to each of the three controversial research projects.

In Chapter 6, John P. Conrad, formerly director of research for the Bureau of Prisons, outlines an ideal, comprehensive program for conducting research into the causes of and possible preventive mechanisms for violent and aggressive behavior. He begins with a sketch of the boundaries of present scientific knowledge about violent behavior. There is little real understanding of the phenomenon of recidivism, the plausibility of current deterrence mechanisms, or the effectiveness of rehabilitation programs. With these and other limitations of present knowledge in mind, Conrad delineates the major research that is called for in this domain, describing those areas of research under the categories "basic" and "applied." He holds that much of the political controversy and ethical objection that emerged with earlier attempts to study the phenomena he cites could have been avoided by establishing a few qualified centers, under government auspices and with federal funding, for research on violence. Conrad concludes by exhorting the public to remember that the fundamental causes of violence, rooted in human nature and social organizations, are beyond the reach of criminal justice. Because the most important questions about violent crime all arise within the context of intrapsychic dysfunction and social disorganization, it should not be expected or advertised that the research program he proposes—although important—will yield the key to any significant alteration in the phenomenon of violent crime.

In the final chapter Thomas M. Scanlon, a philosopher, analyzes the theoretical underpinnings of the claims made by the researchers whose projects were halted. Their central claim was that as scientific researchers they had a special entitlement to protection from interference and criticism of the kinds they had experienced. Scanlon argues that a discussion of the justification of claims regarding this sort of academic freedom requires an analysis of the kinds of harms that might result from research. The question is one of distinguishing when control of research is justified by harms that might occur, and when control of research should not be allowed because it will be dominated by partisan interests. After identifying two different sorts of harms that might result from research—direct consequences of the research process, and indirect harms stemming from the dissemination of the knowledge yielded by research—Scanlon notes that the justifiable control of research is much more problematic in the second sort of case. He concludes with a positive argument contending that at least in some cases, researchers should be held responsible for the harmful applications of their research.

Although we make no claims to have covered all the issues raised by the controversies that erupted over these three research projects, we hope this volume will prompt further reflection—both by scientists and by the concerned public—on those issues we have addressed and others as well.

WILLARD GAYLIN
RUTH MACKLIN
TABITHA M. POWLEDGE

Contents

PART I INTRODUCTION TO THE PROBLEMS

CHAPTER 1

Pitfalls in the Pursuit of Knowledge

WILLARD GAYLIN AND RUTH MACKLIN

RESEARCHING VIOLENCE

Few issues in recent years have so exercised the American public as has violently aggressive behavior. It does not require election rhetoric to document the fact that "crime in the streets" holds a central position in the concerns and consciousness of the average citizen. It dominates the front pages of our daily newspapers and is an omnipresent feature on television's evening news. All arguments over prisons, incarceration, and concepts of criminal justice are infused with the explicit as well as the implicit sense that we or our children are no longer safe in the public spaces. The wanton and seem-

WILLARD GAYLIN • President, The Hastings Center, Institute of Society, Ethics, and the Life Sciences, 360 Broadway, Hastings-on-Hudson, New York 10706. RUTH MACKLIN • Department of Community Health, Albert Einstein College of Medicine, 1300 Morris Park Avenue, Bronx, New York 10461.

ingly gratuitous violence that characterizes so much of urban life—exaggerated through fear beyond its actual incidence—has reached a point where chronic anxiety is a constant companion of those who brave the public spaces at night.

It was inevitable that this situation would attract the attention of a number of social and biological scientists, who postulated that it might be possible to identify factors predisposing toward violence and to define methods of controlling violent behavior by technological means—biological or psychological. In an age when the social scientist has often been accused—with some justification—of a certain amount of dilettantism in his selection of research areas, it should have seemed responsible, logical, and reassuring for the social sciences to address their research efforts to this area; and indeed, that is how this new orientation was first perceived. In the middle to late sixties—no doubt spurred by the anxiety of the confrontational politics of that time—there was a great deal of enthusiasm for such inquiry. It commanded legislative and scientific support, elicited significant research funds, and was looked upon by many as an enormously promising venture, both scientifically and socially. One decade later that research had been radically curtailed, funds had been withdrawn, the researchers themselves had been personally attacked, and understandably, turned their interest elsewhere. The entire field of biological, sociological, and psychiatric research on violence was in full retreat.

Why did it happen? Certain answers seem evident from the start. There was no question that the whole issue became embroiled in a number of other disputes surfacing at the same time: the growing public concern over scientific research and its technological applications; the disillusion with the scientific optimism that dominated so much of twentieth-century thought, and that began to be eroded with the dropping of the atomic bomb and the recognition of the ecology disaster; the eruption of debates over public participation in and community control of all scientific decision making; and finally, the ultimate fear, which seemed to transcend all others, that the research and the technological capacity with which we were dealing might end up being used by those in power to control legitimate social protest.

This retreat from a promising and needed research area in behavior studies concerned us in itself, and beyond that, as an example of problems that were erupting in other areas of science. It was the paradigmatic nature of this problem that captured the attention of The Hastings Center, and motivated us to the research reported in this book.

THE RESEARCH GROUP AND METHODS

The Behavioral Studies Research Group of The Hastings Center was established to examine the ethical, legal, and social problems arising from scientific attempts to understand, control, modify, or manipulate human behavior. It began its work with a concentration on technology because, invariably, it is technology that attracts attention. Our first series of studies was a survey of the primary technological means available to control behavior: electric stimulation of the brain, psychosurgery, drugs, and psychological techniques of behavior modification. From work in this area it became apparent that although technology aroused public anxiety and captured the public imagination, the distinction between the implantation of an electrode and the implantation of an idea was not always as great as it seemed or even in the direction that one might have thought (which is the more reversible, for example). We therefore made analogies between these technological methods and more traditional methods of control, such as education, counseling, and the like. Eventually, we did specific studies on the use of behavior control techniques in total institutions (prisons, mental institutions, and institutions for the mentally retarded).

Following this analysis of the available techniques and current practices for influencing behavior, we began to identify a number of broad conceptual, ethical, and political issues that cut across the technical boundaries. Whether we started with psychosurgery or the education of the preschool child, certain fundamental philosophical concerns emerged; for example, the notion of consent, and the related problems of voluntariness, freedom, and coercion.

Put schematically, the following problems have been carefully studied by the Behavior Control Research Group.

Control of Behavior by Psychosurgery

This study allowed us to look at the ways in which efficiency of a proposed technological intervention can be measured, and at the scientific debate over the merits of such interventions. It also enabled us to contribute to public debate on the extent to which such matters should be regulated, in the form of testimony before Senate subcommittee hearings.

Control of Behavior by Drugs

This study made possible a focus on modes of therapy and social control by the use of widely available and accepted drugs. The widespread use and acceptance of mood-altering drugs creates a social context quite different from that of psychosurgery.

The Use of Modes of Behavior Control Drawn from Psychology and Psychiatry

In this study we were able to introduce still another contrast. Whereas the use of psychosurgery and drugs involves a direct intervention into the body, these psychological methods aim at behavior change by techniques that do not invade the body.

The Use of Behavior Control Techniques in Total Institutions

Whereas the three earlier studies examined the technologies and techniques for their own sake, this study examined their use in the special context of closed and total institutions. In particular, we examined their current use in maximum security systems, and the proposed future use of such techniques, that is, behavior control techniques for the control of violence.

Therapy and Social Control

A major tension that emerged from all the earlier studies was whether and to what extent it was possible to distinguish therapy (aimed at curing or benefiting an individual) and social control (aimed at promoting the welfare of society). After conceptualizing this distinction, we examined the question of developing criteria to make the distinction socially and ethically sound.

Alternatives to Incarceration and Institutionalization

The temptation and the prospect of using behavior control technologies to facilitate the release of people from prisons and other total institutions—that is, using behavior control technologies that might monitor the brain waves of released inmates or parolees, as well as detect their geographic location—has been an important recent development. We studied both the technological alternatives to institutionalization and the special ethical and legal problems raised by these prospects.

Autonomy

The meaning of individual freedom and autonomy, especially in the face of techniques that can bypass reason and individual choice, was a fundamental ethical problem arising in all our earlier studies. It bore on problems of informed consent, the social context of autonomous decisions, and the extent to which self-determination should be a primary criterion for deciding on the use of behavior control techniques.

That, in brief summary, is the range of issues we had addressed prior to the research on which this book is based. One study in particular drew most of these themes together and was the immediate source of the idea for the proposed new project.

The Boston MBD Drug Controversy

In mid-1972, a controversy erupted in Boston over a research project that proposed to test, in the public schools, the efficacy and side effects of three psychotropic drugs on learning difficulties and behavioral disorders in children. The struggle aroused heated opposition involving a coalition of community groups opposing the project, as well as researchers from the Massachusetts Department of Mental Health and Boston State Hospital, who were conducting the study and the National Institute of Mental Health, which funded it. Ultimately, the research project was discontinued and a state law passed regulating research on psychotropic drugs with students.

The Boston conflict was not unique. It resembled numerous episodes in recent years where the aims and priorities of researchers appeared to diverge from those of nonscientific communities. In such cases, despite the mechanisms set in place to review the ethical and scientific merits of proposed biomedical and behavioral research, controversy overflowed the institutional channels, rapidly becoming politicized and sharply polarized. Fetal research, psychosurgery, genetic screening, drug testing in prisons, and the use of aversive conditioning have all provoked intense political confrontations—as have, of course, issues such as abortion and euthanasia. Sometimes these controversies have generated new institutional forms for debating the questions—for example, the 1975 Asilomar conference on the risks of recombinant DNA research, and the National Commission for the Protection of Human Subjects. In other cases, the controversies have flowed, often precipitously, into existing institutions such as legislatures and courts.

The use of psychotropic drugs to treat children said to have learning disabilities, functional behavioral disorders, or minimal brain dysfunction (MBD) was another in the list of issues sharply dividing sectors of the public from the scientific community. Critical questions arose: Were these categories diagnostically sound? Did they risk harming children through the process of labeling? Did they divert attention from the inadequacies of schools to the individual child and obfuscate issues of social derivation with medical concepts? Indeed, is such treatment the best and sometimes the last chance for many children? These questions have been a continuing source of debate, both within the biomedical community and between it and local community groups, public interest groups, and individuals. They were at the heart of the Boston controversy.

The Boston study was initiated in 1971. The principal investigator was Dr. Albert DiMascio, director of psychopharmacology at the Massachusetts Department of Mental Health. The project was designed to examine how a limited course of treatment with psychotropic medications affected a variety of symptoms observed in functional behavioral disorders of children. Effects (and their duration) were to be measured in terms of behavior observed at home and in school, academic achievement, and intelligence-test performance. The research also sought to establish dosage ranges and side effects, and to relate the efficacy of different medications to different patterns of dysfunction and pretreatment characteristics. The study involved a double-blind, controlled comparison of three active psychotropic medications—Valium, Melaril, and Ritalin. These were to be administered for a twelve-week period to 160 boys from six to twelve years of age. At the end of twelve weeks half of the children were to be changed to placebo, and all would continue on either the medication or the placebo for another eight weeks. The selection procedures involved referral by schools to mental health clinics within the catchment area of the Boston State Hospital, screening by the clinics, and referrals to the project itself, where further screening was to take place. Only children in need of help and likely to benefit were to be allowed in the study, and both parents had to consent.

From April 1971 to May 1972 the project was reviewed and approved by a number of individuals and agencies. It received wide media coverage in Boston and was discussed with school and community groups in the catchment area. In June, however, a group outside the area, the Fort Hill Mental Association, voiced criticism of such research in general, and soon a coalition specifically opposed to the project had emerged. The coalition's position paper and Dr. DiMascio's reply centered on such questions as the riskiness of the drugs; the adequacy of diagnostic categories; informed-consent procedures; treatment services and follow-up evaluation; and the role of the schools. A series of meetings and correspondence from December 1972 to the fall of 1973 dealt with possible revisions in the study but failed to resolve the issues. By October 1973 only eleven children, two of whom were black, had been evaluated and treated in the study and nineteen more had been evaluated but not treated.

At that point the state commissioner of mental health directed his department's Human Rights Committee to conduct a special review of the project. In January 1974 the Human Rights Committee found that the project had been properly reviewed and approved, that selection of children was not biased in terms of minority or poverty groups, that the requirements of informed consent had been met, and that the study was safe. The committee concluded that the project was not in "gross violation" of its subjects' rights but that it should nonetheless be discontinued and redesigned because insufficient numbers had been studied to achieve its potential benefits and because involvement of the school authorities might introduce subtle coercion. In the face of this continuing opposition—and much personal abuse—Dr. DiMascio decided to terminate the study. Meanwhile, legislation regulating the experimental use of psychotropic drugs for research in public schools had been passed by the state legislature and signed into law. Its chief effect was to prohibit the administration of psychotropic drugs to students for purposes of clinical research on their efficacy—although it did *not* prohibit their general use. In other words, in the state of Massachusetts it is currently legal to dispense drugs to students in schools, but not all right to test whether they are harmful or beneficial—a typical case of foolish, panic legislation.

On February 13 and 14 of 1976, the Institute of Society, Ethics and the Life Sciences brought together many of the major actors in the Boston controversy; for two days they discussed the recent events with members of the institute's Behavior Control Research Group and other participants.[1]

This research model was then seen as a potentially useful device to examine another area where needed research into human behavior produced suspicion, anxiety, and hostility—the study of violence. Three of the most publicized attempts to bring scientific knowledge to bear on violent, antisocial behavior were aborted because of a variety of public pressures and concerns. We decided to combine these three case studies as the focus of a general inquiry into the problems of doing research on violence. The background to these explosive situations came to our knowledge as they were occurring; a brief outline of events follows. These are the facts as we outlined them—*before* embarking on our project.

The Boston XYY Controversy

In the middle and late sixties studies of the chromosome complement of inmates in mental and penal institutions revealed a higher than expected frequency of an extra Y chro-

---

[1] See "MBD, Drug Research and the Schools: A Conference on Medical Responsibility and Community Control," Special Supplement, *The Hastings Center Report* 4 (June 1976).

mosome among these males, and suggested a correlation between aggressive or antisocial behavior and the XYY genotype. Given this evidence, some investigators felt that it was important to study the development of newborns with the XYY genotype. One such study was begun in 1968 by Dr. Stanley Walzer (a child psychiatrist) and Dr. Park Gerald (a medical geneticist), both of Harvard University, at the Boston Hospital for Women. Their study screened all newborns within two days of birth for three different types of chromosomal variations, and involved a follow-up of these children's psychological development.

A great deal of criticism was raised against the XYY segment of the study. Concern was expressed over the possible risks of labeling and thus stigmatizing children with the XYY genotype. Was the risk warranted in light of the benefits of new knowledge about the condition? Questions were also raised concerning confidentiality of medical information and the requirements for informed consent by parents. Underlying much of the concern was the question of whether or not the XYY genotype was a disease, and whether it did have behavioral correlates. Drs. Jonathan Beckwith (of Harvard Medical School) and Jonathan King (of MIT), both molecular geneticists, were the chief critics of the study and, in addition to raising the above issues, contended that the very notion of genetic origins of antisocial behavior is a myth.

When the issue came before a review committee at the Harvard Medical School and then before the medical school faculty, both groups approved a continuation of the study. However, because of frightening personal pressures, Walzer voluntarily ended the screening program in June 1975, although the follow-up developmental study of those children already in the program continued.

Behavior Modification Programs in Prisons

In February 1974 the government withdrew funds from a number of behavior modification programs with prisoners. The first action, taken by the Federal Bureau of Prisons (Norman Carlson, director), was directed against Project START in Missouri (Special Treatment and Rehabilitation Training; Alfred Scheckenbach, professional consultant). The aim of the program was the alteration of behavior of particularly unmanageable prisoners through operant conditioning techniques. Later that month the Law Enforcement Assistance Administration (LEAA; Donald Santorelli, administrator) decided to withdraw funds from all anticrime legislation passed under the Nixon administration for behavior modification programs. Other institutions affected were the federal facility at Butner, North Carolina (Martin Groder, designated director) and the one at Patuxent, Maryland (Harold Boslow, director; Arthur Kandel, assistant director). This cutoff of funds also affected the UCLA Center for the Study and Reduction of Violence (see below), which the California arm of the LEAA had agreed to fund.

The basic issue remaining unresolved was that of both the ethics and efficacy of using behavior modification in the criminal justice system. The American Psychological Association spoke out against banning its use, claiming that such a ban would result in the use of more primitive methods of treatment. The Children's Defense Fund and the Senate Subcommittee on Constitutional Rights were critical of the LEAA funding, not because they objected to the use of behavior modification *per se* but because of the potential abuses of the technology and the need for more careful investigation. The House Subcommittee on Courts, Civil Liberties and Administration of Justice had several hearings on behavior modification in prisons at which Carlson and Groder testified.

The Hastings Center organized a conference on "Behavior Control in Total Institutions" (December 1973)[2] which brought together representatives from these institutions as well as psychiatrists, criminologists, and lawyers with experience in prison work. That conference began to formulate

[2]See Peter Steinfels, "A Clockwork Orange—Or Just a Lemon?" *The Hastings Center Report* (April 1974); and David J. Rothman, "Behavior Modification in Total Institutions," *The Hastings Center Report* 5 (February 1975).

some of the ethical and legal issues raised by the use of behavior control techniques in prisons, such as goals of treatment, problems of management, rights of prisoners and informed consent, and the general problems of the efficacy of rehabilitation through incarceration.

UCLA Center for the Study and Reduction of Violence

In the spring of 1973 a controversy arose over a proposed center for the study of violence at the University of California at Los Angeles. According to Dr. Louis J. West (a psychiatrist and medical director of UCLA's Neuropsychiatric Institute, and acting director of the center at that time), the purpose of the center was "to study the pathologically violent individual with a view toward earlier diagnosis, treatment and prevention of violent behavior, and its consequences." Among the proposed studies were to be investigations of child abuse, suicide in relation to drug abuse, sex offenders, as well as other types of violent behavior. The center was to be jointly funded by the State Department of Health (Dr. J. M. Stubblebine was director of health at that time) and the California Council for Criminal Justice (CCCJ; Robert J. Lawson was executive director). Dr. Robert Litman, a USC psychiatrist, had been proposed as director.

Concern was voiced from several areas over the possible use of psychosurgery at the center, the respect for requirements of informed consent, and the persecution of minorities. Dr. Isadore Ziferstein, a psychiatrist, was one of the leaders of the opposition to the center. A hearing was held before the State Senate Subcommittee on Health and Welfare, at which time West and Stubblebine were advised to set up a public group of overseers. A subsequent hearing recommended to the CCCJ not to allocate the requested funds for the center. The major concern at the subcommittee (as well as critics such as the Committee Opposing Psychiatric Abuse of Prisoners, the NAACP, and NOW) was the apparently unresolved issue of the use of psychosurgery at the center. West accused opponents of the center of deliberately feeding on "today's climate of apprehension about the powers of government to corrupt even scientists and doctors."

In February 1974 the LEAA decided to cut off funding for the center. Subsequently, several groups expressed the need for thoughtful consideration of the ethical and legal limits of behavioral technology in this area (notably the Institute for Behavioral Research in Silver Springs, Maryland, which was to organize a behavioral-law unit to address these issues).

THE PURPOSE OF THIS STUDY

Let us reemphasize that our purposes in the study were threefold: first, to survey the present and envisioned ability of sciences to understand and control violent and antisocial behavior; second, to examine in detail the three aborted research projects cited above, seeking to determine the political, legal, and ethical dynamic that led to their demise; and third, to ask how and under what conditions further scientific research on antisocial behavior could, and should, go forward by taking into account the social and ethical problems involved while avoiding the pitfalls displayed by those three earlier attempts.

To be sure, the three incidents we examined were by no means identical in all respects, and indeed the conferences in themselves pointed out how dramatically mere personality differences altered the course of the debate. But there were enough similarities to make them a natural cluster, and where they differed the differences appeared to be instructive.

Moreover, our aim was not simply to study the three cases themselves; a broader goal was to use these studies as a data base for some more general reflections on contemporary scientific research, particularly that research likely to evoke passionate differences of opinion and to raise major social issues.

This project allowed us to examine, in the context of specific research areas, at least the following major issues: public and scientific responses to the use of scientific knowledge for dealing with antisocial behavior; the methods of resolving debates that have great social significance within a scientific community; the changing "contract" between science and society—between the expert and the citizen; the way political pressures are increasingly bearing on scientific research; and the question of freedom of scientific inquiry and the responsibility of science to the public. To us it was difficult to think of any comparable situations where so much of a general nature and so much of a specific nature could be encompassed by an intensive examination.

It seemed logical to us, however, that if we were going to discuss the specifics of research on violence, we must have some introductory comments on the meaning of violence; it quickly became apparent that the definition of the term itself would strongly influence one's political and moral judgments on its control. To that effect, we asked Robin M. Williams, Jr., to summarize the state of our knowledge or confusion on the nature of violence.

Throughout this study it became apparent that there was one special quality that influenced behavior control research. This quality has been referred to elsewhere as "the Frankenstein factor."

> Research that is seen as changing or controlling the "nature" of the species, or controlling behavior will inevitably be perceived with more fear than other equally risky research. . . . Success in behavior modificiation and genetic engineering research is more likely to bring dejection than in other kinds of biological experimentation. Devices that save and extend life aggrandize both the discoverer and man in general with the suggestion that such control of death, although still not the immortality of God, is a cut above the helplessness of the general animal host. Behavior manipulation, on the other hand, reasserts man's kinship with the pigeon, the rat, and the guineapig. The more technological the control devices, the more mechanical the method—the scarier it all seems.[3]

---

[3]Willard Gaylin, "The Frankenstein Factor," *New England Journal of Medicine* (September 22, 1977), p. 665.

When we are aware that there is, on the part of the public, exaggerated sensitivity to research that casts man as the *material* of the research as well as the researcher, there is much that can be done to defuse the inordinate anxiety.

Violence *is* an area that ought to be researched. And we know only too well—from specific statements explicitly made at some of our workshops by major medical school department chairmen—that faced with limited resources and limited time there will be a natural inclination for major research departments to avoid those areas that are going to cause controversy. There are always more subjects to be examined than time allows, and scientists, like other people, will eschew those areas likely to limit their pursuits and to ensnare them in ugly personal and political controversy.

The public at large is not aware of the fact that to the scientist, the subject of research is almost always secondary to the process. A scientist is rarely interested in cancer, schizophrenia, or violence *per se*. What he is interested in is his method: tissue culture, isotope studies, psychoanalytic interviewing, the biochemistry of human emotions—these technologies are his passions, the subject, his interest. And he can take his expertise and apply it to a multitude of issues. The neuroanatomist concerned with plotting the way stations of the brain can be just as intrigued by problems of speech and vision as he can by violence and aggression.

In bringing the principals together at these workshops, it was never our purpose to reopen old wounds but simply to examine the dynamics of controversy in a way that might shed light on anticipated problems in future attempts at research on violence and, beyond that, on all similarly sensitive topics. There is little interest on our part in examining the past, unless we can find some applications to the future.

Our primary concerns are with the ethical issues that underlie the control of research in general. There is a growing awareness of the right of people at large to enter into the decision-making process of the scientific structure. This awareness is not, as some scientists believe, an attack on science, but rather a reexamination of science's traditional exemption from public scrutiny and supervision. All future scientific research in sensitive areas—which may mean all future scientific research—is likely to invite public scrutiny. Whether the research is centered on the control of violence, or the storage of liquid gas, or the disposal of nuclear waste, a series of balanced and often contradictory interests and concerns will inevitably be brought into play. How to involve the public in the decision-making process, which is certainly a public concern, while protecting scientific inquiry from excessive vulnerability to doctrinaire rhetoric was a major part of the general purpose of our study.

All too often in the past we have judged the benefits of an action against immediate or apparent consequences—unaware or unconcerned about the long-range diffusion of the decisions we made into other areas at future times. Dr. Robert H. Ebert, dean of the Harvard Medical School at the time of the XYY controversy, was particularly sensitive to the extending implications the actions then taken might have on the nature of the university. He raised some crucial questions about the—perhaps unintended—consequences of some of these actions:

> —Should there be self-imposed limits within the academic community in the way in which a colleague's work is criticized or is there a larger obligation to society which transcends the niceties of academic life?
> —If there are no limits, is academic freedom compromised since a university can do very little about personal harassment?
>
> Universities have long been the home for dissenters—indeed academic freedom means that members of the academic community have the right to dissent without harassment. Academic freedom was meant to protect individuals but what happens if dissent becomes structured into special interest groups as it has in our larger society? Will the freedom of the individual faculty member be enhanced or compromised? What are the limits, if any, on the obligations of the university to protect the rights of dissent of a special interest group within the university—even the rights of a group that has as its stated purpose

the suppression of the rights of some others within the same institution.[4]

We do not pretend to any complete solutions in this book. The eruption of any public controversy is bound to have multiple and complex causes. There will always remain some doubt about both the underlying reasons, arising from the general social climate, and the precipitating factors that lead to such eruptions. There is always the question of why certain conflicts became politically sensitized at certain times. Was it the fact that all the research involved attempts to control human behavior? Or the fact that technological interventions of one sort or another were proposed or anticipated? Or did the research alarm the advocates of minority groups or prisoners who feared that "law and order" was once again about to be a justification for violation of personal liberties?

At the earlier conference on minimal brain dysfunction it was made clear to us that the question of testing drugs in the schools was no longer viewed by the political opponents of the research—if it ever was—as a major threat to their children. The issue was control of the decision making. And their protest was seen primarily as an announcement that in the future all such issues of research would have to be funneled through *the community leaders*. ("Had they come to us in the first place . . ." was a phrase that echoed through that meeting with its implication that the research might have been permitted had the "community" been consulted.)

The truth of this statement was confirmed in one of the most ironic follow-ups to our study. After the proposed violence center in southern California had been scuttled, in great part because its methods were deemed "too vague," its ambitions "too grandiose," and its methods "too general and ill defined," a bill carrying the name of Willie Brown (the same

[4]Correspondence dated September 2, 1980 from Robert H. Ebert, M.D., dean of Harvard Medical School at the time of the controversy, to Dr. Willard Gaylin.

Willie Brown who was a chief opponent of Dr. West and his study) was introduced in the California Assembly, proposing the creation of "the California Commission on Crime Control and Violence Prevention." It requested an original $500,000 grant for the study of "the root causes of violence in our society." This modest proposal announced that

> The areas of study of the commission shall include, but shall not be limited to, the following: (a) The birthing process; (b) The parenting process; (c) Nutrition; (d) Touching; (e) Feelings and emotions; (f) The human body; (g) Self-esteem; (h) sex role stereotyping; (i) Sexual repression; (j) The effects of television; (k) Powerlessness; (l) Poverty; and (m) Prejudice.

This limp and ludicrous set of general topics, with no supporting methodology, passed through the California state legislature with flying colors. Obviously, the question, as Humpty-Dumpty observed a long time ago, seems only to be "Which is to be master, that is all."

Any understanding of the factors involved in these and future cases of public conflict will depend on our ability to scratch beneath the surface of what is reported in even the most respectable publications. In examining these three examples, our major concern was to gain a more general understanding of the processes by which such conflicts arise and how they may be resolved. There are numerous other disputes now arising out of developments in science and technology that will continue to engage the public consciousness and arouse public anxiety. Currently, the debates about nuclear versus other sources of energy, euthanasia, and the many issues surrounding mandatory or even voluntary genetic screening seem to dominate the discussion. But the future will bring us other issues as yet unanticipated as research brings us knowledge as yet unknown. With knowledge come new possibilities. And the new always generates anxiety—potential for good suggests potential for harm. Yet the scientific enterprise will go on. We will—we must—we should continue to expand our knowledge of ourselves and our environment. We must find ways to help the public enter the decision-making process while still protecting the rights of researchers to scientific inquiry. This study was designed as part of our contribution to that end.

CHAPTER 2

Legitimate and Illegitimate Uses of Violence

A Review of Ideas and Evidence

ROBIN M. WILLIAMS, JR.

INTRODUCTION

It is possible to take the position that no violence is ever legitimate under any circumstances. It is possible to take the position that all violence is legitimate. Both views are rare. Most people most of the time do make some distinction between legitimate and illegitimate (or nonlegitimate) acts of violence. In addition, there is often an overlapping but distinct discrimination between justified and unjustified violence; for example, a particular act of violence may be judged legitimate

ROBIN M. WILLIAMS, JR. ● Department of Sociology, 323 Uris Hall, Cornell University, Ithaca, New York 14853.

("he had a right to do it") but not fully justified under the circumstances ("but he *shouldn't* have done it"). It is immediately evident that the relations between the two distinctions, although real and important in everyday affairs, are complex and often ambiguous. The main axis of contrast is between *social right*—"validated" by law, status, custom, or general acceptance—as opposed to *moral justification*—validated by appeal to religious precepts, ethical principles and reasoning, or consensual moral judgments. A legitimate but immoral act may be performed by a duly invested incumbent of a legally established position. An illegitimate but moral act may be carried out by a principled opponent of an evil political regime. In this chapter, we must put aside a fuller conceptual analysis. Instead our primary task is empirical: we seek to find out what main orientations actually do exist, and how beliefs and evaluations concerning violence vary at different times and among different subsections of the societal community.

Evaluations of violence do vary radically across times, places, and circumstances. It is also clear that beliefs and evaluations—cognitive definitions, and appraisals of desirability—are strongly interdependent. Our positive evaluation of a particular type of action may be so intense that we are unwilling to conceive of that action as "violence," if we regard violence as subject to negative evaluation. Or, our acceptance of a definition of violence that includes "infant malnutrition caused by poverty" can lead us to an increasingly negative evaluation of the current distribution of income in our society. It is in this context that we can say that the primary legitimating or delegitimating process is very often *definitional* or *classificatory*. (The making of public definitions and classifications, therefore, is a primal political act.) A decisive step is taken when we answer the question: Is or is not a particular act or type of conduct "violence"? Here as elsewhere in the social world the activities of identifying, labeling or naming, and classifying are of the utmost importance. A rose that we name skunk cabbage may *not* smell as sweet as before, and we live in an age of semantic wrenching in which many conventional distinctions are being blurred, eroded, or even reversed in meaning.

In recent months I have read commentaries that say that illnesses and injuries incurred by workers in industry represent capitalistic violence, and that the deaths thereby resulting are homicides committed by corporations. During the later phases of the war in Vietnam, antiwar rhetoric equated the collectively organized and "obligatory" killing carried out by soldiers with "murder"—which it surely is not by any customary, legal, or sociological criteria. We hear of the violence done to our minds by advertising. Some black leaders have referred to poverty among black people as violence stemming from institutionalized racism.

A crucial first step, then, in establishing the legitimacy or illegitimacy of violence is to decide whether any specified type of conduct is to be regarded as violence or not violence. The definitional problem raises a large number of interesting and consequential questions. Must violence be physical—an overt act intending to cause or actually causing direct injury to persons or property? Or may the action and its effects be symbolic, as in the voicing of insults or in character assassination by the spreading of damaging rumors? Must violence be intentional? To be violent, must an act inflict immediate and direct damage? Or may the effects be long-term and indirect? Is it a violent act when a corporation executive authorizes the storage of highly toxic wastes in a manner that decades later increases the risks of cancer in a human population? Are OPEC officials engaged in violence when they raise the price of petroleum to levels that reduce fertilizer supplies to poor countries and thereby increase malnutrition and famine?

The questions continue. Is an act violent only if the initiating actor is aware that it will cause damage or injury? Is failure to remove a known and controllable cause of injury to be regarded as a form of violence? One may think of black lung among coal miners, cancer among workers in chemical plants, brown lung in cotton textile manufacturing, or exposure to radiation from nuclear weapons tests or from nuclear power plants. The general question is whether acts of omission, when an actor knows that the omission will result in the continuation of conditions that cause injury, can properly count as a form of violence. In conventional language, such behavior is not called violent. Should it be?

In general, scholarly works seem to have chosen relatively narrow definitions. Thus Hofstadter and Wallace[1] define violence as acts that kill or injure persons or destroy property. According to Grimshaw,[2] "social violence is assault upon an individual or his property solely or primarily because of his membership in a social category." Again in general, usage seems to favor a restrictive conception: the clearest cases of violence are those acts that cause physical damage, are intentional, are active rather than passive, and are direct in their effects. For other types of coercive or destructive conduct, other terms may be preferable—for example, Hofstadter and Wallace[3] use the term "force" to refer to acts that "prevent the normal free action or movement of persons, or inhibit them through the threat of violence." Similarly, many nonviolent but damaging acts may fall under the broader rubric of "aggression,"—for example, efforts by verbal means to destroy a person's reputation, to undermine his relationships with other persons, or to defame the symbols he holds sacred. Thus Sanford and Comstock[4] urge a threefold distinction: the *behavior* of (1) "violence" and (2) "social destructiveness," and the *motive* of (3) "aggression."

In what follows, we focus on direct physical violence. Our interest is in the ways in which such violence is legiti-

---

[1]Richard Hofstadter and Michael Wallace, eds., *American Violence: A Documentary History* (New York: Alfred A. Knopf, 1970), p. 9.

[2]Allen D. Grimshaw, ed., *Racial Violence in the United States* (Chicago: Aldine, 1969), p. 2.

[3]Hofstadter and Wallace, p. 9.

[4]Nevitt Sanford, Craig Comstock, eds., and associates, *Sanctions for Evil* (San Francisco: Jossey-Bass, 1971), pp. 2–3.

mated or justified or otherwise rendered socially acceptable or tolerable. Especially important in many ways will be those types of actions in which direct harm is done to persons by individuals who receive positive social sanctions for carrying out such actions. To anticipate, we shall see that the overwhelming bulk of the most destructive violence consists of organized conduct that is socially permitted, or encouraged, or enjoined as a right or duty. Most violence is not deviant behavior, not disapproved conduct, but virtuous action in the service of applauded values.

HOW PREVALENT IS VIOLENCE?

There is no point in an elaborate documentation of the somber facts about the incidence and prevalence of violence. At least a brief summary will be useful, however, to place our present concerns in appropriate perspective.

There are crucial differences between collective violence and individual violence.[5] For example, those persons who commit violent crimes differ greater in personality characteristics from persons who serve in wartime military forces. Individual violence tends to issue from persons who have difficulty establishing satisfactory group ties and enduring interpersonal relationships, who frequently clash with established authority and group norms, and whose violence is often self-defeating and self-punishing. In contrast, "good soldiers" are highly responsive to demands for social conformity, readily adjust to giving and receiving orders, have

[5]For present purposes we shall consider all organized violence to be collective, although some collective violence is relatively unorganized as in crowds and in diffuse rioting. By "individual violence" we mean acts of violence carried out by individuals without reference to a collective plan or coordinated effort. Of course, there will be intermediate cases—for example, assassinations or acts of sabotage carried out by isolated individuals who nevertheless see themselves as participants in a mass movement.

strong affiliative capacities, and function reliably as loyal members of groups.[6]

Although accurate and detailed data do not exist for most of history, there is no doubt that the forms of violence most destructive of lives and possessions are collective rather than individual and organized rather than diffuse or haphazard. The most important organized-collective forms include international wars, revolutions, guerrilla wars, insurrections, rebellions, political purges, genocide, strikes with violence, vigilante actions, pogroms, riots, sabotage, political executions, and assassinations.

Most conspicuous and massive are the violent conflicts that take place between armed forces of political societies, whether ancient empires, tribes, feudal domains, principalities, or modern nation-states. Such tragic encounters are not episodic "interruptions" of some normal condition of peaceful relations. They do not come "out of the blue" into a world of consensus, exchange, cooperation, friendship, and stability. Rather, large-scale conflicts must be considered normal in the sense of high incidence and prevalence throughout history, in all parts of the world, and among peoples of all major cultures.

> Quincy Wright's monumental analysis dealt with some 278 major wars from the War of the Roses to the close of World War II and with 30 additional large-scale international "hostile incidents", 1946–1965.[7] [By 1970, the total of wars since 1484 that properly can be called major had increased to about 315.] War-connected deaths from World Wars I and II probably were close to 90 millions. Between 1945 and 1962 alone, "unconventional

---

[6]Louise Jolyan West, comments in "Researching Violence: Science, Politics and Public Controversy," Special Supplement, *The Hastings Center Report* 9 (April 1979): 5.

[7]Quincy Wright, A *Study of War*, abridged by Louise L. Wright (Chicago: University of Chicago Press, 1964), Quincy Wright, "War," in *International Encyclopedia of the Social Sciences*, 16th ed., ed. David L. Sills (New York: Crowell Collier and Macmillan, 1968), pp. 453–468.

warfare" occurred in 35 of the 104 nations in existence at the latter date.[8] And more people have been killed in civil wars within nations than in wars among nations.[9] With a current world average of about three major outbreaks of collective violence per year, it is not unreasonable to suppose that the grievous inventory as of the year 2000 will continue to justify Sorokin's earlier characterization of the 20th as "the bloodiest century."[10]

A sober appraisal of the conditions of actual societies and their interrelations strongly suggests that frequent wars are more likely than continuing peace.[11] Neither the disappearance of national states nor the establishment of something called world government, whatever it might be, would preclude large-scale collective conflict, including armed violence. Furthermore, it is quite conceivable that aggression in the form of direct physical violence could cease while conflict nevertheless continued with deadly results. If conventional violence were to be replaced somehow by denial of access to oil or food, casualties inflicted might well exceed those that result from conventional warfare.[12]

From 1480 to 1941, the number of major battles fought among European powers alone was over 4,700, or about 10.5 battles per year over the centuries. From 1900 to 1939 the estimated number of "small" wars (300 to 3,200 fatalities) was over 500, or 12.5 per year.[13] Under the glorious Louis XIV, France was at war for 32 of the 44 years of his reign. From 500 B.C. to 1925, the histories of Greece, Rome, Austria, Germany, England, France, the Netherlands, Spain, Italy, and

[8]Janus K. Zawodny, ed., "Foreword" to "Unconventional Warfare," *Annals of the American Academy of Political and Social Science* 341 (1962): viii.

[9]Lewis F. Richardson, *Statistics of Deadly Quarrels* (Pittsburgh: Boxwood Press, 1960).

[10]Pitirim A. Sorokin, *Social and Cultural Dynamics*, vol. 3, *Fluctuation of Social Relationships, War and Revolution* (New York: American Book Company, 1937).

[11]Wright, "War," p. 466.

[12]Robin M. Williams, Jr., "Resolving and Restricting International Conflicts," in *Armed Forces and Society* (forthcoming, 1981).

[13]Richardson, pp. 32–50.

Russia (including Poland and Lithuania) exhibit a total of 967 major interstate wars.[14]

The destructiveness of some wars that are little known in the United States is a somber reminder of organized human ferocity. The Taiping Rebellion, which lasted from 1850 to 1864, resulted in an estimated twenty million deaths from military actions, mass executions, disease, and war-connected famine. The Lopez War of 1865 to 1870 involved the military forces of Paraguay against the combined armies of Brazil, Argentina, and Uruguay. The casualties in Paraguay apparently amounted to an incredible 80 percent of the total population and as much as 90 percent of the adult males.

Genocide, narrowly defined as "a structural and systematic destruction of innocent people by a state bureaucratic apparatus,"[15] may have accounted for the deliberate killing of upward of forty million human beings in this century. The instances totaled in this estimate include Nazi Germany, the USSR from 1929 to 1946, the Ottoman Empire, Colombia, Uganda, Malaysia, mainland China, Brazil, Nigeria, Ruwanda-Burundi, and Indonesia among others.

Collective violence within nations in the form of riots is extremely common. According to official data from the Home Ministry, Hindu–Moslem conflicts in India from September 30, 1965 to September 30, 1967 produced 411 recorded riots; from 1947 to 1970 there probably were at least 1,000 such riots, involving many dead and wounded and great destruction of property. From 1961 to 1968 the United States experienced 341 major urban riots ("civil disorders").[16] From 1948 to 1960, it is estimated, some 200,000 persons were killed in the en-

---

[14]Sorokin.

[15]Irving Louis Horowitz, *Genocide, State Power and Mass Murder* (New Brunswick, N.J.: Transaction Books, 1977), p. 18.

[16]Seymour Spilerman, "The Causes of Racial Disturbances: Tests of an Explanation," *American Sociological Review* 36 (1971): 431.

demic violence permeating the rural society of Colombia.[17] The amorphous and pervasive pattern of violence developed its own momentum, and the recurrent killings came to be marked by fantastic elaborations of cruelty in inflicting deaths. (Gino Germani in commenting on the study speaks of "the atrocious imagination displayed in creating new ways of imposing death").[18] Eventually the *violencia* came to constitute a more or less stabilized—quasiinstitutionalized—mode of behavior.

Over against these reminders of the ubiquity and magnitude of collective violence we must set the records of individual violence—of homicide, manslaughter, rape, assault, arson, vandalism, and numerous lesser varieties of attacks on persons and their belongings. In the United States, arrests for "violent crimes" in 1976 constituted 5 percent of all arrests; to these for present purposes we may add burglary and motor vehicle theft (8 percent), "other assaults" (5 percent), and vandalism and arson (3 percent).[19] Thus by the widest characterization, about one-fifth of arrests deal with "violence" —but only one-tenth concern direct attacks upon persons. Because of serious defects in reporting and classification, the official statistics vastly understate the amount of crime. In the case of violence against persons, underreporting is especially great for forcible rape and aggravated and simple assaults,[20] particularly among members of the same family. According

[17]German Guzman, Orlando Fals Borda, and Eduardo Umaña Luna, *La Violencia en Colombia: Estudio de un Proceso Social* (Bogota, Colombia: Tomo 1, No. 12, Monografias sociologicas, Facultad de Sociologia, Universidad Nacional, 1962).

[18]Gino Germani, review of German Guzman, Orlando Fals Borda, and Eduardo Umaña Luna, *La Violencia en Colombis: Estudio de un Proceso Social*, in *American Sociological Review* 29 (1964): 434.

[19]Elmer H. Johnson, *Crime, Correction, and Society* (Homewood, Ill.: Dorsey Press, 1978), p. 11.

[20]Ibid., p. 23.

to the official data for 1976, violence against persons occasioned some 800,000 (estimated) arrests. Many recent studies[21] show that a very large amount of violence occurs daily within the confines of the nuclear family.

Additional documentation is not needed. Human affairs are marked by frequent violent encounters. Some violence is condemned by common consent; in other instances, violence is socially condoned, approved, or regarded as obligatory. Whence the differences?

HOW VIOLENCE IS RENDERED LEGITIMATE

All societies develop beliefs and evaluations that in some sense are considered to legitimate or justify violence. (We do not say "belief systems" or "value systems," for that would severely prejudge one of the important questions we may wish to consider.) Rarely indeed are people content merely to accept any kind of behavior as a sheer fact and nothing but a fact; almost always there is some interest in evaluation of social behavior as good or bad, desirable or undesirable, proper or improper, necessary or unnecessary, and so on.

"Legitimations" are of many widely differing kinds. Among the borderline cases are *explanations* in the sense of "making understandable" or "making plain" behavior that would otherwise be inexplicable, incomprehensible, bizarre, crazy. Such explanations translate sheer *behavior* into *conduct*.

Other explanations take the form of justifications that give *extenuating conditions and interpretations* that may render condemned conduct acceptable or tolerable—that reduce culpa-

---

[21]Suzanne K. Steinmetz and Murray A. Straus, *Violence in the Family* (New York: Dodd, Mead, 1974); Richard J. Gelles, *The Violent Home: A Study of Physical Aggression between Husbands and Wives* (Beverly Hills, Calif.: Sage, 1974); Ray E. Helfer and C. Henry Kempe, *The Battered Child* (Chicago: University of Chicago Press, 1968); David G. Gil, *Violence against Children: Physical Child Abuse in the United States* (Cambridge: Harvard University Press, 1970).

bility. The behavior in point is not fully legitimate but it is no longer fully deviant or subject to ordinary social sanctions.

One form of exculpation is the claim that the violent actor *did not intend the act* or did not intend to have it produce such damaging results. The violent act was an accident or mischance, it was intended only to scare or to "teach a lesson," and the degree of injury was neither intended nor foreseen. A special variant of such "justifications" is that the actor was *morally incapacitated* by alcohol or other drugs. More deepgoing is the claim of *uncontrollable* (but understandable) *emotion*—grief, moral outrage, horror.

Violence that, undefended, would be open to condemnation may be "justified" by diffusion of responsibility—the leader has the full responsibility, the person who threw the first stone is responsible, everyone was doing it. Individual responsibility may be *systematically* transferred to a collectivity—what Redl[22] calls "depersonalization through the tribal dance." The person dons a special identity (symbolized by paint, feathers, masks, uniform) and acts as a representative of the norms of a group.

The research on "blaming the victim" and the "Just World" orientation illustrates the crucial role of *definition* and *classification* in judgments about oppositional behavior. For example:

1. Behavior that is regarded as random, incoherent, non-purposive, incomprehensible is classified as "crazy," "nutty." It is then seen as without systematic meaning or consequences.

2. Behavior that is defined as coherent, regular, understandable is classified as meaningful and consequential. It tends to be attributed to the agent who is behaving. Hence it is worthy of attention, and of being taken seriously. If the behavior in question is violent conduct on the part of persons

---

[22]Fritz Redl, "The Superego in Uniform," in Sanford *et al.*, pp. 93–101.

in positions of authority, it tends to engage an initial pre-
sumption of purpose and legitimacy.

A radical solution for the problem of legitimacy is *denial*
that a given set of acts is properly classified in a socially suspect
or disapproved category. Thus, as we shall see in more detail
later, many Americans simply deny that physical injury inflicted by police on suspected offenders represents "violence"
at all. A related defense against charges of illegitimacy is to
*exclude the persons injured from the universe of morally protected
entities.* The object or target of physical aggression or force is
rendered fair game by being defined as not a member of the
moral community. Thus it is justifiable to destroy the property
of a soulless corporation or a religious heretic, to kill those
who are monsters or inhuman because of their abominable
acts or traits, or those who are "mere animals" (coons, pigs,
rats, lice, etc.), or those whose political views are unthinkably
heinous (Huns, communists, fascists, traitors).

Activities of justifying and legitimating violence shade
over gradually into activities that obscure, mystify, or otherwise redefine acts of violence. Thus in the Vietnam conflict
one did not kill the enemy soldier—one "wasted" or
"zapped" him. In 1979 a member of the Oklahoma legislature
who introduced a bill to require castration or other surgical
procedures to be performed on the male genitalia of rapists
described the requirement as "asexualization." Kulaks during
the revolutionary period after 1918 in the USSR were not
murdered, they were "liquidated."

Many of these accounts of violence lie in a vague borderland between legitimate and illegitimate "reasons," as well
as between justifiable and nonjustifiable conduct. For example,
there often is a

> twilight zone between justifiable and excusable homicide. [But]
> justifiable harm is always deliberate and intentional, never in-
> advertent, unintentional, involuntary, or unknowing as is typ-
> ical of excusable harm.[23]

---

[23]Hugo Adam Bedau, "Rough Justice: The Limit of Novel Defenses," *The
Hastings Center Report* 8 (December 1978): 10.

When violence is not denied, defined away, or explained as nonculpable on the various grounds just reviewed, its defense enters into the realm of positive justifications. Prominent among the positive legitimating grounds is that of *defense against attack* or credible threat of attack, or defense of the necessities of survival either for oneself, one's family, or other persons. Similarly strong and pervasive is the legitimating claim of *retributive justice*. Even ancient *lex talionis*, the law of revenge *or* retribution, when it matches injury for injury, pain for pain is a moderating or softening code in comparison with the utterly merciless, blind, raging lust for revenge that underlies it.

The annals of the past as well as the daily news of the present are filled with the records of virtuous bigotry, holy wars, justifiable homicide, sanctified cruelty, censorious and punitive piety, obligatory revenge, and retributive justice. A major finding of a 1969 survey of American men was that the more an individual believes in retributive justice, the higher the levels of use of force by police he will advocate or accept.[24] The high frequency and widespread prevalence of obedient aggression and conscientious violence are alone enough to make us wary of the assumption that "violence" and "legitimacy" are opposing or even divergent aspects of human conduct. As we shall see, present-day research in psychology and the social sciences provides detailed evidence of the ways in which moralistic convictions can create socially shared legitimacy for violence.

If one has a capacity for empathy with other persons, some of the sufferings inflicted by violence become difficult to manage. At the extreme—burning alive, for instance—the mind flinches away as does the hand from the flame. What "really happens" when the napalm or the incendaries hit the city is probably something that very few persons wish to fully "understand." It is not strange, therefore, that there usually develop various devices for neutralizing, reducing, buffering,

[24]Monica D. Blumenthal, "Predicting Attitudes toward Violence," *Science*, June 23, 1972, p. 1299.

obscuring, mystifying, or otherwise avoiding the direct affective impact of experiencing what violent acts do to the victims. The transformations only very rarely are merely the idiosyncratic psychological maneuvers of individuals. Instead they grow out of socially shared experiences and rapidly become part of the cultures and collectivities.

Such transformations may operate on all the major components of social violence: the act itself, the violent actor, the recipient or object, the immediate situation, the consequences, and the justifying and legitimating beliefs and values. Let us quickly look at a few examples out of many.

The most direct way to reduce undesired negative aspects of one's own violence (including violence carried out by other members of one's collectivity) is to deny that the acts in question are violence. If "violence" is bad, and the acts are good, the acts of which I approve are exempted from the classification. Thus I have not been violent—I just had to "rough up a little" a fellow who bumped into me in the street. I have never assaulted anyone—but I did have to beat up a couple of guys who "really deserved it." It is a violent act for a draft resister to burn his draft card, but it is not violent for police to use clubs on rioters.

The violent actor may transform himself by claiming lack of autonomy, knowledge, or capacity:

> I didn't know he had a weak heart.
>
> I was only following orders.
>
> He had a gun in my back, he would have shot me if I hadn't pushed the maniac out the window.
>
> The Devil made me do it.
>
> I was too drunk to know how hard I hit him.
>
> A man can't control his rage when he finds another man violating the sanctity of his home.

If sheer denial is challenged or does not adequately serve to reduce psychological dissonance, the object of violence may be transformed in ways that make the violence more acceptable. Basically, the victim is blamed: (1) He "was asking for it," that is, was provocative, acted in a manner certain to elicit violence, or (2) the target is outside the realm of socially protected objects, for example, is not really human, is a deadly enemy of all decent people, is uncontrollable by nonviolent means, is utterly evil.

People who strongly believe in a Just World tend to derogate the victim of unprovoked aggression—indeed, the greater the aggression, the more the victim is derogated.[25] If our society is just, the victims *must* have provoked the aggression, deserved their fate; it follows that the objects of violence inflicted by the Good Authorities (police, etc.) must be bad persons.[26]

Reevaluation may reduce the imputed seriousness of the consequences of the violent acts: "They don't feel pain like we do"; "She'll get over it in a few weeks"; "Children have to learn to take it"; "Fighting develops strength of character."

Biologistic justifications for war have been very popular in the Western world ever since the ideas of "struggle for existence" and "natural selection" captured the field of attention. It was an easy step from a vulgarized Darwinism to the notion of a social (or societal) survival of the fittest. This social Darwinism could be used and was used to justify laissez-faire industrialism. But its more biologistic version was used to justify war: war was a way of eliminating the physically, mentally, and morally weak.[27]

It is a short step from defining groups or categories of people as outsiders, aliens, or otherwise radically *different*

[25]Melvin J. Lerner, "Observer's Evaluation of a Victim: Justice, Guilt, and Veridical Perception," *Journal of Personality and Social Psychology* 20 (1971): 127–135.

[26]Myron Rothbart, "Achieving Racial Equality: An Analysis of Resistance to Social Reform," in *Towards the Elimination of Racism*, ed. Phyllis A. Katz (New York: Pergamon Press, 1976), pp. 356–357.

[27]For a vivid picture of such doctrines, circa 1928, see Pitirim A. Sorokin, *Contemporary Sociological Theories* (New York: Harper & Brothers, 1928), pp. 309–356.

from the ingroup to evaluating those who do not belong to "our" society as inhuman and evil. Thus genocidal societies are vehemently ethnocentric and nationalistic. The ethnocentrism and nationalism not only accentuate an intense "sense of difference between those who belong and those who do not, but also the inhumanity of those who do not belong, and thereby the rights of the social order to purge itself of alien influence."[28] The more intense the sacred quality of the ingroup and its culture, the greater the likelihood that total destruction of its "enemies" will be advocated and accepted.

> Hitler's rise to power was based on his understanding of what people needed and wanted most of all, and so he promised them, above everything else, *heroic victory over evil;* and he gave them the living possibility of ridding themselves temporarily of their real guilt.[29]

The dilemma of a policy of nonviolence toward another party is always that its success depends on some important measure of mutual acceptance. Against the overwhelming force of an adversary who is fully willing to commit genocide, pacific means are of little avail. A Hitler or a Stalin never tires of victims. It is true that nonviolent resistance often succeeds in acquiring the helpful intervention of third parties, but millions of victims give silent testimony to its failures. The basic difficulty in unilateral disarmament is that one's opponent may lack one's own aversion to violence, leaving "a maldistribution of pacifism in which the excess is on the side of the peoples most devoted to humane values."[30]

Violence may be presented as justifiable because it is a last resort, after all other means have been tried and have failed,

---

[28]Horowitz, p. 66.

[29]Ernest Becker, *Escape from Evil* (New York: Free Press/Macmillan, 1975), p. 117.

[30]Inis L. Claude, Jr., review of Klaus Knorr, *The Power of Nations,* in *Political Science Quarterly* 91 (1976): 571.

to remove a deadly threat or to redress injustice. The "exhaustion of other means" is, of course, one of the main criteria traditionally invoked for a "just war." The criterion of deadly threat can be subsumed under the doctrine of self-defense. The rectification of injustice is a special case of justification in terms of "higher values." Taken together the three elements of the "last resort" argument can be combined in many specific forms. One of the most conspicuous is the contention, in an instant case, that violence is necessary now to avoid greater violence: a war to end wars; to get rid of the gun, we must pick up the gun; it is our duty to kill those who will continue to kill others. Again, if *our* power is sacred—because it protects and advances all the values we hold dear—then a threat to that power is a deadly threat. In this sense, all wars are "holy wars": as Becker has said, both as "a testing of divine favor, *and* as a means of purging evil from the world at the same time."[31]

Over and over we find that when violence is accepted or approved, the most frequent claims are that violence is a necessary means for rectifying injustice[32] or that it is an inevitable reaction to intolerable conditions.[33] To justify violent attacks upon government, it is always claimed that the government is corrupt, oppressive, traitorous, immoral;[34] against illegitimate authority, the justifying ideology holds, violence becomes legitimate.

A recently prominent special set of justifications for violence intended to produce social change might be called "violence as redemption." The basic contention is that violence

[31]Becker, p. 115.
[32]"The spread of a tendency to justify violence for the achievement of what is regarded as justice is a fact; witness the triumph in the United Nations of the view that the legitimacy of force depends not upon its defensive function but upon the multilaterally determined worthiness of the cause it is alleged to promote" (Claude, p. 571).
[33]Grimshaw, p. 433.
[34]Ibid., p. 523.

is necessary to liberate and restore the autonomous personality of persons who have been oppressed by illegitimate power. Violence becomes more than acts that are instrumentally effective in gaining political power; acts of violence represent "man recreating himself"—they restore the lost human dignity of the oppressed.[35] At the extremes, revolution becomes a vast exercise in emotional therapy—a collective expression of frustration, deprivation, grief, and rage. Terrorism may be said to be a necessary outlet for political frustration. In response to such a justification, a psychiatrist has said:

> Where the murder of civilians was first justified in the name of higher moral purposes (national liberation), then for political effect (world-wide publicity), it is now simply a psychological necessity.
> "The descent down this ladder of moral discourse is as chilling as it is subtle."[36]

Violence used by the state against those who challenge its rules and its power from within finds its ultimate reach in genocide—the systematic killing of whole peoples within a nation. In this century,

> genocide is a fundamental mechanism for the unification of the national state. That is why it is so widely practiced in "advanced" and "civilized" areas, and why it is so incredibly difficult to eradicate.[37]

JUSTIFYING AND LEGITIMATING VIOLENCE: THE AMERICAN CASE

We have seen that violence may be rendered socially tolerable, acceptable, or praiseworthy by an impressive array

---

[35]Frantz Fanon, *The Wretched of the Earth*, trans. Constance Farrington (New York: Grove Press, 1966).
[36]Charles Krauthammer, "When murder serves as terrorists' therapy." Letter, *New York Times*, April 15, 1979, p. 16-E.
[37]Horowitz, p. 73.

of transforming procedures. The following are the main types of social definitions that thus domesticate violence.

1. *Neutralization* by definition and classification: essentially violence is rendered permissible by defining it as "not violence."
2. *Justifiable* violence: the behavior in question is acknowledged to be violent and implicitly undesirable, but it is excusable either because of special extenuating circumstances of knowledge, ability, mental or emotional condition, or other constraining factors, or by reason of higher values ("acceptable reasons").
3. *Rightful* violence as a legitimate means to attain goals or to protect values: violence as a socially validated claim or prerogative.
4. *Obligatory or dutiful* violence: violence is positively valued as a means to destroy evil, to express or develop virtues, to demonstrate values.

These generic definitions and evaluations are widely found across time, space, and cultures. What are the particular forms and prevalences in the United States?

First, there are strong traditions of approval of violence. Violence within the family is widely approved in the form of physical punishment (spare the rod and spoil the child).[38] Vigilante justice has been frequent. The death penalty is tenaciously advocated. The mass media devote enormous attention to violence, often in glorified forms. Violence is frequently regarded as necessary and justified in the interests of *retributive justice* and of *self-defense*. Blumenthal found that attitudes of approval for the use of violence as a means of social control were closely correlated with approval of retributive justice and violence used in self-defense; rejection of

---

[38]See Robert L. Sadoff, ed., *Violence and Responsibility: Individual, Family, and Social Aspects* (New York: Halsted Press/Wiley-Interscience, 1978); also Steinmetz and Straus: On the legitimation of "normal violence" within the family, see Gelles, pp. 59–61, 114, 166.

violence as a means of social control, on the other hand, was less closely related to attitudes of "humanism" or "kindness" or of ranking rights of persons over property rights.[39]

Second, there is enormous support for violence as a means of social control by established authority, but much less approval of violence as a means for bringing about social change. Blumenthal refers to justifying and exculpatory beliefs as "rationalizations" that enable people to hold positive attitudes toward violence.

> Among other things, they include the need to defend oneself, the tendency to exact retribution, the predilection to believe one's friends can do no wrong and one's enemies deserve no quarter.[40]

But a primary justification is *social control*. In general, approval of violence for social control goes along with approval of the values of self-defense, retributive justice, material rather than humanistic considerations, and rating of property over persons.

In *Ingraham* v. *Wright*, the Supreme Court on April 19, 1977 held that corporal punishment of children as a disciplinary means in the schools is not cruel and unusual punishment under the meaning of the Eighth Amendment. The protection of the amendment, therefore, does not extend to children who may be thus disciplined in the school. Corporal punishment remains a normatively supported means of enforcing rules and requirements of educational authorities.[41]

The legitimacy of states and governments means that those who govern successfully claim the *right* to govern;[42]

---

[39]Blumenthal, pp. 1296–1303.

[40]Monica D. Blumenthal *et al. Justifying Violence: Attitudes of American Men* (Ann Arbor, Mich.: Institute for Social Research, University of Michigan, 1972), p. vi.

[41]Irwin A. Hyman and James H. Wise, eds., *Corporal Punishment in American Education: Readings in History, Practice, and Alternatives* (Philadelphia: Temple University Press, 1979).

[42]Dolf Sternberger, "Legitimacy," *International Encyclopedia of the Social Sciences*, 9th ed., ed. David L. Sills (New York: Crowell Collier and Macmillan, 1968), p. 244.

ultimately this right means the use of coercion, thus of force and violence.

Violence used for social control by political authorities is strongly supported in the United States—for example, ". . . it is widely held that knowledge of the state's right to use violence is an important restraint on criminal behavior."[43] Most of the collective violence in American history has not been directed against the state but has been used by politically conservative or reactionary groupings against the disadvantaged elements of the polity.[44] Most of the deaths that occurred in the urban civil disorders of the 1960s resulted from the use of force by the police and the National Guard; so indiscriminate was such official violence that many bystanders were killed, some in their own homes.[45] A national survey of 1,374 adult males in 1969 showed that about one-half said that shooting by police was "almost always" or "sometimes" a good way to handle campus disturbances—and 19 percent said that the police should shoot to kill student protesters.[46] In the same survey, 30 percent approved of police shooting to kill in handling ghetto riots.

Third, so strong is the emphasis on authority and social control that acts of dissent and nonconformity tend to be thought of as "violent" whereas violence by police against challengers (student protesters, looters, draft-card burners) is often denied as violence. In a national sample, almost identical proportions of American men defined as violent "draft-card burning" (58 percent) and "police beating students" (56 percent)—and 35 percent were not willing to call violent the act of "police shooting looters."[47]

Fourth, violence typically is not accepted as a means necessary to bring about desirable social changes. Again, the analysis by Blumenthal et al. showed that among white males,

[43]Blumenthal et al., p. 7.
[44]Hofstadter and Wallace, p. 9.
[45]Blumenthal et al., p. 3.
[46]Blumenthal, p. 1297.
[47]Ibid., p. 1301.

although 90 percent agreed that some changes are necessary, less than 10 percent said that protests involving property damage and deaths are necessary to produce the desirable changes.

CONCLUSION

Our discussion has been deliberately austere—no doubt pedestrian—in the interest of concise presentation. We have said little about either the psychological or the ethical complexities that are treated by other contributors to this volume.

Some of the sociopsychological processes, however, lie near the surface of the empirical materials. Thus we have seen how omnipresent is the giving of "moral reasons" for, especially, collective violence. Nothing seems easier than to develop the conviction that those who oppose our purposes and who block the satisfaction of our desires are immoral. The most deadly "guided missiles" in everyday life are the aggressive acts that are powered by the secret alliance of superego and id. Violence is *one* way to seek mastery over "evil." But the evil of others often lies in the eye of the beholder, and much of it actually lies in oneself. This uncomfortable, often intolerable situation frequently can be resolved by the familiar processes of repression and projection. Given at the same time genuine and important differences in values and beliefs, what was initially a practical opposition over limited issues easily grows in to a struggle of Good and Evil.[48]

The miracle of organized society is not that there is so much impulsive or spontaneous interpersonal violence but that there is so little. And the tragedy of organized societies is that the enforcement of norms and the maintenance of power leads so regularly to virtuous and obedient violence.

Ernest Becker[49] has shown how those who threaten our "immortality"—our sense of infinite duration, power,

[48]Cf. Becker.
[49]Ibid.

value—can be regarded as infinitely dangerous. A system of culture—of beliefs, values, symbols, rituals—is the guarantor and source of our immortality; hence culture is sacred. Those who threaten our culture, therefore, threaten our omnipotence, our immortality, by threatening its sacred sources. Hence those who oppose our culture are both infinitely dangerous and evil—and the more successful their attack, the more evil they are. Against utter evil, desperate measures must be taken. To destroy the evil, violence may be essential.

As Camus has said, all absolute virtue is homicidal. Absolute virtue in the sense of closed and total commitment to a local and transitory ideology? Perhaps, but unless human beings can defend their fragile selves against the absolute terrors of existence by positive means—in the world of love, work, and play—they will inevitably take up arms against the sea of troubles that all of us must encounter. The constructive mastery of finitude is a necessary part of our mastery over violence. Individual insight and effort alone are not sufficient, and the restriction and resolution of violent conflicts requires a sophistication of social processes to match the complexities on which we have here only touched in passing.

PART II THREE CASE STUDIES

CHAPTER 3

How Not to Study Violence

TABITHA M. POWLEDGE

This is a tale of three plans for studying violence and what happened to them. It is a complicated and dispiriting story, with few villains and no heroes, lacking happy endings (or even any endings at all) and full of lessons troubled and troubling. It may be useful to think of it as three morality plays, but because they are contemporary morality plays, the right and wrong of things in them is often unclear.

Except where noted, the material in this chapter is drawn from three unpublished documents, long chronologies of the events in each of the three case studies under examination in this volume. Working under a grant from the National Science Foundation, I assembled those chronologies in 1977

TABITHA M. POWLEDGE ● Center for Science and Technology Policy, New York, New York 10006.

Like any true stories of the seventies—and these are inescapably stories of the seventies—these began in the sixties, possibly as early as December 11, 1961, when two Army helicopter companies arrived in Saigon, but certainly no later than November 22, 1963. The United States became—it seemed almost overnight—a country torn by violence, at home and abroad. Some of it was political, some criminal, and the distinction was often ignored. Being occupied by violence, the country was also preoccupied by it. Explaining it became a national obsession; perhaps there was hope it could be explained away. Economically, times were felicitous. A president had promised guns and butter. It now seems by hindsight that we took some of the money for guns and tried to buy not butter but salve. If we studied violence, perhaps we would discover its causes and—we seemed really to believe this—its cures.

---

and 1978, drawing mostly on an immense amount of primary source material (memorandums, reports, letters, broadsides, and long tape-recorded interviews with many of the principals) and also some secondary accounts (chiefly contemporary newspaper and magazine articles). All of the original documentary and recorded materials (and the chronologies compiled from them) are stored in the archives at The Hastings Center, which initiated the study, sought and received NSF funds for it, and whose employee I then was. On those few occasions when material in this account comes from elsewhere, the source will be footnoted. I have spoken of the immense amount of source material; it would not have been available to me had many of the disputants, on both sides, not given me complete and open access to their files and scrapbooks, often supplemented at length by interviews and subsequent correspondence. In addition to being time-consuming, for many of them the process of recollection was painful and difficult, and I am more grateful than I can say. Nor—with one exception—were any restrictions put on my investigations. The exception was Harvard Medical School, which gave me access to files on the deliberations of some of its internal committees assessing the XYY research project on condition that I not quote them directly, unless I could obtain them from another source.

THE PROJECTS

The Center at UCLA

Or so Louis J. West thought when he was developing plans for the administrative entity first known as the Center for Prevention of Violence, later given the somewhat less ambitious name of Center for the Study and Reduction of Violence. The immediate impetus, however, was the brutal on-campus rape and murder of a student at the University of California at Los Angeles, where West was director of the Neuropsychiatric Institute (NPI). He concluded that "there should be an organized major research program to deal with all these related issues at a great university, that UCLA was the place, and that the time was as soon as we could engineer it."

The other impetus came from the State of California itself, in the person of James M. Stubblebine, state director of health and former director of mental hygiene who, in conversations with his wife in early 1972, became convinced that it would be desirable for California to do research into how to prevent violence. In the spring of 1972 he explored the possibilities with a number of institutions, but came away from a meeting with a group of UCLA people impressed with their potential for doing this sort of work. West remembers a meeting in August 1972, to discuss the future of a state hospital for mentally disturbed offenders, at which the idea that the university should study individual violence came up. Said West some years later:

> To my surprise, Stubblebine perked up at the idea that there should be research. Furthermore, the other people in the group were very supportive of this proposal, which had been prepared in a rough way prior to the meeting. And Stubblebine asked whether we at UCLA would be willing to organize a research enterprise along this line, if the State could provide funds for it. I told him that this was exactly what we were trying to do. . . .

At the time, the availability of funds for this kind of work
from the National Institute of Mental Health and other sources
was zilch. The Nixon administration had been very heavy-
handed with psychiatry in general, and with this kind of thing
in particular. . . . There was nothing available for child abuse
then; there was nothing available for rape. It seems like only
yesterday, and now there's lots of money for these things, but
at that time it was virtually impossible to get any research funds
for these things. . . . So this possibility from the State was very
welcome. . . . At that time, NPI belonged to the Department
of Mental Hygiene of the State . . . so I was getting most of my
budget from Stubblebine anyway. In the past I had also gotten
research funds from that agency, except that latterly they had
also been cutting down research funds. Governor Reagan was
not a big supporter for mental health research, any more than
President Nixon was. But I pointed out to Stubblebine that
Reagan had gotten a lot of political mileage out of the rising tide
of violence within the State, and here was a chance for him to
put his money where his mouth was, so to speak, and to start
something.[1]

A fourteen-page document entitled Center for Prevention
of Violence and dated September 1, 1972 appears to have
functioned as a preliminary-draft grant proposal and was one
of the major sources of the ensuing controversy, even many
months and years after it had been replaced by other versions.
It says the project's goal is "the reduction of violence" and
states five objectives: to understand the cause of all pathologically violent behaviors; to develop techniques for prevention,
intervention, "postvention," and treatment and rehabilitation
of the violent; to educate mental health and law enforcement
professionals about both symptoms of potential violence and
its prevention; to develop methods of deflecting aggressive
impulses into other forms of expression; and to disseminate
public information to aid "the community to cope more effectively with violent and violence-prone people." The document described four major areas in which the center would

[1]Author's interview with Louis J. West, M.D., director of the Neuropsychiatric Institute of the University of California, Los Angeles. Interview
conducted December 1977.

conduct research (epidemiological, biological, psychological, and animal models). It also discussed in a vague and general way the possibility of remote monitoring of subjects by electrode implantation in their brains. Among names on a list of possible researchers to be associated with the center was that of Frank R. Ervin, newly hired as a professor of psychiatry at UCLA and coauthor, with Vernon Mark, of the controversial book *Violence and the Brain*, seen by many critics as the central apologia for psychosurgery.

Establishment of the center was proposed in Governor Ronald Reagan's State of the State message in early January 1973, but got little public attention until Earl W. Brian, Jr., the state's secretary for health and welfare, formally announced it on January 13. The center was described as part of a Reagan package for reform of California's mental institutions, correctional system, and health care delivery system. According to a brief article in the *San Francisco Chronicle*, Brian said more than a million dollars would be invested in the center in fiscal 1973–1974, and that the center should be discovering the causes and cures for violent crime by mid-1975. He also said that it was a possibility that prison inmates might be used as volunteer research subjects "in such a center to solve the mysteries which trigger such violence as hijackings and the recent New Orleans mass slaying."

According to West,

> that was when the trouble began. . . . I was ingenuous in this regard. I felt triumphant that I had, in the face of the known practices, policies, and attitudes of the Nixon and Reagan administrations, succeeded in getting funds.[2]

At about this time Isidore Ziferstein, associate clinical professor of psychiatry at UCLA, got a call from one of the members of the Committee Opposing Psychiatric Abuse of Prisoners (COPAP), an informal intraprofessional group in Northern California, alerting him to plans for the center. When he got a look at the September 1 document, he says,

[2]Interview with Dr. West.

"I almost fainted." He objected to the scientific design, which he characterized as "very poorly conceptualized," to the brevity of the document, and to the discussion of violence and the brain and electrode implantation. Ziferstein has remained one of the most outspoken of the center's opponents throughout the public controversy and to the present day.

Not knowing that controversy was about to erupt, on January 22 West wrote to Stubblebine a letter headed CONFIDENTIAL, a letter that became so central in the dispute that it will be quoted in full.

> I am in possession of confidential information to the effect that the Army is prepared to turn over Nike missile bases to State and local agencies for non-military purposes. They may look with special favor on health-related applications.
>
> Such a Nike missile base is located in the Santa Monica Mountains, within a half-hour's drive of the Neuropsychiatric Institute. It is accessible but relatively remote. The site is securely fenced, and includes various buildings and improvements making it suitable for prompt occupancy.
>
> If this site were made available to the Neuropsychiatric Institute as a research facility, perhaps initially as an adjunct to the new Center for Prevention of Violence, we could put it to very good use. Comparative studies could be carried out there, in an isolated but convenient location, of experimental or model programs for the alteration of undesirable behavior.
>
> Such programs might include control of drug or alcohol abuse, modification of chronic antisocial or impulsive aggressiveness, etc. The site could also accommodate conferences or retreats for instruction of selected groups of mental health–related professionals and of others (e.g., law enforcement personnel, parole officers, special educators) for whom both demonstration and participation would be effective modes of instruction.
>
> My understanding is that such a direct request by the Governor, or another appropriate officer of the State, to the Secretary of Defense (or, of course, the President) would be most likely to produce prompt results. Needless to say, I stand available to participate in any way that might be helpful.[3]

---

[3]Correspondence dated January 22, 1973 from Dr. West to California's director of health, James M. Stubblebine. A copy of the letter is on file at the Hastings Center.

Stubblebine, however, recognized the potential explosiveness of such a site. In his reply, he argued that the base should not be part of the proposed center because the subject was

> so delicate, so sensitive that everything about it must be available for public scrutiny and participation as well as the highest order of respectability.
>
> To be doing something at some secret base in the mountains would by some people be interpreted negatively and create potential opposition that we don't need.[4]

In February West sounded out John Seeley, a sociologist at the University of California, Berkeley, about joining the project. West knew Seeley had an intrinsic interest in the subject through the sociologist's work on alcoholism, but he also knew that Seeley had a very strong interest in ethical aspects of research and was hopeful Seeley would keep an eye on such matters in the center project.

The UCLA student newspaper, the *Daily Bruin*, reported February 16 on a meeting between members of Students for a Democratic Society and people from the NPI, held in response to an SDS leaflet distributed on campus claiming that Dr. Ervin[5] had been given a grant of more than $100,000 by the Justice Department to "develop psychosurgical techniques to control undesirable behavior in individuals who are believed to have damaged brains." At that meeting West denied that Dr. Ervin had received such a grant, and in a February 27 letter to the *Bruin* denied that Dr. Ervin was involved in any of the projected studies at the Violence Center.

> Furthermore, psychosurgery has never once been considered as part of this program . . . the only procedure currently being contemplated by the UCLA violence research group on an experimental basis for prison inmates is transcendental meditation.

---

[4]A copy of this letter is on file at the Hastings Center.
[5]The honorific "Dr." will be awarded Frank Ervin throughout this narrative in order to distinguish him from another major actor with the same surname, the North Carolina Democratic Senator Sam Ervin. No relation.

On Valentine's Day, Edward M. Opton of COPAP wrote
to Charles Young, chancellor of UCLA, opposing establishment of the center, partly on grounds of Dr. Ervin's participation. The letter argued that the project was of doubtful
merit and politically explosive. Opton continued,

> at a bare minimum there ought to be public debate and some
> input from concerned and knowledgeable groups to counter-
> balance those who advocate behavioral-medical programs
> which—however inadvertently—could inhibit crucial freedoms
> we now enjoy.

The letter also asked for a meeting on the center.

SDS was mistaken about Dr. Ervin's involvement in the
center, or perhaps they were instrumental in preventing it.
The brief mention in the September 1 document was the clos-
est he came. That can be explained as a grant-proposal writer's
urge to sprinkle requests with well-known names, thus en-
hancing their chances of acceptance, an extremely common
practice. In an interview with the *Los Angeles Herald Examiner*
some months later, Dr. Ervin said he, newly arrived at UCLA,
was asked by someone on the center's staff if he would be
interested in some of the proposed projects; he replied that
he would, and gave permission for his name to be used in
the proposal. Dr. Ervin's connection with the center appears
in retrospect never to have gone beyond that, though it is of
course impossible to know whether he would have become
more involved had the center ever really come into existence.
According to Opton, deletion of Dr. Ervin's name in subsequent proposals did not mollify the center's opponents but
instead made them believe the proponents were devious.

SDS was not, however, mistaken about the center's
source of funds; they were to come largely from the Law
Enforcement Assistance Administration (LEAA), an arm of
the Justice Department. The LEAA had been created in 1968
as a way of distributing federal money to local law enforcement agencies. (By the time the Carter administration and the
Congress were contemplating disbanding the agency in the
budget-cutting fervor of the spring of 1980, the LEAA had

disbursed more than $7 billion on projects ranging from police hardware to computerization of cases in the criminal justice system. Its history was always checkered and controversial, but its imminent demise prompted the *New York Times* to editorialize [on April 15, 1980], "More realism at the outset about what the agency could accomplish might have produced a sounder program then and better appreciation of its genuine achievements now.") The LEAA's involvement, however, triggered the intense interest of the other Ervin, the Democratic senator from North Carolina, the powerful Bill-of-Rights-minded chairman of the Committee on the Judiciary, Subcommittee on Constitutional Rights. On March 22 Sam Ervin wrote to the LEAA administrator asking for clarification of the use of LEAA funds for research into violent behavior. He wanted to know whether the agency had copies of the California proposal and whether any of the work on the project was to be performed by Dr. Ervin; he also asked for copies of any guidelines the LEAA had covering its research projects involving human subjects.

The following day the NPI issued a press release about its intention to establish the center, denying that any surgical procedures were contemplated, and giving assurances that ethical concerns would be paid special attention, partly because UCLA already had in place review procedures for work with human subjects. A story based on that release appeared in the *Los Angeles Times* the next day, March 24. It was in this story that West was quoted as saying he first got the idea for the center after the assassination of John Kennedy in 1963.

Seeley formally joined the staff about then, though he had been conferring with West by telephone about the developing political difficulties for several weeks. In the ensuing months he functioned as an in-house critic of the proposed research projects and participated in development of several drafts of the grant proposal.

On April Fool's Day, an article in the *San Francisco Examiner* described the controversy over the center and quoted Stubblebine as conceding that there might be some psychosurgery there, though on a "selected basis" for "curative reasons" only. Stubblebine also said a system of safeguards would be set up to ensure the rights of inmates and all other research subjects.

On that same day the grant proposal was officially submitted to the California Council on Criminal Justice (CCCJ), the state-level distribution point for LEAA money, under the federal omnibus Crime Control and Safe Streets Act of 1968. The formal applicant was the State of California Health and Welfare Agency; West was listed as project director, and the application was signed by Brian. The total amount requested was $1 million, of which three-fourths was to come from the federal government through the LEAA. The proposal described the projected organization of the center, which was to include a task force on Law Enforcement, Law and Ethics to develop guidelines for the ethical use of predictors of violent behavior in the event such reliable predictors were indeed developed by research at the center. It also described six broad research projects: a survey of violence in California; a study of the determinants of violence; a study of the biological aspects of violence; prevention and treatment models of violence against children; development of prevention models for serious sex offenders; and development of prevention models for violence in the schools.

Shortly thereafter, COPAP stepped up its anticenter campaign by issuing a "memorandum on the Center for the Study of Violent Behavior." It charged "This Center is, in short, a laboratory for the Department of Corrections and law enforcement officials with the diaphanous veneer of UCLA used to make it appear to be a respectable university research facility." The memo described and listed the group's objections to several drafts of the proposal for the establishment of the center.

On April 11 the Committee on Health and Welfare of the California state senate held the first public hearing on the center. The senators urged the center's leaders to conduct their research openly every step of the way and to set up a public group of overseers to guide the research and forestall any more suspicions. At these hearings West repeated his denial that any psychosurgery was planned, but Stubblebine again contradicted him slightly by saying, "We should not deny the benefits of medical science to those who need treatment." The center's projected total first-year budget was said to be $1.5 million, half to come from the state's proposed budget for health and welfare.

But opposition to the center was developing in the state assembly, in the office of the chairman of the Ways and Means Committee, Willie Brown. That opposition was led by Steve Thompson, a health and welfare consultant to the committee, who was concerned about development of the center because of a previous encounter with West, in which he believed West had argued for reproductive restrictions on the mentally ill. In interviews in 1977, Brown and Thompson both said they never opposed the idea of research on violence *per se*, but only what they felt to be lack of safeguards in this particular proposal and its location at UCLA. Said Brown,

> If it had been at Langley-Porter [the neuropsychiatric institute at the University of California, San Francisco], with the proper controls, we probably would not have even opened our mouths. . . . We were not opposed to the basic idea. . . . It would be ludicrous for us to oppose research on violence and the causes thereof.

Thompson said he, too, had no objection to the idea of the research, "but that it ought to have more careful people involved. And why couple it with this [Reagan] administration?"

At the end of April, California Attorney General Evelle Younger asked for authorization to establish a special review committee for the project. The review committee was to have representatives from the California Medical Association, the state bar, the LEAA, a mental health organization, and others. The report was to be made public, public hearings were to be held, and the CCCJ was to make a decision about funding on the basis of that information. The *Los Angeles Herald Examiner* interview with Dr. Ervin, in which he denied active involvement with the center, appeared a couple of days later.

In May opponents of the center were very active. At the American Psychiatric Association meeting in Honolulu, for instance, four doctors, among them Ziferstein, handed out a broadside arguing that the main problem with such a center was that violence as a social phenomenon was deemphasized, whereas the biology or psychology of certain individuals was highlighted. The flier also expressed concern that neurosurgery would indeed be used, and that prisoners and patients in mental hospitals would serve as subjects for such surgery. The whole project was seen as increasing the danger that psychiatrists would be used as agents of social control. Ziferstein later said he handed out between 10,000 and 20,000 fliers of this sort at professional meetings over the next few months.

Representatives of COPAP held a press conference opposing establishment of the center and arguing that psychosurgery was indeed planned there. A spokesman for Stubblebine replied that he "now declares 'flatly, unequivocally and totally' that the project's researchers will neither sponsor, support nor undertake any psychosurgery."

The following day the state senate Health and Welfare Committee held another public hearing and took testimony from several opponents of the center, including Fred Hiestand, an attorney with Public Advocates, Inc., a law firm representing the NAACP, the Black Panthers, NOW, the Mexican-American Political Association, and the California Prisoners Union. The chairman of the senate committee, Anthony Beilenson, expressed concern about plans to finance the center, and asked "whether the Center might simply be a way to continue and expand experimental programs already under way for which federal funds are now lacking."

On May 10 LEAA administrator Donald E. Santarelli replied to Senator Ervin's March 22 letter, enclosing a copy of the grant application for the center and saying that the proposal had not yet been reviewed by the LEAA.

A couple of weeks after the hearing six members of the state senate Committee on Health and Welfare wrote the executive director of the CCCJ, saying they believed many ques-

tions needed to be resolved before any public money was
approved for the center. The letter expressed worry over a
number of points: whether the center would be independent
of state control, vagueness of the project proposals, adequacy
of safeguards for experimental subjects, whether funds would
be diverted from other areas of the Health Department
budget, and lack of peer review. It concluded, "We believe
that approval of the proposed Center by the California Council on Criminal Justice would be ill-advised at this time."

But the center's proponents were not idle either. Toward
the end of May a press briefing on the center was held at
UCLA. Among the handouts were a four-page fact sheet on
the center, issued by the state Department of Health Office of
Communications, which denied that surgery of any kind
would be used. West gave an interview in which he expressed
his worry at the opposition of the state senate committee and
offered assurances that several scientific review groups would
be supervising the center's work, including a national scientific advisory committee. West also wrote to Beilenson in
defense of the center, pointing out that on July 1st the NPI
was to be transferred from the state to UCLA (an administrative transfer that had been in preparation for some time,
and that had no particular connection with the center). Therefore, he argued, "all control of the Center and its various
projects will be exercised only by the University." He continued to offer assurances of procedural safeguards, some of
which he described, and also discussed funding questions.

But in mid-June John Gardiner, the director of research
operations for the LEAA, wrote to the CCCJ expressing serious reservations about the proposal to establish the center.
The letter was critical of the planned staff, expressing surprise

> that no specialists of national stature are involved. For the few
> people on the project staff assigned research roles there is little
> evidence of established research ability of the kind or level nec-
> essary for a study of this scope.

As for the research content of the proposal, Gardiner argued
that no hypotheses or methodologies were presented, and

noted dryly that "the bibliography contained in the proposal is a mixture of items which suggest that the staff may not be totally familiar with the state of the art in this area." His letter also said that past experience led him to believe that the creation of research centers "spanning a wide scientific area may be the least cost-effective structure over the long run."[6] In addition, the formal proposal was ambiguous about the intent to perform psychosurgery; Gardiner suggested that the CCCJ expressly forbid it. He also indicated dissatisfaction with the specified outside review and evaluation procedures.

Also by then, in a *Los Angeles Times* interview headlined "Watergate Dims Hope for Center on Violence," West was expressing gloom over the future of the center. The Watergate revelations, he was quoted as saying, had resulted in suspicion of the center's motives. Still, on June 25, the NPI issued a program plan for the coming year that included a précis of the projected work of the center and several attachments, including an endorsement of the project by the medical director of the American Psychological Association, a copy of UCLA policy on protection of human subjects, a protocol for submission to human-use review committees, and a description of the organizational structure and projected research at the center.

But at the end of June, the state legislature wrote into the preamble to the governor's budget a specific prohibition against the use of any funds for the center (from the state or from other sources) without prior approval of the legislature. According to Steve Thompson that action effectively killed the center project, although he said that if the university had wanted to pursue it, it probably could have. "It was not really the legislature that scotched it. The proposal was withdrawn somehow; it kind of just died."

Over the summer, the Northern California Psychiatric

[6]Correspondence dated June 12, 1973 from John Gardiner, director of the Research Operations Division of the LEAA, to Robert Lawson, executive director of the California Council on Criminal Justice. A copy of this letter is on file at the Hastings Center.

Society and the ACLU of Southern California formally protested establishment of the center in letters to the CCCJ. West continued his communication with Beilenson in a letter in which he said the proposal had been endorsed by the Faculty Council of the UCLA School of Medicine, the Psychiatric Advisory Panel of the California State Medical Association, the medical director of the American Psychological Association, and the Los Angeles City Council. As supporters he also cited the chancellor of the university, the dean of the medical school, Anthony Amsterdam of Stanford Law School, and Wendell Lipscomb, a black psychiatrist.

At the end of July the center's proponents achieved a victory of sorts; the CCCJ held a hearing and voted to approve funds for the center. That, of course, was simply the first step; approval was still required by the state legislature and the Justice Department. And the opposition continued, numerous, vocal, and broadly based. Anticenter testimony at the hearing was given by two prisoners' unions, the Black Panthers, the American Friends Service Committee, the Federation of American Scientists, and COPAP, among others.

Sometime that summer—just when is unclear—a meeting between proponents and opponents of the project was held at Huey Newton's apartment in Oakland. (Newton, head of the Black Panthers, was at that point a fugitive.) Accounts of what went on at that meeting differ markedly. Among the opponents gathered there were a number (estimates range from five to thirty-five) of people (variously described either as representatives of concerned groups like the California Prisoners Union, NOW, and the Panthers, or as Newton's hangers-on). Representing the proponents were West, Seeley, and Stubblebine. Opponents raised questions about psychosurgery, involuntary experimentation, and the possible use of shock treatment. They also expressed concern over whether or not the program would study violence among whites as well as blacks.

In interviews several years later, recollections of the outcome of the gathering varied. Stubblebine believes "this meeting absolutely killed this project forever and ever." West, however, says he got a strong impression that Newton was prepared to support the center. So does Seeley, who says he had proposed to Hiestand that one way out of the dilemma might be to write into the budget (in which there was said to be a good deal of room) a substantial amount of money, perhaps $100,000, for opposition groups. That would enable them to have meetings and hire their own publicists and lawyers to voice publicly any disapproval of particular projects the center undertook. Seeley said the proposal was well received at the meeting, and that West was lionized. Seeley quoted Newton as saying, "This West is not nearly as bad as he is made out to be." The proposal to fund the opponents, however, was dropped. Hiestand later recollected that the opposition recommended some procedural safeguards, including an informed-consent procedure and a decision not to pay people for participating in the research. According to Hiestand, West objected but Stubblebine did not.

Throughout the rest of the summer and fall, the controversy appeared to sputter and be on the verge of dying. A task force of the Southern California Psychiatric Association met with several staff members of the NPI at West's home. In September it recommended against the project. In November Brian issued a press release using the recent slaying of nine people in the California town of Victor to argue for establishment of the center and blaming the legislature for blocking the proposal. He was quoted as saying

> I am compelled to make a public plea for quick action by the legislature when they reconvene in January. Sixty-two people have died in barbaric mass slayings; many more have died in individual murders. I implore the leadership of both parties in the legislature to move, and move quickly, on these urgently needed programs.

After the first of the year in 1974, however, the controversy renewed itself when Senator Ervin wrote Santarelli that the information he had received about the center "indicates that programs were being contemplated for the Center that raise profound moral and constitutional questions, and it would be extremely desirable for LEAA to conduct a comprehensive review and evaluation. . . ." The letter continued:

> The use of human subjects in biomedical and behavioral research raises several fundamental constitutional and ethical questions, and I believe LEAA must develop guidelines adequate to protect fully the constitutional rights of the subjects of LEAA-funded research in these areas. Of particular concern is a lack of needed supervision of biomedical and behavioral research projects that receive funds directly from LEAA through the block grant system.

The letter went on to ask a great many detailed questions about the LEAA's guidelines and its review procedures, some of them aimed at the UCLA Violence Center but many of them about the agency's funding of violence research in general. It averred that such research programs

> raise important questions which must be resolved by both LEAA and Congress. There is a serious issue of whether the federal government should be in a position of financing programs posing such extraordinary challenges to human freedom and dignity at all. Certainly LEAA ought to conduct a most searching inquiry before committing its funds to such a project, whether by discretionary or block grant. If, after such inquiry, LEAA were to support such projects, it ought first to develop stringent and exacting requirements for the control and maintaining of these experiments. As you are aware, HEW and the Congress are now subjecting the question of federal financing of human behavioral research to close scrutiny. A series of guidelines on the ethical and administrative standards have been developed, both in legislation and in regulations. I believe that LEAA ought to consider a moratorium on the further use of its funds for these purposes until it develops guidelines at least as comprehensive as those now under consideration by Congress and HEW. These guidelines should provide for specific approval by a special committee on research and ethics within LEAA and the Administrator's Office of any project, whether funded by block or discretionary grant, in the field of human behavioral research. These projects also should be subject to both institutional control and

review and to prior approval by local, ethical committees as well.[7]

At the end of January West disclosed in an interview in the *Daily Bruin* that the center would no longer be conceived of as an independent administrative unit, but rather as part of UCLA's Laboratory for the Study of Life-Threatening Behavior, already in existence. The interview quotes West as saying that the establishment of a new center is not the best approach for two reasons. One was that it is administratively complex and time-consuming. The second was that

> it suggests building something new and different, involving activities unlike anything gone on before. This is not the case. The Center was mainly a device to get funding for faculty already working in these areas who were not able to develop their work for lack of funds.

The interview also quotes West as saying,

> The LEAA will give $50 million this year, and most of it will go to the police . . . some of that money can be used for research if it can be connected with "prevention of crime." We stretched that point and said acts of violence by mentally, emotionally unstable people qualify. . . . It is a better use of the money to study certain kinds of violent behavior in a medical setting than to buy computers or weapons for the police.[8]

In February the student government at UCLA decided to hold a referendum on the Violence Center, although Chancellor Young said the referendum would have no effect on his decision about whether or not to ask for funds for the center. "I would pay no attention to what the referendum says student attitudes on the Violence Center are," he said. The referendum was "based on obviously very bad information."

[7]Correspondence dated January 13, 1974 from Senator Sam Ervin to LEAA Administrator Donald E. Santarelli. A copy of this letter is on file at the Hastings Center.
[8]"Plans for Acquiring Missile Base by Violence Center Fail", *Daily Bruin*, January 25, 1974.

About 4,500 students voted in the referendum, twice as many as had voted in the preceding year's regular student government election. The vote was roughly 60 percent against the center.

But two weeks before the referendum, on Valentine's Day, the LEAA had announced a ban on the use of LEAA funds for psychosurgery, medical research, behavior modification, and chemotherapy. The following day, the *Washington Star News* reported on the announcement and its probable effect on the center proposal, which was said to call "for the experiment to be carried out at an abandoned Nike missile site in the hills near Los Angeles with $750,000 to be supplied by the State and $750,000 by LEAA." The far more accurate story in the *Los Angeles Times* also reported that the fund cutoff appeared to terminate plans for the center. It quoted from Senator Ervin's January letter to Santarelli, and also quoted a California LEAA spokesman as saying that the directive sounded as if it would kill the idea for the center.

In the *Congressional Record* for February 19, Senator Ervin took credit for the February 14 announcement about restrictions on LEAA funds, saying that

> until strict and comprehensive mechanisms guaranteeing informed consent and the individual privacy, self-determination, and dignity of human subjects of experimentation have replaced the Federal Government's present slipshod methods of funding such projects, such experimentation should be halted. The announcement by LEAA was especially gratifying to me because it came 4 weeks after I sent a detailed 6-page inquiry to LEAA expressing my concern that LEAA's review structure was woefully inadequate. . . . I further expressed my view that "LEAA ought to consider a moratorium on the further use of its funds for these purposes until it develops guidelines at least as comprehensive as those under consideration by Congress and HEW." I am pleased LEAA has accepted my suggestion. . . . It is high time we found out about how many and what kinds of biomedical and behavioral research projects involving human subjects are now being conducted under Federal auspices and just what review procedures and protections for

rights are provided. LEAA found the answers to such questions sufficiently difficult, or perhaps embarrassing, so that it terminated its involvement in such research altogether.[9]

In a February 16 broadside issued by the National Caucus of Labor Committees, West was "officially indicted" by an "Operation Nuremberg" committee in San Francisco for "crimes against humanity." The broadside charged West with being "a long-time CIA operative,"[10] repeated the Nike missile site accusation, and said he would use brainwashing techniques on prisoners, particularly those from Vacaville.

A February 20 *New York Times* article credited the Children's Defense Fund with successful coordination of the efforts to stop development of the center. David Bazelon, chief judge of the New York Court of Appeals (who had been listed as one of the center's advisors) and Diane Bauer, a former newspaper reporter then on the Children's Defense Fund staff, had journeyed to California several months before to investigate the controversy and conduct interviews with many of those involved. According to Seeley, and Opton concurs, Bauer was chiefly responsible for carrying back to Washington and putting into shape the material that eventually influenced Senator Ervin enough so that the whole project was brought down.

The controversy continued to dwindle, though it occasionally experienced a brief flare-up. The anticenter student referendum took place at February's end. In mid-March, the *San Francisco Chronicle* carried an advertisement headed "A

[9]*Congressional Record*, February 19, 1974, p. S1803.
[10]According to the *New York Times* of Aug. 2, 1977, West had studied LSD in the 1950s with money from the Geschikter Fund for Medical Research, a foundation that served as a channel for CIA research funds. According to the *Times* article, West knew of the CIA connection. It is not clear whether the Operation Nuremberg Committee actually knew about this work as early as 1974, whether its allegation, which was not specific, was based on other information, or whether it was simply name calling.

Statement Against Racism," signed by many academics and condemning the center.

Shortly after 9:00 A.M. on April 11, about a dozen people entered the NPI and barricaded themselves inside West's office. Police removed the demonstrators and three of them—all UCLA students—were arrested. On the same date an article by Ziferstein appeared in the *Los Angeles Times,* as a commentary on a feature story on the center controversy that the *Times* had printed March 21. In the article, Ziferstein argued that successive changes in a series of proposals for establishment of the center meant that "a serious credibility gap had developed, and many reputable behavioral scientists concluded that these successive changes in the proposals were in reality 'launderings' in response to criticisms and protests."

On May 1 an article in *Psychiatric News,* official newspaper of the American Psychological Association, described the center controversy and said that West still intended to seek funding. A pamphlet dated this same month and emanating from UCLA described the "Project on Life-Threatening Behavior." It briefly noted some aspects of the controversy over the Violence Center and said that a revised version of the proposal was being prepared for submission to the National Institute of Mental Health. It described some of the research work contemplated, listed the titles of twenty-one such studies along with their principal investigators, and included a "National Advisory Council" listing of a number of well-known names in jurisprudence, biological psychiatry, and violence research. The pamphlet also included a copy of an affidavit dated February 1, 1974, signed by West, that affirmed that the project contemplated no surgical procedures of any kind, no experimentation on prisoners, and "no noxious conditioning procedures or punitive behavior modification," and that no investigations involving human beings would be carried out without review.

Later that month, Chancellor Young defended the idea of the center at a University of California Board of Regents meeting. But the center itself was dead. Interestingly, however, at least some of the projects planned for it survived because West was successful in getting other funding for them. In an interview in 1977 he said,

> We've got $250,000 to do one of the most minor projects in that collection there, the crosscultural study on Qat, which is a drug alleged to cause violent behavior in Yemen. A lot of the work on the hyperkinetic children is going forward with support from other sources.

He also said that work on alcoholism and the training of people to help rape victims was being pursued.

Justice and Behavior Modification

The beginnings of behavior modification programs in the federal prison system can be traced to a midsixties program at the National Training School for Boys (a facility for youthful federal offenders) devised by psychologist Harold Cohen. In the program, called Contingencies Applied to Special Education (CASE), Cohen was trying to accelerate learning in small groups of people who had previously been resistant to learning of any kind. According to John P. Conrad, who was director of research for the Bureau of Prisons (BOP) in the midsixties,

> this program was extremely influential in the Bureau of Prisons. The director at that time felt that this was the most hopeful thing that he had going for him. . . . He was anxious to develop models where expertise in behavior modification, using Cohen's paradigm, would be extended as widely as possible. As a researcher, a person who had to take an empirical point of view about this, I could not see that there was any carry-over value in this at all. A follow-up, which was done on people who had gone through the CASE program at the National Training School for Boys and then who had gone back into the community . . . simply didn't show that any positive results over a long period of time had been achieved. I found that my pointing this out was not exactly what anybody wanted to hear; most people wanted to hear that you really do get good results. . . . What you have to understand at this time was that all of

us, myself included, were hoping that the prison could indeed be transformed into a sort of hospital for the disease of criminality, and that some kind of treatment would be possible for converting people who were law violators into people who were good citizens and non–law violators.

In the late 1960s Conrad, by then chief of the Center for Crime Prevention and Rehabilitation at the LEAA, encouraged Cohen to develop other behavior modification programs for consideration for LEAA funding. The LEAA was genuinely interested at this point in doing research on how to improve corrections, Conrad says, but Cohen was never able to get together a proposal "that made any sense to me or anybody on my staff." During Conrad's first two years at the LEAA (he left in 1969), behavior modification was dormant.

> Finally, a decision was made that it was not the province of the National Institute of Law Enforcement and Criminal Justice [the research arm of LEAA] to do studies having to do with psychological or psychiatric intervention, because we didn't have an adequate staff of psychologists and psychiatrists to be able to evaluate the usefulness of the projects, and that, properly, this kind of research should be reserved for the National Institute of Mental Health. That's where it has been ever since, I think. To the best of my knowledge, LEAA has not engaged in any research of this kind.[11]

(The LEAA had, however, apparently funded other kinds of violence research. In response to a 1972 request by the indefatigable Senator Ervin, the LEAA administrator disclosed in a letter dated October 27 that the agency had made a grant to the Neuro Research Foundation of Boston, headed, among others, by Dr. Ervin. The grant was "an effort to develop a testing procedure to determine the extent of neurological and biological dysfunction in a violent prison population. It was anticipated that the test and survey so developed would yield diagnostic and predictive methods for creating a medical classification of violent people. Such a classification might or would provide a method of measuring the potential

[11]Author's interview with John P. Conrad.

for violence in individuals within the criminal justice system, to the extent that violence might be due to medical or biological causes. Due to administrative problems with the grant, it was terminated prior to completion.")

In the early 1970s, according to Robert Levinson, who came into the BOP central office in 1965 as the BOP's first chief psychologist, the BOP tried to apply some of the Cohen techniques when faced with the problem of what to do with a group of prisoners who were

> assaultive and disruptive. We had a number of these people scattered around in various institutions. We got the idea of setting up a unit to deal specifically with these kinds of people in the early '70s.

This idea eventually generated the Special Treatment and Rehabilitation Training (START) program.

START was a BOP demonstration project for dealing with adult-male offenders in long-term segregation; it began in September 1972 at the Federal Medical Center in Springfield, Missouri. The designers of the project thought of it as a typical behavior modification program that rewarded good behavior rather than punished bad behavior. Its critics and some of its participants thought otherwise. Located in a maximum security building, the program involved several different levels through which an inmate could progress, on the basis of a "good day" system in which he was rated in twelve different areas such as personal hygiene, conduct, politeness, and relations with the staff. Placement into the START program was from any other prison in the federal system and was involuntary. Among selection criteria were "repeated inability to adjust to regular institutional programs," "repeatedly displayed maladaptive behavior," and "has been aggressive, manipulative and resistant to authority." The prisoner must also have been, at the time of transfer, in the sending institution's segregation unit. According to the BOP, a participant could successfully complete the program in eight or nine months.

Another planned use of behavior modification was at the Federal Center for Correctional Research, a BOP project at Butner, North Carolina, which had been on the drawing boards for more than a decade. Originally called the Center for Behavioral Research, Butner was conceived as having two main components: an inpatient psychiatric facility to supplement the one at Springfield, and a research unit that would attempt to evaluate various sorts of rehabilitation programs that might be used with prisoners. Research plans for Butner were largely formulated by psychiatrist Martin Groder, who had achieved some success with a behavior modification program in the federal prison at Marion, Ohio. The research portion of Butner was originally designed to house 200 prisoners drawn from various federal prisons in the eastern United States, all of whom were to be randomly assigned to a number of different experimental rehabilitation programs including group therapy, psychodrama, and yoga.

Toward the end of 1972 Senator Ervin had asked Norman Carlson, director of the BOP, for information about both Project START and Butner. Just after the first of the year, 1973, Tom Wicker's column in the *New York Times* described the plans for Butner. He noted that a large number of people in corrections were not sanguine about prospects for improving prisons, and quoted one critic as worrying that Butner might be aimed at "politically oriented troublemakers" and might constitute an effort to restore tranquility in prisons by isolating such prisoners.

At about the same time the National Prison Project (NPP), a prisoners' rights organization sponsored by the ACLU Foundation, Inc., began to receive mail from prisoners in the START program. According to Matthew L. Myers, an NPP staff attorney, the NPP received letters from between 50 and 80 percent of the people in the START program, complaining about the deprivations they were undergoing and the punitive nature of the program, and containing accusations that they were being shackled to beds. "We received too many letters from prisoners in the START program to ignore," he said.

On February 8 Carlson replied to Senator Ervin's December 21 letter, saying Butner had two purposes: the provision of psychiatric services and the development of "more effective correctional treatment programs." He also said that

> programs will be devised which enable individuals to better cope with the demands of free society. Those program elements which appear to be successful in achieving this objective will be made known to other federal, state, and local correctional institutions.

Enclosed with the letter was a copy of the BOP's policy statement on research.

> We are very much concerned with the rights of individuals who are participants in research projects. Accordingly, we have incorporated into our policy statement standards which emerge from the Nuremberg trials and the statement of the Surgeon General regarding investigations involving human subjects.[12]

On February 19 Arpiar G. Saunders, Jr. and Barbara Milstein, NPP staff attorneys, went to Springfield, interviewed virtually every prisoner in the START program, and talked to several BOP officials responsible for the program at the time. "They came back appalled at what they had seen," Myers said. "They did, in fact, encounter several prisoners who had been shackled to their beds for substantial periods of time, who had not been permitted to go to the toilet or do all those normal sorts of things." The deprivations they encountered, he said, were much more severe than in any other segregation unit in the federal prison system. The NPP decided to act swiftly because, although the program seemed to be different from that of any other segregation unit, it was hard to see why these particular prisoners had been selected. An additional worry was that the program was both involuntary and indefinite. The NPP wrote a lengthy letter of protest to the director at Springfield and began working with the

---

[12]Correspondence dated February 8, 1973 from Norman Carlson, director of the Bureau of Prisons, to Senator Sam Ervin. A copy of this letter is on file at the Hastings Center.

START prisoners to develop litigation. Several of the prisoners had already brought suit, and ultimately the NPP consolidated a number of those cases.

Throughout the late winter and spring Senator Ervin peppered the BOP with letters requesting elaboration and further information.

In one communiqué the BOP denied that it had developed "plans to implement programs which are directed specifically at the treatment of homosexuals"; in another it said:

> Such procedures as psychosurgery, the use of massive dosages of drugs, and other similar approaches will *not* be permitted at the Butner facility. Extreme treatment techniques, such as these, are counter to the policies and procedures of the Bureau of Prisons and are not acceptable in any of our facilities.

By early fall the NPP, the court, and the prisoners agreed on the issues in the START case: the question of procedural due process (should prisoners be allowed to challenge the facts on which placement into START was based?); whether the program interfered with basic First Amendment freedoms; whether it made any difference if the program was experimental (would consent be required, because of the nature of the deprivation?); and whether the program was doing things in the name of treatment that would not be allowed in the name of punishment. The court appointed three of its own experts to evaluate START.

On November 27 Ralph H. Metcalfe, Illinois congressman, asked the General Accounting Office to investigate both the START and the Control Unit Treatment (CTP) programs. His concern was prompted, he said, by several letters from prisoners at the Marion facility, where CTP was in use.

> While I am deeply concerned that the Civil Rights of these inmates be protected, I believe that this can be accomplished through the proper Congressional Committee which has jurisdiction in this area. At the same time, however, I am also concerned about the cost effectiveness of these programs.

The CTP (formerly CARE, the Control and Rehabilitative Effort Program) was set up by the BOP as a long-term segregation unit following an inmate strike at the Marion penitentiary in July 1972. According to policy guidelines issued by the BOP in June 1973, the purpose of the CTPs was to help the inmate change his attitude and behavior so that he could return to a regular institutional program. Transfer was involuntary, from other forms of segregation, and involved prisoners who were believed to pose a serious threat to other inmates or staff. According to the guidelines, the CTP was to include counseling, a progression system through which the inmate could pass, and activities such as work, education, and recreation. According to the BOP, the difference between START and the CTPs was that the CTPs were intended chiefly for dangerous inmates who required close control. CTPs were in operation at Marion, at the young adult facility at Lompoc, California, and in the prison at Milan, Michigan. The time passed in a CTP was supposed to be no longer than a year.

At year's end, the regular meeting of The Hastings Center's Behavior Control Research Group was devoted to the subject of "Behavior Control in Total Institutions," and it focused on prisons. Among those at the meeting were representatives from START and Martin Groder, director-designate of Butner.[13]

Senator Ervin's lengthy letter to Santarelli asking for a moratorium on LEAA funding for behavioral research (quoted extensively in the UCLA Violence Center discussion) was written January 14, 1974. It had been preceded on January 11 by a letter from Lawrence M. Baskir, chief counsel and staff director of the Ervin subcommittee, to Gerald Caplan, director of the National Institute of Law Enforcement and Criminal Justice, saying that LEAA funding for behavior modification experiments

> is a problem which greatly concerns us, and which we'd like to see LEAA take a strong position on . . . personally, I find this program both very disturbing and morally complex. I'd like to

---

[13]For an account of this meeting see Peter Steinfels, "A Clockwork Orange—Or Just a Lemon?" *The Hastings Center Report* (April 1974) 10–12.

stir your interest and see if there is some way we can work together on it.

On January 24 Caplan replied:

My instinct is that the government ought to proceed very cautiously, but probably not ban *all* efforts in the field; however, I do feel strongly that LEAA does not have special expertise in the area, should probably stay out of it altogether, and that the logical agency to carry the responsibility is NIH.

On January 19 the Subcommittee on Courts, Civil Liberties, and the Administration of Justice of the House Judiciary Committee, chaired by Robert Kastenmaier of Wisconsin, issued a report critical of the START program. That same day the BOP announced that, for economic reasons, it was closing START. Said Levinson several years later,

We probably did not do a good job in getting the word out about what the program was. It got construed as brainwashing and shackling people to beds, and all sorts of wild and woolly horror stories. Whether we could have done anything to get across a more positive image of the program, I don't know, but we probably could have tried harder than we did.

START was abandoned, he said, because it was just taking too much of everybody's time. Carlson concurs:

We kept it going for, oh I guess a year-and-a-half or two years, and then finally gave up on it out of frustration. The frustration consisted partly of the controversy and partly because it didn't meet all our expectations as far as results were concerned. I think it did make some headway with some individuals, but it was no panacea; it wasn't going to solve all the problems. . . . I think if I could have had demonstrated to myself that it was more effective than it was, more successful than it was, then I would have gone on with it.

Simultaneously, Senator Ervin had been carrying on an epistolary exchange with Groder, pressing him for more details on his plans. Groder appeared before Senator Ervin's subcommittee January 25. On February 12 an article in the *Washington Post* announced that the BOP was dismantling Project START for economic reasons. But, the article said, despite its claim that financial factors doomed the START program, the Federal Bureau's decision comes just a week after a court-appointed panel of independent penologists declared the program punitive—not rehabilitative—and said it should be shut down.

The chairman of the committee to evaluate START was Cohen, designer of the original behavior modification project at the National Training School for Boys, who asked the court to close START and instruct the BOP to design a new rehabilitative program for prisoners in long-term segregation.

On February 14 the LEAA issued its press release (previously referred to) announcing an end to the use of its funds for psychosurgery, medical research, behavior modification—including aversion therapy—and chemotherapy. The American Psychological Association issued a press release critical of the LEAA funding decision the next day. According to the APA,

> behavior modification involves a large number of procedures some of which are clearly abhorrent to psychologists as well as to the public. Other procedures, however, are humane, benign, systematic, educational, and effective. Psychologists have been in the forefront in developing and approving such procedures and applying them. The banning of these procedures will result in a regression to outmoded, unsystematic forms of inhumanity in prisons that have characterized society's past treatment of its criminal offenders. The LEAA action, in equating all behavior modification with the "Clockwork Orange" type of aversive conditioning, thus results in an injustice to the public and to prison inmates. The LEAA action will tend to stifle the development of humane forms of treatment that provide the offender the opportunity to fully realize his or her potential as a contributing member of society. The APA urges a reconsideration of the valuable educational methods of behavior change and at the same time, the development of procedures to protect the rights of inmates against arbitrary and misguided forms of treatment.

Articles in the *Washington Post* and many other papers described the LEAA's announcement; several of the stories pointed out that the LEAA decision came shortly after that by the BOP to abandon START. In a *New York Times* article

Leslie Oelsner pointed out that the LEAA ban covered only that agency's funding and not that of any other government agencies (which would, of course, include the BOP):

> Beyond that, there was some question as to how the ban would be enforced. The LEAA concedes that it does not know how many behavior modification projects it is financing. In addition to not resolving the basic issues raised by the critics, such as the ethics and efficacy of using behavior modification in the criminal justice system, the Law Enforcement Agency's action, to some observers, raised a new concern: the possibility that the effort to avoid abuses in behavior modification might go too far, so that any potentially good use of the method might also be lost.

The story also described the APA's opposition and commented,

> to some extent the present impasse is the fault of the proponents of behavior modification themselves, for often they have given little thought to the sociological or legal ramifications of the methods they have been developing.

In a letter to the editor appearing February 26 in the *New York Times*, B. F. Skinner argued that

> whatever the merits of the decision to withhold Federal support of behavior modification in prisons through the use of drugs, shock, or emetic therapy, or psychosurgery, it was a tragic mistake to include behavior modification through management of the prison environment. . . . Whether we like it or not, the behavior of prisoners will continue to be modified by the world in which they live. . . . It is possible for prisoners to discover positive reasons for behaving well rather than the negative reasons now enforced, to acquire some of the behaviors which will give them a chance to lead more successful lives in the world to which they will return, to discover that the educational Establishment has been wrong in branding them as unteachable and for the first time to enjoy some sense of achievement.

The following day, Kastenmeier's subcommittee held hearings on behavior modification programs in the BOP. Among those testifying was Carlson, who noted that

> the term "behavior modification" has been misconstrued by a number of groups and individuals as a sinister effort to coerce

offenders through techniques of psychosurgery, brainwashing, and other mental and physical abuses. It has been alleged that the Federal Bureau of Prisons has used and is continuing to use psychosurgery and various forms of aversive therapy to bring about changes in offenders committed to custody. For the record, let me state unequivocally that the Federal Bureau of Prisons never uses and does not countenance the use of psychosurgery, electroshock, massive use of tranquillizing drugs, or any other form of aversive treatment to change behavior.

Carlson also said,

> We have no plans to discontinue the use of behavioral modification techniques as I have mentioned. As a matter of fact, we will continue to use them as indicated where we feel it appropriate to motivate offenders to get out of segregated units and take advantage of opportunities prior to their release. We have no plans to use the START program as such, but we certainly will use in the future, where applicable, the techniques which we think have some very promising potential.[14]

Carlson reiterated that the economics of the START program was the primary reason for stopping it.

At the end of February, the NPP turned its attention to prison projects funded indirectly by the LEAA through its system of block grants to states, the same sort of grant system that had been employed for the UCLA Violence Center. Saunders, the NPP staff attorney who had investigated START, wrote to both the governor of Virginia and Santarelli, protesting the Contingency Management Program (CMP), a behavior modification project then in operation in the Virginia prison system, more than half of whose support was contributed by LEAA grants. The program was administered by four psychology professors and used positive reinforcement techniques. It was voluntary and involved a token economy

---

[14]Testimony of Norman Carlson, director of the Bureau of Prisons, U.S. Department of Justice. "Oversight Hearings: Behavior Modification Programs in the Federal Bureau of Prisons," a hearing before the Subcommittee on Courts, Civil Liberties, and the Administration of Justice of the House Committee on the Judiciary. Hearing transcript, February 27, serial no. 26. Government Printing Office, 1974.

system in which the inmate earned credits for appropriate behavior such as personal hygiene, neatness, cooperation, and completing lessons. To Santarelli he said, "The project clearly falls within the category of behavior modification and, in accordance with the recent LEAA announcement, funding must be immediately terminated."

An article in the March 11 *Time* magazine described several behavior modification programs in prisons, saying, "The programs are all the rage—and outrage—in U.S. penology today." It detailed the controversy over Project START and the LEAA's announcement about its funding procedures, noting that "LEAA grants can easily be salvaged by state administrators with wit enough to re-christen their programs."[15]

Complaining that his earlier letter had gone unanswered, Saunders threatened legal action in a mid-March letter to the Virginia governor and Richard N. Harris, director of the Virginia Division of Justice and Crime Prevention, the funding arm of LEAA in that state. Harris replied immediately,

> The Division of Justice and Crime Prevention is not taking any steps to dismantle the projects being operated under the [LEAA] grant awards. The guidelines developed by the Law Enforcement Assistance Administration do not prohibit the award of block grant funds to programs such as the ones being carried out in the Virginia prison system. The LEAA guidelines state that it is inappropriate for the states to fund projects involving any aspect of psychosurgery or projects involving the use of "medical research." The programs in operation in the Virginia prison system do not fall under either of these two categories, and, therefore, the award of funds for the programs referred to in your letters is considered to be proper and to be allowable under the LEAA guidelines to which you refer.[16]

---

[15]"Behavior Mod behind the Walls," *Time*, March 11, 1974, pp. 74–75.

[16]Correspondence dated March 19, 1974 from Richard Harris, director of the Virginia Division of Justice and Crime Prevention, to Arpiar Saunders, Staff attorney for the National Prison Project of the American Civil Liberties Union. A copy of this letter is on file at the Hastings Center.

On May 13 Saunders wrote to Thomas Madden, LEAA general counsel, describing a visit he made to the CMP program at two Virginia prisons. The letter noted,

> We believe that CMP, while it may not violate the guidelines (as clarified) is a poorly designed and poorly implemented program which only contributes to the dismal state of affairs within the Virginia Department of Corrections. It is our position that CMP should not be refunded. No matter how well designed and/or implemented, sophisticated piecemeal overlays on a correctional system that lacks the capacity to provide even minimal vocational and educational services to its subjects are doomed to fail.[17]

At the same time, Liberation News Service distributed an article describing the dismantling of START. It quoted one of the prisoners who filed the suit as saying,

> The decision by the Bureau of Prisons to dismantle START is a partial victory, but also a ploy by the government. This was done because they know we're bound to win in court. And they hope by dismantling it, they will not get a bad decision about behavior modification and similar mind control programs, so they will be free to give it another try later. But we are continuing our legal struggle against START to get the decision so other prisoners can use this to legally attack their similar type programs and to attack Butner, N.C. when it is finally put in effect.

The article went on to describe the plans for Butner and said,

> Despite the fact that Butner is due to open at the end of 1974, Groder in all his statements and interviews, has repeatedly changed his description of what exactly will take place there. Some people say it's because he hasn't decided yet; others say it's because he knows what's going to happen there, but wants to be evasive. . . . Those in the research section, will include prisoners with what the prison system has defined as "major character disorders" who have engaged in "deviant and/or violent behavior." Read that incorrigibles, troublemakers and rad-

---

[17]Correspondence dated May 13, 1974 from Arpiar Saunders, staff attorney for the National Prison Project of the ACLU, to Thomas Madden, general counsel of the Law Enforcement Assistance Administration. A copy of this letter is on file at the Hastings Center.

icals. . . . Butner will only hold prisoners from institutions on
the East Coast . . . which certainly suggests the establishment
of other institutions like Butner in other parts of the country.[18]

By June 18 LEAA had issued a new Guideline on "use
of LEAA funds for psychosurgery and medical research,"
which canceled the February 14 Guideline. The June Guideline said it was LEAA policy

> not to fund grant applications for medical research or for the
> use of medical procedures which seek to modify behavior by
> means of any aspect of psychosurgery, aversion therapy, chem-
> otherapy (except as part of routine clinical care), and physical
> therapy of mental disorders. . . . This guideline is not intended
> to cover those programs of behavior modification such as involve
> environmental changes or social interaction when no medical
> procedures are utilized.

On July 15 the federal district court issued its decision
memorandum and order on the START program, noting that
START's termination made many of the legal issues moot,
but that the issue of an inmate's transfer without any sort of
hearing was not affected by the termination since such situations were likely to recur. The court concluded that an inmate
transferred into START or into a similar behavior modification
program—which, on the facts, involved a major change in
the conditions of confinement—is entitled, at a minimum, to
the type of hearing required by the recent United States Supreme Court decision involving disciplinary confinement of a
state prisoner.

Constance Holden described the controversy over Butner
in an early August article in *Science:*

> The chief concern is not what Groder plans, but what, given
> the institutional pressures of the prison system, the Butner fa-
> cility will evolve into. Many reporters and critics who have
> questioned Groder find him to be distressingly vague on such
> matters as research protocols, selection methods for prisoners,

---

[18]"Prisoner 'Behavior Modification' Spreading," Liberation News Service article as it appeared in the *African World*, May 13, 1974, p. 11.

and ethical guidelines. Groder appears to be deliberately trying to keep things flexible and open-ended.

The story said Angela Davis staged a demonstration in Raleigh to protest

> what she assumed would be psychosurgery and brainwashing of political radicals at the Center. . . . More moderate critics fear that even if all goes well at Butner it may open the way elsewhere for the involuntary commitment of prisoners to rehabilitation and therapy, as well as expansion of programs into the touchy and ill-defined area of behavior modification.[19]

A feature article in the *Washington Post* of August 11 described the CMP in the Virginia prison system and the NPP opposition to it. An NPP spokesman was quoted as saying that the director of the program "seems to have an idealistic notion that his program is going to make prisoners better people. All he is doing is helping the prison make them more docile." Criticisms about how truly voluntary the program was were also aired. The warden of the prison was quoted as saying that the program should be compulsory.

> The inmates have too much control over the program. They can drop in and out. It's a Mickey Mouse program for ten-year-olds. The only reason they cooperate is the ice cream and the Cokes. If they were forced to cooperate, the counselors would be much more effective.[20]

The NPP kept up its anti-CMP pressure, including its threat to sue, for several months. Finally, on October 29, Virginia decided not to re-fund the CMP program, partly because of a negative recommendation by the Virginia Division of Justice and Crime Prevention.

In November, Senator Ervin's subcommittee issued "Individual Rights and the Federal Role in Behavior Modification," its report on the subcommittee's continuing investi-

---

[19]Constance Holden, "Butner: Experimental U.S. Prison Holds Promise, Stirs Trepidation," *Science*, August 2, 1974, pp. 423–426.
[20]Bob Kuttner, "Virginia Prison Tests Behavior Modification," *Washington Post*, August 11, 1974, p. R1.

gation into behavior modification since 1971. It included a review of legal and constitutional issues, particularly those pertaining to work done on prisoners, a description of behavior modification techniques in general, and some descriptions of specific prison programs. It asserted that many government agencies were funding behavior modification programs, among them HEW, the Justice Department (through both the BOP and the LEAA), the Veterans Administration, the Defense Department, the Labor Department, and the National Science Foundation. It compared programs at Justice with those at HEW, saying Justice

> has made virtually no effort either to provide the necessary monitoring of research projects or to resolve important questions relating to individual liberties. This conclusion is inescapable in view of the policy innovations made in response to legal challenges and other objections to Department programs.[21]

The report noted that it was the plan to fund the UCLA Center for the Study and Reduction of Violence that first brought the committee's attention to all LEAA behavior research programs. It also pointed out:

> One major factor behind the inadequacy of LEAA's ability to protect the rights of human subjects of its funded research projects is the philosophy behind the agency. Established as a revenue-sharing mechanism for local law enforcement agencies, LEAA distributes grants on a decentralized basis. A product of the "New Federalism," its basic philosophy is the decentralization of government control over local law enforcement matters, and a minimum of authority is maintained over individual grantees. This is true even in the case of so-called discretionary grants that are administered directly by LEAA. Because it depends primarily on indirect means of providing funds for individual research projects, the agency has never developed the extensive review mechanisms and guidelines necessary for the adequate protection of the rights of human subjects.[22]

---

[21]"Individual Rights and the Federal Role in Behavior Modification," Committee on the Judiciary, United States Senate, November 1974, p. 31.
[22]Ibid, p. 37.

At about the same time, the LEAA decided to set up a task force to draft proposed guidelines for the LEAA's role in behavior research. The task force met a few times in the following months, but apparently issued no formal report of its work and eventually dwindled out of existence.

On April 3, 1975 Groder called a press conference at which he read a letter of resignation sent to Carlson that same day. It said "the philosophical and operational turn you and the Bureau of Prisons have taken is antithetical to my philosophy and my commitment to corrections." The letter also accused Carlson of "secret, adverse actions you have taken against me and the proposed Federal Center for Correctional Research." The immediate impetus for the resignation was Carlson's decision to relieve Groder of responsibility for Butner and transfer him to Springfield.

The first substantive response to Groder was an April 14 interview with Carlson that appeared in the *Washington Post*. Carlson described his changed views on the purpose of prisons, said that he was in the process of reevaluating a number of activities and programs, defended Groder's transfer to Springfield, denied that the transfer indicated a change of mission for Butner, but also said some of its programs might "be changed from some of Dr. Groder's plans, now that he is leaving."

Writing in the May 23 *Science*, Constance Holden described the charges

> that Butner would be used for a variety of unsavory techniques that have been accumulated under the rubric of "behavior modification." In fact, behavior modification—which among professionals commonly denotes positive reinforcement for approved behavior—and not the opposite—negative reinforcement or aversive conditioning—was not among the programs planned for Butner. One authority believes Butner had simply become too much of an "embarrassment" to BOP and a change was in order.

The article also described Carlson's change in philosophy, strongly influenced by an LEAA study that "concluded that no programs of rehabilitation provided solid evidence that such things worked." Also influential was Norval Morris's *The Future of Imprisonment,* which advocated the recognition of prisons primarily as agents for "deterrence and incapacitation." Noting that the Academy for Contemporary Problems had published a set of principles the previous year based on the assumption "that there are no methods of changing people that are both of predictable effectiveness and essentially acceptable; also that some people really need to be locked up to protect society," the article quoted Groder as saying that this was a step back, that "policy-makers want to buy the idea that 'nothing works,' so that they can get on with the grand old business of repression." There were others, the story said, who believed the rehabilitation idea was being abandoned without having really been tried, that politicians were already latching on to the current attitude of retrenchment—fostered and fed by rising crime rates—to call for harsher penalties, particularly for violent crimes.

The General Accounting Office (GAO) issued its report, "Behavior Modification Programs: The Bureau of Prisons' Alternative to Long-Term Segregation" in early August. On the cover it said:

> One approach to handling problem prisoners is to keep them segregated—often for extended periods—from the rest of the prison population. The Bureau has attempted to avoid such segregation by "behavior modification" programs which are aimed at making prisoners more amenable to institutional disciplines and receptive to the Bureau's rehabilitation activities. However, the Bureau has not effectively managed these programs nor adequately assessed their overall operation and result.

The report said a total of 23 inmates were assigned to START during its 18 months of operation, and the maximum number of inmates assigned it at any one time was 15.

> START's accomplishments are unclear. BOP has not fully assessed START in its various ramifications and consequently has not used the experience to the extent possible to develop better correctional or treatment approaches.

Both START and the CTPs, according to policy guidelines, were to change the behavior of inmates in long-term segregation so that they could be placed in a prison's general population to participate in regular programs and activities. As far as we could determine, the programs differed little, if at all, in their approach to modifying inmate behavior. START's approach, called behavior modification, measured an inmate's progress by his movements through several program levels with specified behavioral requirements as his goals. While not using the term "behavior modification," a CTP included a progressive system and established clearly observable goals to motivate the inmate and measure his progress.[23]

The GAO study said that CTPs were used at Marion and at the young adult facilities at El Reno, Leavenworth, Lompoc, and Milan.

Among the GAO's recommendations were these comments:

BOP wants an inmate to change disruptive and/or dangerous behavior so that he can be placed in the prison's general population and participate in regular prison programs and activities.

In our opinion, the effort has not been well managed. BOP did not assess the characteristics of the inmates it had in long-term segregation and, consequently, did not identify the extent to which CTPs were needed. In addition, it has not assessed CTP operations and results. It terminated START because of a lack of eligible inmates; yet, any difference between the specified selection criteria for START and the CTPs was difficult to determine. Also, START's specified behavior requirements and progress criteria were more consistent with BOP policy than were those of the retained CTP at Marion.

BOP needs to give more centralized attention and direction to developing and/or operating long-term segregation units. It should use the experience gained from START to determine if major improvements are needed in the establishment, testing, and evaluation of new or different programs.[24]

---

[23]Comptroller General, "Behavior Modiciation Programs: The Bureau of Prisons' Alternative to Long-Term Segregation" (GGD-75-73), pp. 9, 23.
[24]Ibid, p. 33.

The report went on to recommend to the attorney general that the BOP examine its general policy on long-term segregation, its existing policy guidance, its procedures for oversight, and new treatment approaches. Since the BOP said START was abandoned because not enough inmates were appropriate to make it worthwhile, the report argued that the "BOP needs to know, at a minimum, the number and characteristics of inmates to determine the appropriateness of the program before committing its resources to developing and implementing it."[25]

On September 3, Metcalfe described the GAO report and said,

> the Federal Bureau of Prisons has been nothing short of irresponsible in its administration of its behavior modification programs. I have asked that these programs immediately be discontinued unless, or until, the Bureau can justify their necessity and document their effects upon inmates.

The Boston XYY Controversy

In 1961, Sandberg et al. reported in Lancet their discovery of the first XYY man.[26] His extra Y chromosome was discovered by accident in the course of a routine investigation undertaken because his child had Down's syndrome. The following year W. M. Court Brown, also in Lancet, discussed

---

[25]Ibid, p. 34.

[26]A. A. Sandburg, G. F. Koeph, T. Ishihara, and T. S. Hauschka, "An XYY Male," Lancet 2 (1961): 488–489. The genes of most organisms are organized into individual packages called chromosomes, with a characteristic number for each species. Human beings have forty-six in each body cell except eggs and sperm, which have half that number. Gender is determined by the sex chromosomes, called X and Y; females have two X chromosomes and males have an X and a Y. Errors in cell division can result in extra chromosomes in each cell. The XYY man has an extra Y, or male-engendering, chromosome, and the XXY man has an extra X, or female-engendering one. The latter may develop enlarged breasts at puberty (a treatable condition known as Klinefelter's syndrome) but is still a male. Such men are often infertile and somewhat retarded. The clinical consequences of the XYY condition are still—as we shall see—a matter of considerable dispute.

criminal responsibility in people with abnormal sex chromosome numbers, saying some anecdotal material might "raise the whole problem of whether such individuals could be held in law to suffer from a diminished responsibility by virtue of their abnormal constitution."

Stanley Walzer, a Harvard child psychiatrist, in 1963 began a two-year residency in genetics. Walzer had previously seen two patients who were XXY and homosexual, and he became interested in studying the effect of that abnormality on behavior.

According to Park Gerald, professor of pediatrics at Harvard Medical School and chief of the Clinical Genetics Division, Children's Hospital Medical Center, the idea for the study arose before it was even known that XYY existed with significant frequency in newborns. The study was not originally an XYY study at all, but an XXY study.

> We wanted to identify such individuals in order to learn more about the genetic determination of sex. . . . What we wanted was a population of individuals who had altered genetic aspects for their sex determination, and the one readily available that we all knew existed was the individual with XXY who is overtly a male, but who is genetically in effect somewhat intermediate between female and male, and to use this population to inform us about the relationship between genes and sex in the area of behavior. . . . To put it in simple-minded terms, the question I asked Dr. Walzer to pursue as a research problem was "Tell me why it is that boys supposedly like trucks and girls like dolls, and is this an acquired or genetically-determined characteristic?" . . . It is known, for instance, that 20 percent of boys as they enter first grade have reading difficulties, while many fewer females entering first grade will have reading difficulties. What is this difference between boys and girls? Is it hormonally-dependent, environmentally-influenced, or genetically-determined? Would these boys have more dyslexia, like boys would have, or less dyslexia, like girls would have, or intermediate? [The XXY boy] is a male by all social characteristics, but his genes are in effect intermediate between male and female. So, in a sense, he is an admixture of both. What will his genes do about his behavior?

But it was not until two years later that Walzer began to examine the chromosomes of randomly selected, normal-appearing newborns in Boston. This pilot study ended in January 1969 and involved only a chromosome survey, no follow-up. In this original pilot study, the number of female chromosome abnormalities that turned up was so small that Walzer and Gerald decided to concentrate on males. At about this time, newborn chromosome screening was beginning to be done at several institutions around the world. "It was a recognized approach," according to Gerald.

On Christmas Day, 1965, in an article entitled "Aggressive Behaviour, Mental Sub-Normality and the XYY Male," Patricia Jacobs and her colleagues described a chromosome survey "of mentally sub-normal male patients with dangerous, violent or criminal propensities" in a state hospital in Scotland, eight of whom (3.5 percent of the hospital's population) possessed an additional Y chromosome. By this time, twelve case reports of XYY males were in the literature, and although the population prevalence of this chromosome abnormality was unknown, it was widely assumed to be considerably less than the 3.5 percent turned up by the Jacobs study. Their brief report concludes,

> At present, it is not clear whether the increased frequency of XYY males found in this institution is related to their aggressive behaviour or to their mental deficiency or to a combination of these factors. We are attempting to elucidate this problem. (P. Jacobs, M. Brunton, M. M. Melville, and W. F. McClermont, *Nature*, p. 1351-1352)

According to Gerald, publication of the Jacobs study, which caused a stir among both medical professionals and the public, did not increase his nor Walzer's interest in doing the research because at that time their impression was still that the newborn incidence of XYY was very low. The XYY abnormality did not appear early in their study, and they were a little startled by all the talk elsewhere. "For some reason," said Gerald, the people who were in opposition to this study don't give a damn whether we study X<u>X</u>Y individuals; it's only XYY that attracts their attention. . . . To me, it demonstrates that their arguments are only dictated in order to achieve a political end, and they have no real interest in the children as such. . . . I think it's because XYY is a newspaper-potent item and X<u>X</u>Y is not.

Court Brown reviewed the XYY findings in 1968. He concluded,

It is fair to suggest . . . that our knowledge of the range of phenotypes associated with a 47, XYY complement is possibly far from complete, and that in concentrating on males with grossly antisocial conduct, as currently is being done, we may be guilty of biased selection. . . . There are so many unknown factors that the sorts of estimates that have been made in this review have to be regarded with considerable circumspection. In the end there can be no substitute for an extensive and prolonged study of newborn children. . . . Many of the problems posed by the 47, XYY male can only be satisfactorily answered by their identification at birth and their surveillance from birth onward. In this way it will become possible to assess what are the chances of any liveborn XYY male developing extreme behavioural aberrations, and, of course, if these risks are ultimately shown to be substantial, then preventative measures through adequate training are only likely to be effective in infancy and early childhood.[27]

But the XYY condition had begun to emerge in courts of law. In that same year:

- An Australian was acquitted of murder on grounds of insanity after a prison psychiatrist testified that he was unable to tell what he was doing when he killed his landlady because "every cell of his brain" was abnormal by virtue of his extra Y chromosome. Since there were several other pieces of medical evidence introduced to demonstrate the defendant's distraught state

[27]W. M. Court Brown, "Males with an XYY Sex Chromosome Complement," *Journal of Medical Genetics* 5 (1968): 341–359.

of mind, it is not clear how important this particular testimony was.

- A French XYY man on trial for murder was convicted, but a reduced sentence was given. His attorney had claimed his client's extra Y chromosome rendered him not criminally responsible for his behavior. The court appointed an expert panel to review the defendant's mental condition, and the chromosome evidence is thought to have influenced their report.

- Richard Speck, convicted of the brutal murder of eight student nurses in Chicago, was repeatedly reported in the press to be an XYY man. His attorney denied that that was the case, and medical evidence to the contrary was published twice, but the reports continued to appear.

- An XYY man in Britain pled guilty to the manslaughter of his four children. His plea of diminished responsibility by reason of mental abnormality was supported by all the medical reports, though his abnormal chromosome constitution was never mentioned. He was ordered sent to Broadmoor.

- In Maryland the following year, however, Carl Ray Millard was denied permission to use his XYY chromosome pattern as evidence of legal insanity in both a local circuit court and the state court of special appeals; he was convicted of armed robbery.

The Center for Studies of Crime and Delinquency of the National Institute of Mental Health held a two-day conference on the XYY chromosome anomaly in mid-1969. According to the conference report, written by the center's chief, Saleem Shah,

> Conferees were generally critical of the lack of information in many of the institutional and neonatal survey reports about the characteristics of the population studied, criteria used for the selection of the subjects, and details concerning various study procedures . . . the dangers of using such meager and inadequate data on the occurrence of the XYY karyotype for crucial

> decisions involving the welfare of individuals or groups or for
> social policy decisions were the recurring theme during the
> conference . . .
>   On the basis of available studies, a general statement which
> could be made is that the individuals with an XYY chromosome
> anomaly in comparison to XY males, appear to incur some in-
> creased risk of developing behavioral problems. However, there
> is no reason to believe that an XYY male is inexorably bound
> to develop antisocial traits or behavioral problems.

The conference outlined major gaps in knowledge and
their attendant research needs. Among the latter were more
accurate incidence and prevalence data, information about
the effects of various environmental influences, and a deline-
ation of the relationship between the XYY condition and social
behavior. Methodological considerations were also of concern, such as characteristics of the survey population, variations in sample size, and the question of double-blind studies
("there was general consensus that the requirement of scientific rigor in such research needed carefully to be balanced
with proper concern for, and protection of the rights and
welfare of the research subjects as well as those of the parents
of the infants studied"). Also taken up were such legal and
ethical issues as informed consent, privacy, and confidentiality. Among the conference participants were Park Gerald,
John Money, Stanley Walzer, Herman Witkin, and Saleem
Shah.

In early 1970 an article by Diane Bauer, then a reporter
for the *Washington Daily News,* disclosed a plan to screen
15,000 boys in Maryland for the XYY chromosome pattern.
Funded by the Center for Studies of Crime and Delinquency,
the study was to be administered through Johns Hopkins and
to include surveys of two main test groups over three years:
6,000 boys from Maryland's juvenile jails, and 7,500 from a
group of largely poor, black families enrolled in a free medical
program at Hopkins. The projected study aroused considerable controversy and was opposed by such groups as the
Maryland Civil Liberties Union.

Later that year (1970), in an article in the *American Journal* of Psychiatry, G. R. Clark and his colleagues compared XYY and X$\underline{X}$Y men and found little difference "between their behavior and criminal records." They concluded that "XYY men have been stigmatized falsely and that their involvement in crimes and antisocial behavior may not be significantly different from the normal individuals" (G. R. Clark, M. A. Telfur, D. Baker, and M. Rosen, pp. 1659-1663).

In midyear Walzer began screening all male newborns at the Boston Hospital for Women for their chromosome constitution. From January 1970 this work was supported partly through a grant from the NIMH's Center for Studies of Crime and Delinquency, but the LEAA was also interested in the possible criminal propensities of people with chromosome abnormalities. Its 1971 annual report describes a grant of just under $80,000 to a researcher at Massachusetts General Hospital for a survey of fingerprints in both the general and prison populations. From the abstract:

> The association between violent behavior and sex chromosome aberrations has been known since 1965. . . . Screening via fingerprints offers an inexpensive and efficient method to establish the incidence of chromosomal aberrations. Fingerprints may very well prove to be a better predicter of behavior than a blood sample culture—the usual method of determining chromosomal aberrations.

This blithe hope—luckily for us all—has proved unfounded.

Scientific disagreement about the behavioral effects of such abnormalities continued. In the March 1972 *Archives of General Psychiatry*, a review of Gardner and Neu concluded, "The extra Y chromosome does have an apparent effect on behavior, and should be considered a factor in assessing a defendant's responsibility in a court of law."[28]

In the January 12, 1973 issue of *Science*, Ernest Hook, of the Birth Defects Institute, New York State Department of

[28]Lytt I. Gardner and Richard L. Neu, "Evidence Linking an Extra Y Chromosome to Sociopathic Behavior," *Archives of General Psychiatry*, 26 (1972): 220–222.

Health, published "Behavioral Implications of the Human XYY Genotype," a major review that is still regarded as important and authoritative. He concluded,

> there is a definite association between the XYY genotype and presence in mental-penal settings, but both the nature and extent of this association are yet to be determined. Discovery of an extra sex chromosome in a male hardly predicts antisocial behavior with the confidence, for instance, that the observation of trisomy 21 (the chromosome pattern associated with mongolism) predicts mental retardation. This raises a serious dilemma for the physician as to whether and how to advise the parents when a sex chromosome abnormality is detected in a male infant or child in whom the diagnosis has not been suspected clinically.[29]

Shortly after the New Year in 1974, Science for the People, an organization on the left dealing in intramural radical critiques of science, got wind of the study. Science for the People had been organized as Scientists and Engineers for Social and Political Action (SESPA) in 1969. After Jonathan King, now associate professor of biology there, joined the MIT faculty in the early seventies, he was taken to a meeting of the group by a colleague who was a member. He said,

> It was immediately clear to me that these people operated at a higher level of valuing human beings, just from the way they listened, than anything I was used to in the scientific community. I just immediately recognized that what was going on here was important, and so I joined in.

Previously he had gone to occasional demonstrations, but he had never organized anything and never been part of any organized political activity.

> I think that lots and lots of people in Science for the People were simply people who had become scientists out of a little bit of idealism. They didn't want to go to law school, and they didn't want to go to medical school, and they didn't want to go to business school, and they'd become research scientists.

---

[29]Ernest B. Hook, "Behavioral Implications of the Human XYY Genotype," *Science*, January 12, 1973, pp. 139–150.

They got involved in Science for the People out of good hearts and Christian conscience, and then developed politically within Science for the People through the activities they took part in. Nothing will politicize a person quicker than when they are doing something out of conscience and they get labeled the radical left. . . . We were being painted as these political radicals. I was no political radical; I was just a well-meaning . . . I just didn't like to see bad things happen. I then was radicalized by being labeled a political radical, because then you saw this move to isolate people who were going against the status quo.

At a meeting in February King heard the Walzer study described by Jonathan Beckwith, professor of microbiology and molecular genetics at Harvard Medical School, also a Science for the People member. Beckwith said he wanted to raise the issue before the appropriate Harvard committee, but preparation of the case would require some work; King volunteered. Already interested in the race/IQ controversy, he went to the library and started reading up on XYY. "The emphasis on the relationship between the extra chromosome and criminality wasn't supported by the data I read"; as for the Hook article, "I thought that although there was a certain amount of evenhandedness in the handling of the data, the conclusions weren't borne out by the presentation of the argument."

On February 26 A. Clifford Barger, Robert Henry Pfeiffer Professor of Physiology at Harvard Medical School and chairman of its Commission of Inquiry (the Barger committee), replied to a medical student's inquiry about the newborn karyotyping in Boston by explaining that the commission could only open an investigation into a study on receipt of a formal written complaint, and suggesting that an appropriate first step would be an informal presentation of the critics' objections.

On May 29 Beckwith, as a representative of an ad-hoc group associated with the medical school, only a few of whom were Science for the People members, lodged a formal complaint with the Barger committee against the newborn karyotyping at the Boston Hospital for Women. The complaint listed several objections.

We do not believe that anything approaching truly *informed consent* is obtained from the parents. The Hospital gives no hint that a primary aim in conducting the test is identification of suitable subjects for research. . . . No mention is made of the possible hazard and risks that informing parents of the abnormality may entail. . . . Once an infant has been identified, Dr. Walzer solicits the family's continued participation in the study. He gradually discloses the full nature of the "disorder" (as he sees it) to the parents. As a result, most or all parents are made to suspect that their child may develop violent or aggressive behavior. This information obviously is likely to have serious effects on their behavior toward the child and result in a self-fulfilling prophecy. The consent procedures of the hospital clearly fail to protect the rights of parents who do not want to be caught in the screening net. Those parents certainly have a right not to know that their son is XYY, especially in light of the fact that the claims for deviant behavior of XYY individuals have dubious scientific validity and have been widely contested. . . . If the parents reject continued participation in the study, they reject the assistance and counseling that go with it. The researcher has in effect sought out the parents, raised a matter of serious concern, and then offered help. This may constitute subtle coercion. . . . Aside from the harmful effects on the individuals participating in the study, we [also] fear that there is a strong likelihood that the results of such studies might be used to support unwarranted discrimination against XYY individuals, in general.

When he heard about the complaint, Gerald said he was startled that people would raise the issue without first speaking to him about why he was involved in the study and why he was interested in doing it. "It's the kind of thing that happens to the other guy, never to me. . . . I thought this whole thing was just a house of cards; I couldn't believe what it was all about."

The Barger committee decided that a complaint about a research project was properly the province of the medical school's Human Studies Committee, chaired by Dana L. Farnsworth, and in early June requested the Farnsworth committee to review it.

In the August *Pediatrics*, Martha F. Leonard, Gail Landy, Frank H. Ruddle, and Herbert Lubs published a prospective study of eleven young children with sex chromosome abnormalities, only three of whom were XYY. It noted, "Up to the age of two-and-a-half years there is no clear trend of excessive size or difficult, or aggressive behavior, both of which have been emphasized in some adult studies." In this study parents were not informed about their children's chromosome abnormalities, because of "the real uncertainty in 1967 regarding the significance of the XYY abnormality and the effect of such knowledge and uncertainty on the parents and on the parents' view of the child." The paper concluded, "A range of developmental levels and personality has been demonstrated in these . . . children, and one cannot predict developmental potential from a knowledge of the genetic constitution."[30]

One of the major annual events in medical genetics is a week-long state-of-the-art seminar in Bar Harbor, Maine every August. That year Park Gerald reported on the birth incidence of male chromosome abnormalities, assessing it at roughly one in 500 male births (including both XXY and XYY boys). Richard Knox reported this estimate in the *Boston Globe,* and quoted Gerald as saying,

> It is unquestionably true that there is an increased incidence of XYY among individuals in certain mental-penal institutions. But our evidence so far indicates it is wrong to characterize these individuals as more aggressive. Instead they appear to be more impulsive. When they're happy, it's almost a rampage of happiness.[31]

Another report on the Bar Harbor meeting appeared in the September 6 edition of *Medical World News,* a publication for professionals. It quoted Gerald as saying,

> I'd like to see XXY and XYY get the same massive attention Down syndrome receives. We've marshalled our energies to

---

[30]Martha F. Leonard *et al.* "Early Development of Children with Abnormalities of the Sex Chromosomes: A Prospective Study," *Pediatrics* 54 (1974), 208–212.
[31]Richard A. Knox, "Sex Chromosome Defects in Males Found More Prevalent Than Suspected," *Boston Globe,* August 8, 1974, p. 5.

take care of children afflicted with it—now let's take care of these children, who are equally diseased.

The first article on the Boston XYY screening appeared in the September issue of *Science for the People*, the SESPA publication. The article argued:

> The wave of XYY studies is not an isolated incident of bad science but rather a reflection of a general political and social-economic climate. More and more we find that pseudo-science is being used to explain away social problems. . . . A theory of genetic determinism for criminal behavior comes in handy for an administration which spends more money on war (is this criminal?) than for the liberal social programs of the sixties. Although a correlation between genetic constitutions such as XYY and criminal behavior is not a scientific fact, it gives pseudo-scientific backing for the current ideology of "blaming the victim."[32]

A sidebar to this article described the formation of a genetic-engineering group of SESPA, organized around the XYY issue, and said,

> This is a good starting point for ongoing national action because a similar study is being conducted in Denver. We expect to turn local and national press on to these issues so that a wide range of the public will become informed.

It also said,

> We felt that the benefits of stopping the research would indeed outweight any harm which might be done to the few children now under study. In fact, we have much greater fear of the harm Dr. Walzer has already done by the information given to the parents.

In early September Walzer wrote Farnsworth a letter in which he described the informed-consent procedure and said,

> Long before Professor Beckwith's concern, both the hospital and our study have been investigating ways of broadening the informed consent, bringing it more in tune with demands of

---

[32]Dirk Elseviers, "XYY: Fact or Fiction," *Science for the People*, September 1974, pp. 22–24.

the times. We instituted individual signed permission slips in late spring of this year.

After some preliminary correspondence Jay Katz, adjunct professor of law and psychiatry at Yale Law School and coauthor of *Experimentation with Human Beings*, sent a brief critique of the Walzer project to Beckwith at the end of the month. It noted,

> In its present form Dr. Walzer's initial approach to the parents is neither straightforward enough nor does it comply with what I consider the requirements for informed consent to imply. Elements of "fraud, deceit," and even "duress and overreaching," proscribed by the Nuremberg Code, are clearly present.

The letter also argued that in order to honor the obligation to inform the parents, from the beginning

> all the possible and probable ramifications of the study be explained to them. Since this project carries so many known and unknown risks, it is advisable that not only a protagonist of the experiment talk with the parents but also that an *intelligent* antagonist do so.

Katz also argued that consent of the parents should not be decisive because it is proxy consent, more often justified in a study "with a possible direct therapeutic payoff. . . . This is not true for this study which has many known and unknown risks and little likelihood of direct benefit to the children involved." He asserted that more work should be done on adults before turning to studies of children, and concluded, "Speaking for myself and on the basis of the information available to me I do not believe that Dr. Walzer's project should be approved at this time."

At about this time, Money and colleagues published in *Clinical Genetics* a comparative study of a dozen each XYY and X X Y men, concluding that the XYY men

> had behavior disability involving a predominance of impulsive acting out and poor long-term planning . . . a greater frequency and diversity of sexual experience and imagery [and] were mobile and more likely to intrude on other people and their property. (J. Money, C. Annecillo, B. van Orman, *et al.*, 1974, pp. 370–382).

In the same journal, Noel and colleagues reported being able to distinguish seven XYY men from twenty-eight normal men with normal chromosomes by means of a blind psychological evaluation that included such standard measures as the Rorschach and the Thematic Apperception Test (B. Noel, J. P. Duport, D. Rebil, I. Dussuyer, and B. Quack, pp. 387–394).

On October 4 the Farnsworth committee met jointly with the Barger committee to take up the question of the Walzer study. The minutes report that results of their deliberations were to be presented to Robert Ebert, dean of the medical school. The researchers described the rationale for the study and the consent procedure, arguing that

> we have always believed that the parents have a legal, moral and ethical right to know about any significant abnormality found in their child and this policy has been rigidly adhered to throughout our study. . . . The most relevant risks relate to the concerns raised in the parents about having a child with a variation and how this knowledge might affect child-rearing. It has become evident to us that the continued contact with the investigator—in an atmosphere of honesty—allows for free communication between the parents and the study. They are able to share their concerns and to receive support and corrective information when doubts or distortions arise. . . . We feel that the honest, free communication and continued presence of the investigator has made the parents relatively comfortable with the knowledge that they have and that this knowledge has not adversely affected the rearing of their children.

Three of the XYY boys in the study

> showed rather prominent behavioral difficulties early in their lives, taxing the coping capacities of the parents. These parents were significantly benefited by our suggested alternatives for more effective coping with their child's behavior.

The researchers also described therapeutic interventions—chiefly speech therapy—with XXY children. Walzer also noted his past contacts with many individuals and groups in an attempt to sort out the ethical issues, including other scientists, lawyers, the district attorney, a federal judge, theologians, parents' groups, groups concerned with medical ethics at both Harvard and Boston College, hospital review committees, and site visitors for the grants. He noted,

> I would further like to emphasize that my studies are not entitled "The XYY Karyotype in Deviancy." They are entitled "Variations in Behavior with Sex Chromosome Aberrations." My original interest was to understand more about the XYY karyotype—about which the literature was replete with ascertainment bias about risks of retardation—threats to role identity—risks to academic and educational failure, etc. With the identification of infants with the XYY karyotype, our study was broadened to include these individuals since we felt that prospective studies from birth offered the best way to understand some of the questions about the possible behavioral implications of this karyotype. . . . The application of . . . a reductionistic schema to the field of behavior genetics has resulted in horrifying consequences, i.e., the YY chromosome disorder results in delinquency or causes specific behavioral correlates. This is completely contrary to what the field of behavior genetics is all about. Behavior genetics is both the study of limits and variability. It studies the limits within which a particular genotype can unfold without pathological consequences. However, it accepts enthusiastically that within these limits a wide range of variability of expression exists. We study really the ultimate limits of variability possible without a pathological phenotype emerging.

He went on to argue the case for informing, follow-up, and early intervention and said,

> In response to the changing times, we have changed our informed consent procedure. I wish to emphasize that it was not the direct response to this inquiry but was a response to such individuals as Norman Fost and to Dr. Kenneth Ryan of the Boston Hospital for Women who intensely felt that such studies as this must be constantly reviewed and revised with an eye to protecting patients' rights.

He concluded with a charge that some of the articles cited as evidence by the study's opponents have not "been honestly represented. I would recommend that you review these articles yourself to clarify this point."

The critics also presented a statement:

> We consider that the study . . . generates such serious risks to the health and welfare of individuals and family involved,

> that it should not be continued. Given all of the criticisms out-
> lined, we feel that the major effort in approaching the issue of
> behavioral problems should be one of changing the social and
> psychological (inseparable) conditions which generate them.
> . . . This criticism is not an attack on academic freedom. Clearly,
> there are limitations on areas of research where there are liable
> to be adverse effects on human subjects. . . . We consider that
> the XYY study under discussion falls under the categories al-
> ready established for scrutiny.

In a separate critique, Harvard molecular biologist Richard Roblin said:

> In my view, the way Dr. Walzer's prospective study of
> XYYs is apparently being carried out raises two major questions:
> (1) Is the "benefit" of the knowledge which may be gained from
> this study greater than the risk to the patients/subjects? (2) How
> ought the informed consent criterion be applied in the case of
> this study? Specifically, does his current description of the nature
> and potential outcomes of the chromosome test, which he gives
> to parents before testing the newborn male infants, enable the
> parents to give an informed consent on whether or not they
> wish to participate in the study?

On the first question he was somewhat equivocal, pointing to
the danger of stigmatization even if a firmer knowledge of the
true consequences of the XYY chromosome complement is
obtained. On the second he concluded, "It seems to me that
the current consent procedure needs to be revised, in order
to minimize the possibility that the parents are left with no
choice but to enter Dr. Walzer's program." He recommended
that study of the six XYY individuals already located continue,
provided the parents and eventually the XYY individual himself consented, that the entire rationale for newborn chromosome screening be reexamined (particularly since studies
from around the world had by that time made available fairly
reliable data on newborn incidence of chromosome abnormalities), and that since the kind of study Walzer was doing
was clearly recognized as experimental rather than routine,
informed-consent procedure should be requisite.

The files at Harvard Medical School concerning the Farnsworth committee deliberations contain two sets of minutes for each of the committee's two formal meetings, one set considerably more organized, detailed, and coherent than the other. There is no indication of who wrote either set, or when.

In the less organized minutes, Beckwith was described as making both the consent and the self-fulfilling-prophecy arguments. The Katz letter was also quoted, and the minutes note parenthetically that Dr. Katz was an HMS graduate. Daisene Wellman, the admitting aide at Boston Hospital for Women who was one of the first people to bring concerns about the study to Beckwith, testified that she handed the consent forms to women in labor, and they had to be signed as quickly as possible; there was no time to read the lengthy explanation, and no one on hand qualified to answer questions. Robert Rosenthal, professor of social psychology at Harvard, testified on the idea of the self-fulfilling prophecy; his prior work on that subject was well-known. He argued that both animal and human work indicated that there was some validity to the self-fulfilling-prophecy argument. Walzer testified that ethical issues had always been uppermost in his mind, but it was difficult to proceed with little or no experience or precedent to guide him. The discussion in this set of minutes is not easy to follow because many of the speakers are not identified by name.

In the second and more organized set of minutes, Rosenthal was described as citing several cases in which expectations of others influenced behavior, but as noting in summary that committee members should make their own interpretations of those data in relation to the Walzer study. The second set of minutes also reflects a number of committee members' concern with the project, particularly the informed-consent procedures, the question of whether or not a double-blind study could be done, and possible restrictive legislation that might come about as a result of the controversy. The minutes do not reflect any formal—or even informal—vote taking. A couple of motions were made but later, according to the minutes, withdrawn.

Shortly after the meeting, Beckwith wrote Diane Bauer, who was by this time working for the Children's Defense Fund in Washington, describing the Farnsworth committee hearing and enclosing some materials on the study. He noted:

> It was clear from the questions asked that people on the committee were unhappy about Walzer's study. Many were trying to come up with modifications that would make it more palatable. Farnsworth indicated to me later that it was likely that the committee would decide either to demand changes or end it (off the record). It is quite possible that when 3 to 4 weeks rolls around they will decide to be much more moderate, but we clearly made a very strong case. After the decision is made, we will attempt to publicize it.[33]

That same day Beckwith also wrote to Katz, thanking him for his critique and asking if it would be possible to use excerpts from it in articles. He also said:

> It is our strong feeling that issues of this sort should be brought to the attention of the public. First, we are anxious to try to dispel specifically some of the mythology that surrounds the XYY story. Secondly, we feel that it is important to show to people that a lot of what is presented by scientists to the press is based on poor evidence. We are interested in the demystification of science in general. Finally, there are other XYY studies of this sort going on (including one in New Haven with a different approach) which the public should know about.[34]

On Halloween, Beckwith wrote Farnsworth:

> I have thought over our conversation of Tuesday and discussed it with other members of our group. It appears to us that there was a fair degree of consensus at the hearing on October 4 that the current informed consent form and procedures are deceptive. This feeling seems confirmed by the fact that the Hospital is preparing a new form and procedures. The only conclusion can be that currently those who do sign the form are doing so under false impressions. We have heard

---

[33]Correspondence dated October 9, 1974 from Jonathan Beckwith to Diane Bauer.

[34]Correspondence dated October 9, 1974 from Jonathan Beckwith to Jay Katz.

reports that mothers are consistently being told that this is a "routine" test.

It seems logical to us that screening at the Hospital should be temporarily suspended, at least, until some resolution of these questions has evolved. Otherwise, parents may be brought irreversibly into the study under conditions which seem now to be generally accepted as deceitful.[35]

The formal Science for the People criticisms of the study were always aimed at structural and procedural aspects, never at the researchers themselves; in fact Walzer was more than once praised for his sincerity and good motives. Nevertheless at about this time a campaign began of personal vilification against Walzer, one that had a profound effect on the course of the controversy, an effect that persists today. Over the next two months, Walzer has reported, he received between twenty and thirty telephone calls at work, probably from only four or five different people, calling him names ("fascist pig," for instance), quoting from documents distributed to the Farnsworth committee, and making veiled threats such as asking him if he had seen his children lately. He says he was frightened, but feared that if he told anyone about the calls, he would have to go to the police, and that it would eventually get into the newspaper. He was afraid of publicity because he did not want to frighten his family; he did not tell his wife and children about the calls until December. When he finally learned of them, Beckwith consistently expressed dismay about the calls and asserted that no one in Science for the People was responsible; Walzer says he believes Beckwith.

The Research Advisory Committee at Boston Hospital for Women also reviewed Walzer's program and informed-consent procedure, asked for changes, and, early in November, "approved the program feeling that the informed consent process was now fully explanatory and allowed the patient to make an informed decision."

[35]Correspondence dated October 31, 1974 from Jonathan Beckwith to Dana Farnsworth.

Dissatisfied with the study's continuation, several of the critics, mostly members of Science for the People, decided to go public. In a November 8 letter to Farnsworth, they defended their action in indirectly providing a woman who delivered a son at Boston Hospital for Women with information critical of the study.

> We feel that these actions are perfectly justified. First, if we are truly concerned about this issue, we cannot hide the information from someone we know who is about to become a victim of the procedure, and even requests more information. Furthermore, we see no reason to consider our opinions, as expressed in the critique, as "privileged documents."

The letter also justified contact with journalist Graham Chedd, which resulted in publicity about the story on WGBH in Boston and, shortly thereafter, an article in the British professional journal *New Scientist*, of which Chedd was then United States Editor. The letter argued that the public had a right to know about these decisions; the formal complaint had been submitted the preceding May and

> it is now over 5 months later and it is still unclear how any final decision is to be made or how long it will take. In the meantime, parents are continuing to be drawn into the study by the same deceptive practices that have been used all along.

As for the arrangements with Chedd,

> At first we were reluctant to go ahead with these suggestions, since our information at that point was that a decision of the Committee was at hand. However, the more recent indications that the process would take even longer than anticipated, and the continuation of the same practices at the Hospital, led us to question our reservations. . . . We never considered that our participation in these hearings should restrict our freedom to speak out in public. Certainly, Dr. Park Gerald felt no restraints when he granted interviews to at least *The Boston Globe* (August 8) and *Medical World News* (September 6) and discussed the XYY issue and the study being done here.[36]

---

[36]Correspondence dated November 8, 1974 from Jonathan Beckwith *et al.* to Dana Farnsworth.

Thus the major objections to the study reached a wide professional audience when, on November 14, *New Scientist* published "The XYY Syndrome: A Dangerous Myth" by Jonathan Beckwith and Jonathan King. It strongly argued the Science for the People case against the Walzer project, concluding:

> Isn't it time that we stopped wasting society's resources on poorly conceived and ideologically influenced studies on the genetic basis of anti-social behavior and, instead, concentrated on changing the social and economic structure which generated most of these problems?

The article was accompanied by a brief sidebar by Chedd describing attempts to stop the study, and saying that Farnsworth replied to Beckwith's request that the screening be suspended until the issue was settled by saying that such a request violated all tenets of academic freedom.

Simultaneously with the appearance of the article, the critics associated with Science for the People issued a press release calling for the end of the Walzer study. The attempt to reach the general public was greatly aided when, on November 15, the *New York Times* published a long story on the controversy by Jane Brody. Brody had been alerted to the story partly through King, with whom she went to high school, and who got in touch with her when the group decided to seek publicity.

The following day, Richard Knox's story describing the controversy appeared in the *Boston Globe.* It concluded:

> Asked if the children exhibited any tendencies toward violent behavior, Walzer said: "Oh, God, no. There has been no tendency toward violent behavior. Let's just say that they have experienced difficulty with certain parameters of behavior. But with help and guidance most of them are doing just beautifully.

The Farnsworth committee met again November 20. A memorandum from Farnsworth setting up this meeting says that its recommendations were to be presented to the full faculty, and also describes the exchange with Beckwith in which Farnsworth said that stopping the study would be an infringement of academic freedom. Once again the Harvard files on this meeting contain two sets of minutes, one of which is more organized and coherent than the other. The more organized minutes note that Roblin asked to be disassociated from the other critics of the study because he was distressed about the publicity. The threats against Walzer are prominently mentioned.

Committee members expressed some distress at the design of the study, and there were suggestions that the developmental study be separated from the screening. One committee member was quoted as saying that, as the study was currently designed, the risks exceeded the benefits and, as an ethical man, Walzer could not continue. The minutes also reflect a general concern in the group about the consent procedure and the risk–benefit ratio.

According to this set of minutes, at one point in the meeting one member moved that the committee declare that, as the study was presently constructed, risks to the children outweighed the benefits. There follows a separate page written in the first person. It appears to be a retrospective account of the vote on this motion and notes that the vote on whether or not risks outweighed benefits was a test of sentiment and not a vote based on the scientific merits of the research. It also says that, because of a proxy vote and an abstention, the vote was ten to nine in favor of benefits outweighing risks. The following page picks up the previous minutes: according to them, a vote was taken on whether or not risks outweigh benefits, and the vote is yes–nine and no–eight.

The minutes also describe a unanimous vote for the desirability of researching behavior genetics, and also a unanimous vote endorsing Walzer's behavior. There is also a single motion with four parts: that behavior genetics is a legitimate field of pursuit, that Walzer's behavior has been exemplary, that there are questions about risks versus benefits, and that these problems can be amended by appropriate changes in the study design. The motion is seconded and then, later in the minutes, there is a record of a vote with two opposed.

The minutes also report a unanimous vote that the controversy should have been kept inside Harvard.

Following these minutes is Farnsworth's own report on the vote, which also says that the experimental design should be modified.

In this file is also a copy of a letter dated October 1, 1974 from Lee Coleman and Philip Shapiro, psychiatrists in California, who had been particularly active there on similar issues. They describe their concern about the Walzer study, and say:

> Perhaps there are ways of further investigating these issues, consistent with the ethics of human experimentation. We feel most sincerely that Dr. Walzer's research, however, is inconsistent with these mandates, and urge your committee to exercise its responsibility to ensure that human experimentation meets the strictest ethical standards.

An article by Barbara Culliton appeared in the November 22 *Science* saying, "Today, no scientist with any experience in the matter actually believes that there is such a thing as a 'criminal chromosome,' but there is preliminary evidence that XYY boys are at risk for developing some rather ill-defined behavioral problems." Walzer was quoted: "This has been a very ugly time in my life. I've even had threatening phone calls. . . . This is like the McCarthy era." David Bazelon, chief justice of the United States Court of Appeals, was portrayed as being concerned that a cult may be growing up around the ethics of human experimentation that may not be good for either patients or medicine.

> Bazelon has always been a defender of patients and believed they had rights before it became fashionable. But now he wonders whether concern may not be getting mixed up with paternalism on the part of some "elitist" scientists who underestimate patients' abilities to cope with complex information and tough decisions.[37]

---

[37]Barbara J. Culliton, "Patient's Rights: Harvard Is Site of Battle over X and Y Chromosomes," *Science*, Nov. 22, 1974, pp. 715–717.

The story also noted that the Farnsworth committee was in the process of preparing its final recommendations, which were to be delivered to a medical school faculty meeting December 13.

On November 26 Farnsworth issued a one-page document saying that the following motions were voted on and approved at the November 20 meeting of the Standing Committee on Medical Research:

> It is the sense of this Committee that research on the genetic base of behavior is important and worthy of pursuit. This feeling was practically unanimous.
>
> It is the sense of this Committee that Dr. Stanley Walzer has shown profound sensitivity and behaved ethically in his studies to-date. This feeling was practically unanimous.
>
> There was some concern on the part of several Committee members that possible risks of the study might outweigh the benefits. . . . It was suggested that the experimental design of the study could be amended as new data are accumulated to reduce further possible risk.
>
> It is also the sense of this Committee that some of the critics of Dr. Walzer's studies may have used methods of questionable validity in an academic community. It was agreed that any faculty member is free to criticize the work of another. The entire structure of the Committee on Human Studies is designed to make this possible. The advisability of using public media as a forum before decisions had been reached was not looked upon with enthusiasm. This feeling was practically unanimous.
>
> During this meeting many Committee members who had some reservations about one or another aspect of the research program expressed their hope that Dr. Walzer and others connected with it would participate in a joint discussion with them that might hopefully lead to greater mutual understanding, lessened criticism and to more effective research results. (Dr. Walzer fully approves this idea and will confer with the Committee at any time it desires.)

An anonymous leader (editorial) in the November 30 *Lancet* entitled "What Becomes of the XYY Male?" concluded:

> On present information, what is the best advice to parents? On the one hand, a tenfold increase in a lifetime risk of committal to a maximum security hospital cannot be regarded as

trivial. On the other hand there is little justification for a pessimistic prognosis if the likelihood of this event is only 1 in 100, and there is no certain evidence that behavioural problems *per se* are more common than in XY males. Precise assessment of any special hazards for XYY males must await the outcome of a prospective study of those identified at birth. If the risk of abnormality is as small as now seems likely, a very large sample will have to be followed, for many years, to obtain this information.[38]

On December 5 Beckwith wrote to Katz asking for "any thoughts you have on possible legal action against this study."

The minutes of the December 13 faculty meeting (with 204 faculty members in attendance) describe only a single item of business: the report of the Farnsworth committee as specified in Farnsworth's November 26 memo. Farnsworth is quoted:

> When concerted campaigns are conducted to stop research work approved by the appropriate committees on human studies (four in all in this instance), the question must necessarily arise as to whether they are, or are not, infringements on academic freedom.

Beckwith replied, repeating many previous criticisms of the study. He argued that it was not possible to say that the study had no bad effects on the children

> when Drs. Gerald and Walzer have already stated to the press that many of the XYY children have exhibited behavioral problems. These may, in fact, be problems that the study itself created. The result of the publicity these statements receive lends strong credence to the stigmatization which XYY males currently suffer.

He also criticized the new consent procedure, the source of the funding (the Center for Studies of Crime and Delinquency at NIMH), and concluded by asking that the study be halted.

Among other opponents of the study present was Alvin

[38]"What Becomes of the XYY Male?" *The Lancet*, November 30, 1974, pp. 1297–1298.

Poussaint, associate professor of psychiatry. He criticized the composition of the Farnsworth committee and recommended that the study be referred instead to the Committee on Human Studies. This committee, which had recently been formulated under HEW guidelines with three lay members, was chaired by Herbert Benson, who was also a member of the Farnsworth committee. Ebert was quoted as saying that the new NIH funding for the study could not go into effect until the Benson committee had approved it. Given the likelihood that the Benson committee would take some time to make a decision, Poussaint asked that the screening be stopped until the issue was resolved.

The minutes report:

> Dr. Benson said that his committee was considering this within three days and he expected a speedy decision on these complex matters. . . . Dr. Benson said that his committee would like a sense of the Faculty about these matters. Dr. Ebert replied that the function of his Committee was to decide. It was not appropriate to take a sense of the Faculty. The Faculty as a whole had not been able to consider this study's scientific values. . . . Dr. [Bernard] Davis said that there was a problem of what was to happen after the Faculty meeting. Would the Benson Committee make a speedy decision? Dr. Poussaint said that the newspapers were very interested in this problem and that is why he had wanted to propose some resolutions for the Faculty. Dr. Ebert said that he would not allow his Faculty to be dictated to by the press.[39]

The faculty then passed a motion declaring that it approved of the procedures followed to review the study.

Following the meeting, there was a press conference featuring both critics and defenders of the study. A press release issued by several of the critics argued that the report of the Farnsworth committee failed to deal with substantive objections raised by the critics.

---

[39]Harvard Faculty of Medicine, Minutes of the Faculty Meeting, called to order by Dean Ebert, December 13, 1974.

Neither the value of research into the genetic basis of behavior in general, nor the sensitivity of the investigator for his patients, nor the behavior of the critics of his study is at issue. It is the "concern on the part of several Committee members that the possible risks of the study might outweigh the benefits," expressed in one of the Committee's motions which is of major importance.

The release criticized the consent procedure, the source of the funding, the possibility of a self-fulfilling prophecy, and the substitution of genetic explanations for society's problems, calling the recommendations of the Farnsworth committee a "whitewash."

Reports on the day's events appeared in the Boston papers and elsewhere. The *New York Times* report, written by Jane Brody, quoted Beckwith as criticizing the Farnsworth committee as inappropriate because it was not constituted according to HEW guidelines which said such review committees should have members from the community at large and hold public hearings. (All the meetings so far had been closed to the public.) The story noted that the new [Benson] committee was formulated according to the new HEW guidelines and had three community representatives, though Beckwith criticized the makeup of that committee too, arguing that one of the "lay" members was a trustee of one of the Harvard hospitals.

True to his word, Benson's committee met on December 16. Gerald and Walzer attended and submitted new documents, but no opponents were present. Several critics of the study complained to Benson about their exclusion, saying:

We feel that there is good reason to conclude that community opinion is not represented by the particular individuals chosen for that purpose to serve with the HMF Human Studies Committee. It seems to us that, in the long run, the Committee could avoid problems now and in the future by following the spirit of the HEW guidelines and including members on it who would bring a *critical* community attitude to it.

That year's edition (1974) of the annual volume *Progress*

in Medical Genetics contained a major review, "The XYY Chromosome Male—or Syndrome?" by Borgaonkar and Shah. Among its conclusions:

> Because of the relatively small numbers, the absence of matched controls and of blind assessment procedures, and the inconsistent findings, there are relatively few psychologic, psychiatric, and behavioral characteristics which clearly and consistently distinguish the XYY males from comparable control subjects. . . . There are very few personality traits which appear to distinguish the XYY offenders and patients from control groups; the few differences which do appear tend to refute the notion that XYY males are predisposed toward aggressive and violent behavior. . . . A wide range of psychiatric and social pathology has been reported, but these characteristics are not remarkably different from those of matched XY males in the same populations. There have been several reports of increased incidence of psychopathic disorders and sex crimes among XYY offenders as compared to XY controls from the same population. . . . Although there is no disputing the very significantly greater prevalence rates of the XYY chromosomal constitution among certain special institutionalized populations, there continues to be uncertainty about the precise way in which the influence of the extra Y chromosome is mediated and the ways in which such factors interact with a variety of environmental variables. In view of the phenotypic heterogeneity which clearly seems to accompany the XYY chromosomal constitution, it would be incorrect to suppose a narrow range of phenotypic variation or that a typical syndrome exists. . . . This review of data on the XYY male does not provide firm or conclusive statements on a number of characteristics. However, it does allow us to conclude that many of the premature speculations about the behavioral predispositions of XYY males toward aggressive, impulsive, antisocial, and violent behavior are *not* supported by a careful analysis of the relevant studies.[40]

Early in the new year, 1975, Carl Ray Millard, who had unsuccessfully attempted to use his XYY condition as a de-

---

[40]Digamber S. Borgaonkar and Saleem Shah, "The XYY Chromosome Male—or Syndrome?" in *Progress in Medical Genetics*, vol. 10, eds. Arthur Steinberg and Alexander Bearn (New York: Grune & Stratton, 1974), p. 202.

fense in a trial for the 1968 armed robbery of a Maryland liquor store, was killed in a two-hour shootout with police.

On January 11 Ernest Hook replied to *The Lancet*'s November leader, "the 1 percent risk of an XYY eventually appearing in a mental-penal setting calculated in your editorial cannot be assumed to be the entire measure of the increased likelihood of future behavioral problems."

On January 15 Arthur Sackler, in a column in *Medical Tribune*, defended the Boston study and Walzer and called the critics "present-day Torquemadas." The Inquisition is a favored image in these disputes; the Toronto *Globe and Mail* later compared Walzer to Galileo.

On January 21 Benson issued a report saying his committee had approved the Walzer study January 14. Science for the People responded by circulating a petition that criticized the committee's composition and their exclusion and requested the dean to reopen the investigation.

The January 31 *Science* published a letter signed by several of the study's critics, describing their objections to the study and to Barbara Culliton's November article. The latter, it said, "does not clearly lay out the nature of the study and its implications, nor the basis of our objections."[41] In that same issue, a letter from Wayne Davis of the University of Kentucky and the Kentucky Civil Liberties Union asserted that the critics'

> view that knowledge is a danger from which the public needs protection is the same force that keeps textbooks out of West Virginia schools and leads to the type of academic McCarthyism that prevents Shockley and others with unpopular interests from fulfilling speaking engagements in our colleges.

The level of intramural acrimony continued to rise. At a Valentine's Day Harvard Medical School faculty meeting with eighty-six members in attendance, Benson reported the verdict of his committee, "that the proposed study had been approved on the basis that its benefits exceeded its risks."

[41]Jonathan Beckwith *et al*. Letter, *Science*, January 31, 1975, p. 298.

Beckwith retorted that 150 people had signed a petition against the research, and moved (1) that the dean reopen the investigation; (2) that a full hearing be given to critics; (3) that the dean appoint to the Benson committee additional members who could represent the interests of the public and of children; and (4) that the Benson committee explain its evaluation of risks and benefits to the faculty. Ebert said that the motion could not be acted on at this meeting. From the minutes:

> He wished to raise the question of the ethics of debating whether a piece of research should be continued when it was known that the research had been passed by all relevant committees of the Faculty. Would this start a dangerous precedent?

Benson described the composition of the committee and said it had been approved by HEW. Leon Eisenberg

> asked who does in fact represent the interests of children if not the Faculty? He was annoyed that there was an imputation that it was of benefit to stop research. Pediatricians and even microbiologists could be excellent spokesmen for children. Dr. Beckwith replied that the Civil Liberties Union or the Children's Defense League would be more appropriate agents. His group had no wish to stop research. Dr. Eisenberg said that he felt that Dr. Beckwith's presentations had been unbalanced.

Ebert said he wished to consult the university's counsel about the faculty's legal right to reopen the matter. One faculty member was quoted as saying he was considering a motion to censure the critics because of their efforts to achieve publicity, and that if other members of the faculty felt similarly they should get in touch with him.

Two weeks later Ebert addressed a memorandum to the medical faculty describing Beckwith's motion, saying "since few members of the Faculty are well-briefed on the particulars of the research under consideration or the criticisms that had been made," he believed a formal debate on the subject at the next faculty meeting would be appropriate.

Walzer, exhausted, had assumed the controversy was ended with the vote of the Benson committee and, having assured his family that that was the case, had gone to Puerto Rico for a rest. He found out about the decision to reopen the investigation by accident, through his wife after his return, and was devastated.

On March 14 the Faculty of Medicine met again, this time with 375 members in attendance. Gerald, rather than Walzer, was the first presenter, because of, Gerald said, the personal abuse and threats that Walzer had been undergoing. His case rested on the fact that the study had been reviewed eleven times at Boston Hospital for Women, eight times at the Judge Baker Guidance Center (Walzer's institutional employer), and at least twice by the Medical School Senior Faculty Fellowship Committee. The NIH had also reviewed it twice.

Beckwith responded that he believed Walzer was sensitive to the issues in his study, more sensitive than many of his supporters. The issue was not research into behavior genetics, or medical research in general, but rather whether this particular study was consistent with HEW guidelines. He described the critics' view of the study and argued that little scientific knowledge could be gained from it. There should either be an attempt to design a double-blind study that might lead to significant results, or to recognize that the study as alternatively designed had too many risks, and to stop it.

Speaking next was Julius B. Richmond, then director of the Judge Baker Guidance Center. He argued against the notion of self-fulfilling prophecy, saying that Rosenthal's work had been widely criticized in the social science literature and, in general, had not been replicated.

Speaking in support of the critics was David D. Potter, a neurobiologist who argued that the composition of the Benson committee was important because it is difficult for employees of an institution to judge its research proposals dispassionately. In addition, he asserted, the Benson committee, like the faculty at the December meeting, had been given an inadequate report of the Farnsworth committee findings. A majority of members of the Farnsworth committee, Potter said, had voted against the study, finding that risks outweighed benefits. "I think," he said, "it is reasonable to ask whether the Benson committee would have found as it did if they had known that the Farnsworth committee, which still has this matter before it, had found against the study."

Benson replied that his committee had discussed the Walzer protocol on October 8, November 12, December 10, December 16, and January 14, and that they had considered all the points raised by the critics. "We simply could not be convinced in our research that much credence could be given to the concept or to the weight of self-fulfilling prophecy." The Benson committee also asked for and received five different revisions of the consent form. Benson did not believe there was an irregularity in reporting the deliberations of the Farnsworth committee, but that the Farnsworth committee had, in fact, voted for the study.

Beckwith replied that he had heard from several members of the Farnsworth committee that there had been a majority vote that the risks of the study outweighed the benefits, and that some of the members of the committee did not understand that a vote was being taken. Ebert argued that the issue was whether or not the Benson committee did consider the merits of the case irrespective of the Farnsworth committee report. Benson replied, "I believe we did." Ebert then said,

> That is the legally constituted committee, and I think the other quite honestly is irrelevant. In view of the lateness of the hour I would ask whether or not you wish to have a period for questions, or whether you feel you have enough information to make a vote on the motion.

The question was then called, and the vote was 199 against the Beckwith motion and 35 for it. (It is not known whether the 141 people in attendance who did not vote were abstaining, or not entitled to vote, or had simply left by that time.)

At the end of the meeting a resolution was introduced that the faculty express "its deep regret at the anxiety suffered by Dr. Walzer and his patients' families"; and its belief that resolution of the issues was impaired when criticisms were presented to the public before they had "been thoroughly debated by those with professional knowledge of their complexity"; and its conviction that efforts to prevent injury were "counterproductive" if they "injure[d] innocent parties and intimidate[d] investigators and their subjects." The resolution was later withdrawn.

A few days later Beckwith wrote to Walzer:

> Now that it appears that the Human Studies Committee decision is final, I would like to express feelings I have had for some time. I have deeply regretted the personal abuse to which you were subjected and the suffering you and your family must have gone through. I have no idea of the source of these attacks and can assure you that it was no one in our group. In our contacts with the press, we constantly attempted to play down the personalities involved and focus on the issues. Clearly, we could have been more careful.
>
> I recognize and have stated before faculty meetings that you have, in fact, shown more sensitivity to the issues involved than many of your supporters. If you feel that it would be at all useful, I, and possibly Jon King, would be interested in meeting with you to talk over any of these issues.[42]

Walzer replied that he and his family

> were deeply appreciative of your note. It really was very kind of you.
>
> Somehow or other a sobering and honorable inquiry rapidly developed into an adversary situation, providing little opportunity for free dialogue between us. It was particularly distressing because I was—and still am—concerned about many of the issues that you raised. What was most lacking was the opportunity for an interchange of ideas between us, leading to more far-reaching answers than the "yes you can"–"no you can't" variety. I truly hope we will have the opportunity soon. I must make my own decisions now and these require more knowledge than I presently have.
>
> Again, my deep appreciation for your most compassionate note.[43]

On May Day, Walzer halted his screening of newborns.

---

[42]Correspondence dated March 18, 1975 from Jonathan Beckwith to Stanley Walzer.

[43]Handwritten letter, undated from Stanley Walzer to Jonathan Beckwith.

His original plan had called for a study group of about forty boys (fifteen each of XXY and XYY and ten controls), a sample size he said was achieved in March. He thought it unwise to stop screening while the controversy was still prominent, so he had decided instead to stop the study in the fall. In April, however, he changed his mind because of the toll taken on his family and because of new action by other advocacy groups, such as the Children's Defense Fund. Of them he said, "They came up here knowing nothing about XYY; they had done no homework, no reading. They were very nice, but they didn't know enough about it to make the accusations they were making." In addition, two staff members of the Children's Defense Fund were interviewing researchers conducting XYY studies in Colorado.

The National Symposium on Genetics and the Law was held at the Copley Plaza Hotel in Boston May 18–20. (The proceedings of this meeting are available in *Genetics and the Law,* edited by Aubrey Milunsky and George Annas, and published by Plenum Press in 1976.) The Boston temperature was in the nineties. On the morning of the first day, Ernest Hook, author of the 1973 *Science* review, argued in very strong language in favor of XYY research; he also coined the word "geneticophobia" to describe the fear that a genetic explanation of a trait, particularly a behavioral trait, will undermine social attempts at positive changes in the environment. His principal discussant was Beckwith. A lengthy and often acrimonious discussion of the XYY situation in Boston and in general ensued and recurred continually for the three days of the meeting.

The fact that Walzer had stopped screening was not widely known until June 20, when Jane Brody wrote about it in the *New York Times,* though she also pointed out that he was continuing to follow up children already in the study. She reported that the timing was also partly because he was "run down by harassment, unrelenting controversy and the threat of further opposition to his work by groups supporting children's rights." The story goes on,

Until he said he was planning to stop screening, a second wave of criticism was mounting under the leadership of the Children's Defense Fund in Washington, working with a number of Massachusetts advocacy groups. William Smith of the Defense Fund said, "We had prepared a draft statement attacking the research, but we didn't have to use it because Dr. Walzer said he would stop screening."

Beckwith was quoted as saying he was "not too happy" about the follow-up being continued, but "at this point, the issue is murkier because he is already involved with the families, so he may have to continue to follow them."

Barbara Culliton described cessation of the screening in the June 27 *Science*, and quoted Walzer as saying

"I hope no one thinks I don't still believe in my research. I do, but this whole thing has been a terrible strain. My family has been threatened. I've been made to feel like a dirty person. And, even after I won with the Faculty, it was clear the opposition would go on. In fact, new groups were becoming involved. I was just too emotionally tired to go on." For example, lawyers for the Washington-based Children's Defense Fund went up to Boston not long ago to question Walzer about his work. Any even tentative thoughts they had about bringing some sort of legal action were, apparently, dropped when the screening stopped.[44]

The story also mentioned the dispute over whether Farnsworth reported the sense of his committee's deliberations accurately.

The following fall the *Harvard Crimson* reported that the Massachusetts attorney general eventually became involved, and although a suit was contemplated, it was never brought because by that time the screening had been stopped.

With cessation of the screening, the controversy was essentially over, though it continued to sputter in public for more than a year. The sputterings still had the capacity to wound, however. In July the *Boston Globe* carried a full-page

[44]Barbara J. Culliton, "XYY: Harvard Researchers under Fire, Stop Newborn Screening," *Science*, June 27, 1975, pp. 1284–1285.

wrap-up of the controversy, which said that the faculty had voted overwhelmingly "against the study." In a letter of apology to Walzer, the reporter said that was a typographical error, and that the copy he turned in had said "against *discontinuing* the study"; but from Walzer's point of view, damage had been done. He had begun to visit each of the families in his study (who by this time, of course, were well aware of what was going on) in an effort to find out how they felt about proceeding. The response, he said later, was "astounding"; the families were deeply upset at the idea that the study might stop. From the beginning, he says, no family has ever quit the study.

The following fall, in an address at the annual meeting of the American Society of Human Genetics in Baltimore, John Hamerton discussed the XYY controversy. Hamerton was that year president of the American Society of Human Genetics but had also done XYY studies in Canada, including newborn screening. He said:

> To me, the termination of the study is of less importance than the means used to bring this about; the ignoring of normally accepted methods of review and the continued harassment of individuals and their families are methods which in an earlier era might have been called "genetic McCarthyism." . . . Beckwith and King are entitled to their views . . . they are not, however, entitled to force their views on others by methods which, at best, can be termed doubtful, and at worst, thoroughly unethical.

The address concludes,

> It seems that there is no scientific basis for the major criticisms made by Beckwith and his group, Science for the People, and that these criticisms are not supported by available scientific data. This raises the question of Beckwith's scientific ability and objectivity outside his own field and his ability to mount valid criticisms of work in human and behavioral genetics, fields in which, so far as I am aware, he has no experience. The whole case put forward by this group is based on a misplaced ideological approach to scientific investigation.

A year later, *Harvard Magazine* ran opposing articles on

the controversy by Davis and by Beckwith and Miller. The Davis article criticized the form of attacks on the study, saying that they raised

> the old problem of how a democracy can protect itself from those who would use freedom of speech to deprive others of significant freedoms—in this case, freedom of inquiry, and the patient's freedom to know.

He also questioned

> whether academic freedom includes the right of a faculty member to carry an academic controversy to the public before it has been adequately explored within the institution, and the right to present an issue of policy in a way that publicly impugns a colleague's reputation.

He continued,

> We must recognize that we are dealing not simply with legitimate dissent. Just as Lysenko destroyed all of genetics in the Soviet Union from 1935 to 1969, Science for the People aims to destroy the field of human behavioral genetics. And we would be naive not to recognize that an opposition to certain ideas underlies its attack on allegedly harmful research activities.[45]

The Beckwith and Miller reply criticized the lack of public participation in the decision at Harvard and the composition of the various committees. It also noted:

> As the XYY case illustrates, the scientist works in a social environment and makes critical assumptions that inevitably color his or her research. The point is *not* that research on human behavior is without value, but rather that such research may become dangerous when social assumptions are subtly incorporated into science without acknowledging their social nature. The results have been falsely presented as "objective science" and finally applied in this disguised fashion to current social problems. In the case of XYY and other behavioral studies, scientists have relied on their "objectivity"—freedom from bias—to justify "freedom of inquiry." But if this scientific objectivity is brought into question and the intimate relationship

---

[45]Bernard D. Davis, "XYY: The Dangers of Regulating Research by Adverse Publicity," *Harvard Magazine*, October 1976, pp. 26–30.

between the scientist and society recognized, this justification for
unfettered research disappears.[46]

In the fall of 1977, Walzer became professor and chairman
of the Department of Psychiatry at the University of Massachusetts. "It was good to go away," he says, "it really was.
I was able to forget this stuff."

REFLECTIONS

The three case studies were selected by Hastings Center
staff with the idea that the controversies they describe would
have characteristics in common, and that from those could
be gleaned some useful lessons. Although that did turn out
to be the case, it is also true that their occasional differences
are instructive. This section will underscore some of those
parallels and divergences; implicit in this exercise ought to be
some lessons for the future.

Politics

At bottom, of course, the projects owed both their existence and their downfall to politics. Politics is, however, an
imprecise and catchall term, and the politics of these controversies were on different levels, in both the formal and informal senses of that word.

Of fundamental importance was national politics. Both
social and political violence were wracking the nation and
appeared to be on the rise in the sixties. The violence resulted
in a succession of national-level task forces and commissions
that often included among their recommendations the need
for more research. A series of Washington administrations
were willing to try a variety of responses to what they perceived as the anxious demands of the citizenry. Congress was
also influential in stimulating the research. According to R. W.

---

[46]Jonathan Beckwith and Larry Miller, "The XYY Male: The Making of a
Myth," *Harvard Magazine*, October 1976, pp. 30–33.

Velde, then acting administrator of the LEAA, the agency agreed to fund the Dr. Ervin–Neuro Research project largely because the late Brooklyn congressman John Rooney, chairman of the subcommittee that oversaw the LEAA and also a powerful member of the House Appropriations Committee, indicated interest in it and even arranged a meeting with the researchers. Said Velde:

> I decided very early on that whatever heat might be generated was a small price to pay for the political support, the appropriations support, that might likely come if this project were funded, from certain quarters on the Hill.[47]

Later, when the controversial nature of the research became more apparent, attitudes reversed. According to John Conrad, the top LEAA administrators all felt

> that during 1971 and 1972 particularly—remember, those were election years—that they didn't dare proceed on a program that might embarrass the President. . . . I think the caution which [they] had on this grant was understandable and in line with the well-known caution of that administration about everything. . . . I don't think [they] could have lost the election for Nixon in 1972, but I don't think they wanted to be accused of losing votes for him, either.

And of course Senator Ervin, one of the most uncompromising strict constructionists of the Bill of Rights ever to sit in Congress, was centrally important in halting both the Violence Center and federal interest in behavior modification in prisons. The influence of national politics on the XYY studies was considerably more subtle, consisting largely of the atmosphere generated by the citizenry's preoccupation with violence. This atmosphere predisposed politicians to look as if they were taking action, and functioned as the central psychological background in all three cases.

Formal politics at the state level was also important, particularly in those cases involving LEAA money, since much

[47]Unpublished transcript of a meeting on behavior modification in prisons at The Hastings Center, April 27–28, 1978, p. 9.

of it was administered through the state machinery. The Violence Center was essentially initiated by Stubblebine, fueled by the opportunistic (and of course utterly absurd) promises of his boss that the center would be discovering the causes and cures of violent crime by the middle of 1975. State-level control over such federal money made possible the continuation of behavior modification programs like those in the Virginia prison system long after the LEAA administrator appeared to renounce his support.

But state politics was also important in bringing down the projects, particularly in California, where powerful legislative opposition developed early and never wavered, and any friends the center had failed to speak up. As Stubblebine put it in a postmortem,

> We did not spend nearly enough time carefully developing the public education which would have brought about greater acceptance of the goals, the personnel, the restraints, the separation of powers, the roles and functions of the different powers—federal, state, and university. . . . Many politicians saw the center as too hot to handle, backed off, and refused to be counted, in part because they were not sure whether the public was behind it or not. California legislators and politicians, in the main, simply sat on their hands. In private, they would say "Yes, it's a hell of a fine idea," but in public they would do nothing.[48]

Although formal state-level interest does not appear to have figured in development of the Boston XYY research project, the possibility that the state attorney general's office might file suit against it was a factor in Walzer's decision to cease screening.

Finally, what might be called informal internal politics of various sorts was also critical: the eternal politics of grantsmanship, the labyrinthine machinations of the buck-passing

---

[48]Transcript of a meeting on the Violence Center at The Hastings Center, February 2–3, 1978, p. 4. Published as "Researching Violence: Science, Politics, and Public Controversy," Special Supplement, *The Hastings Center Report* 9 (April 1979).

Harvard committee structure, the importance of informal networks of people attuned to particular kinds of issues, so that some of the critics were active in more than one dispute. (Those kinds of networks can also be important in other ways: one can only speculate, for instance, that the course of the XYY controversy might have been different had one of the critics not gone to high school with a reporter for the *New York Times*.) But all these informal political factors—including that favorite scapegoat in most contemporary public disputes about science, "the media"—will always be important in such controversies. Details of this kind of internal politics are often interesting and sometimes even illuminating, but since such politics are inevitably present, to say that they were important in these three cases is to assert the trivial.

The Competence of the Researchers

Surely one major factor in the downfall of the Violence Center and the prison projects was the questions they triggered about the adequacy of the study designs and the competence of their designers. The letter from the LEAA research director to the federal agency's California funding outlet is a polite, mildly phrased, but devastating criticism of the Violence Center's plans and its staff, and the worries he expresses were a subtheme voiced by both the legislative and other critics of the center. Similarly, the disappointing record of Project START in actually changing the behavior of prisoners and the lack of focus and precision in the plans for Butner left an impression of ineptness that was very important in determining their fates.

By contrast, competence was not much of an issue in the XYY case. To be sure, the central argument revolved around the adequacy of the research design, but it was an argument about whether self-fulfilling prophecy was a real phenomenon or not, an argument not resolved even today. In this as in other respects, the Boston dispute was a different sort of controversy.

In the case of the Violence Center at least, the importance of questions of competence was acknowledged by both sides. Said Stubblebine: "Why was the center never established? For one thing, there was very poor planning. There were ideals, there was recognition of problems, and some glimmerings of possible solutions, but a plan is something else."[49] Hiestand agreed: "Ultimately it seemed to us that the project was not well thought out, or that someone was misrepresenting it, and that is why we opposed it."[50]

Competing Goals

No doubt much of the apparent disarray of the projects was the result of the failures of competence and even simple human sloppiness, but much was the result of competing aims and motives that were ultimately impossible to reconcile. This was as true of the Boston XYY case as of the other two.

One of Stubblebine's chief reasons for wanting to see the Violence Center come into existence was that he hoped it would result in a kind of list of predictors of violence. How such a list—assuming such a staggering assignment is even possible—would or could have been ultimately put to use was, however, never specified. Some of the possibilities—preventive detention, perhaps—seem to justify the worst fears of the critics. Yet the researchers who hoped to work through the center were by and large interested in doing "pure" rather than applied research, though the grant applications, of course, tried to make a case for the center's usefulness.

Confusion of and conflict over goals is endemic in the prison system because there is no agreement about whether prisons exist to rehabilitate or to punish, as John Conrad points out in chapter six of this book. A tool such as behavior modification—whose stated purpose is behavior change lead-

[49]Ibid.
[50]Ibid.

ing to rehabilitation—can easily be turned to punitive ends and become "cruel and unusual punishment" when the rehabilitative goal is confused with or overwhelmed by the ancient notion of just deserts. The enemies of behavior modification in prisons see this distortion as inevitable, and their conviction that the techniques will always be misused in this way fueled their opposition.

Stanley Walzer began with a relatively uncomplicated theoretical interest in the effects of chromosome abnormalities on behavior. In fact, at the outset he was far more interested in the XXY abnormality than in the XYY, and his study to this day includes both. But his original aim got complicated. The first complication arose through his boss, Park Gerald, who mistakenly thought Walzer's research would elucidate the biological base of sex differences. (This task, were it feasible, would no doubt have proved fully as controversial as the XYY study.)

The Crucial Yet Much-Ignored Role of the Funder

The second complication was the aim and goals of his funding agency, the Center for Studies of Crime and Delinquency of the National Institute of Mental Health. The very name of this funder in some sense begs the questions Walzer wanted to ask. It implies from the outset that chromosome abnormalities must somehow be involved with crime, delinquency, and mental disease. Both Walzer and Saleem Shah, head of the Center for Studies of Crime and Delinquency, argued at a Hastings Center meeting that Walzer's application was assigned to the center almost fortuitously, largely because Shah had already begun to express an interest in the XYY condition by organizing and sponsoring the 1969 meeting.[51] But the fact remains that *somebody*, if only a nameless NIMH

[51]Transcript of a meeting on the Boston XYY controversy at the Hastings Center, November 9–10, 1978, p. 15. Published as "The XYY Controversy: Researching Violence and Genetics," Special Supplement, *The Hastings Center Report*, 10 (August 1980).

administrator, thought the center the most appropriate locus for Walzer's proposal, which means that the mental link between XYY and crime was already in existence.

In fact, the role of the funding agencies in these cases can hardly be overstated. In each of the three situations the core research projects and their goals were deformed to meet what the researchers perceived as the goals of the underwriter. At a Hastings Center meeting on the prison case, psychiatrist Robert Michels observed:

> I think grant rhetoric is a dependent variable, and the independent variable is to whom the grant is mailed. The reason the grants are written the way they're written is that they're mailed to people who won't understand them if they're written more honestly . . . if you get investigators writing grants, to be reviewed by people without scientific training or without familiarity with the technical content of the field, then every biomedical research grant is written to find a cure for cancer, and every prison experimental grant is written to end all crime.[52]

He made the same point even more eloquently at a meeting about the Violence Center:

> A sequence of characters has emerged here. There is an investigator who wants to study something and find out answers. He couldn't care less about violence centers but he wants West, his boss, to get him money so he can do his project. West, who's a good boss, wants to help him and knows that the way to get money is to sell Stubblebine on the fact that the results, with a little bit of exaggeration, will serve some practical purpose for the California justice system. Stubblebine, wanting that practical result and believing in the potential value of research, is going to—with some discount for West's persuasive skills— support the project at that time. But Stubblebine has a selling job too. He has to make sure that the people who have to approve his budget feel that his distribution of resources is appropriate for the practical problems he is supposed to face. By now we are getting somewhere near Governor Reagan.
>
> At that level the distinction so important to West between individual and collective violence might become usefully

---

[52]Unpublished transcript of a meeting on behavior modification in prisons at the Hastings Center, April 27–29, 1978, p. 127.

blurred for political reasons. The project that begins by being aimed at understanding the impact of early childhood experience on later behavior, then becomes a potential way of assessing the safety of returning a battered child to a battering parent, and then becomes a potential tool for convincing the California electorate that the government is doing something important about crime in the streets and social unrest. This convenient political blur then triggers a group of anticonservative forces who are against the proponents of the center because it represents values that the anticonservative group sees as detrimental to their goals for society. The investigator, who only wanted to study white rats, cannot understand why someone is protesting in his office the next morning. I think that sequence isn't implausible.[53]

Although the funders played a crucial role in muddying the project goals in all three cases, they also had an important influence in the area of competence discussed earlier. It was the incompetence of agencies of the Justice Department to adequately review and oversee research more properly the province of the (then) Department of Health, Education and Welfare that was centrally responsible for the mess in the first two cases. The fact that the NIMH—complete with elaborate peer review—was Walzer's funding source is probably one reason why his study design was so defensible, and why it was repeatedly vindicated by review committees. The peer review process can be accused of many things, from bureaucratic torpor to the stifling of innovation and creativity in science, but it probably does at least function to keep some inept research from being done.

If there is a single salient point that emerges from these case studies, it is one that is familiar to virtually anyone who has ever written a grant proposal: the all-important (but often forgotten) part the funder plays in shaping the nature of the research it underwrites. This point applies not just to potentially controversial research, but to *all* research. As Michels told West,

<hr/>

[53]Transcript of a meeting on the Violence Center, February 2–3, 1978, pp. 6–7 (see fn. 48 above).

I have a feeling that the more interesting underlying conflict
was not opponents v. proponents, not West v. Hiestand but
West v. Stubblebine, because although those two are grouped
together here, it seems to me that they are antagonists in some
ways. The San Francisco *Chronicle* reported that more than a
million dollars would be invested and the center should be
discovering causes and cures for violent crime by mid-1975. Dr.
West, that may have served your funder well, but it did not
serve *you* well. At that moment you are being brought into an
entirely different agenda which may be your funder's agenda,
but it is not yours. The lesson may be that the community
groups are going to have to be dealt with, and the lawyers, too,
but the real problem area may be those who you think are your
friends.[54]

Character Assassination, Ad-Hominem Remarks, and Bruised Egos

Personal acrimony always plays a part in controversy,
though its importance is usually underestimated. Bad blood
and hurt feelings were prominent in each of these three cases,
exacerbated them, and kept them from being resolved. West
is a major figure in American psychiatry, no stranger to controversy, and he has therefore by definition made enemies. In
addition, as the chronological account of the Violence Center
controversy shows, he had made a bad impression on legislative consultant Steve Thompson some years before, with
the result that Thompson and his boss, the chairman of a
crucial state assembly committee that held the purse strings,
simply did not trust him. In the prison controversy, Martin
Groder was very angry and felt personally attacked when the
BOP fired him as director-designate of Butner; he called a press
conference to protest the action, and gave indignant interviews. Perhaps the worst torment was undergone by Walzer.
While even his formal public opponents were declaring their
belief in his integrity and good intentions, his telephone was

[54]Ibid, 14.

ringing off the hook with anonymous vilification and sly, sadistic threats against his family.

Adding to the impact of the genuine personal attacks was the fact that all the researchers subjectively experienced substantive criticisms of their research as personal attacks, though at least sometimes that was not what they were. Nor was the derogation all one-sided; the researchers and their defenders often had unpleasant things to say about the opponents as well. The most striking example is Hamerton's astonishing presidential address to the American Society of Human Genetics, which contained a bitter personal attack on Jonathan Beckwith. It was also routine in all three controversies for many of the defenders to characterize the opponents as "leftist" (which was often true), "Marxist" (which was sometimes true), or worse, and their criticism of the research as part of a master plan to create political revolution in the United States.

This point about name calling is not a trivial one. Sociologist Robin Williams Jr. has observed in connection with the Violence Center (but it applies just as well to the other two cases):

> Very conspicuous in this case are derivative controversies and conflicts that emerge directly from the controversy itself, such as the development of public commitments which then have to be defended, a loss of face and consequent psychological repercussions, injurious recriminations, and depths of hurt feelings. One of the prime rules of conflict resolution is not to indulge in these kinds of things unnecessarily, because quite often they are much more difficult to resolve than the initial issues.[55]

The legacy of all the name calling is as Williams prophesied. Although all of the controversies will soon be a decade old, they have left behind a thick and sticky residue of hostility that—particularly in the case of the Boston XYY study—shows very little evidence of abating with time.

[55]Ibid, 17.

The Ostensible Ethical Issues

Taking all the foregoing into account—some of which was explicitly at issue during the courses of the controversies and some of which bubbled beneath the surface—how much merit was there in the critics' major public allegations?

The Violence Center. I doubt that there was any intent on the part of its progenitors (even in state government) that the center serve repressive political ends; allowing a certain discount for the inevitable operation of self-interest, the stated motives were probably close to being the "real" ones. That is not to say that the critics' worries were illegitimate. Given the right political climate, such a center could certainly have been turned to the purposes they feared. Since the future political climate is always unknowable, their opposition was from the outset total and unwavering, and therefore no offers of compromise or plans for procedural safeguards were—or could ever be—acceptable. This style is common to contemporary disputes over the uses of science; one sees it, for instance, in the controversy over recombinant DNA research. Critics employ an argument that is a variation on Murphy's law, such as: "If a piece of scientific research can be used for repression, it will be." It is an impossible argument to assess or deal with at the time, because it can only be resolved by history. The center's critics may, in short, have been right about its ultimate uses.

On the other hand, one could argue that such uncompromising criticism may be a tactical mistake. It may drive such research underground, where it can be more easily misused. Those who worry about political repression might be better served by a highly visible center, replete with procedural safeguards and peer review, one whose work and its social uses are more easily subject to scrutiny.

Does that mean the center should have been established after all? I do not believe so, though my objections are more akin to those voiced by the LEAA research director—inadequacy of research design and of its probable execution—

than because I fear the center would have served as an instrument of fascism. Criticisms based on competence factors were quite justified—and were, interestingly, probably the single most influential group of arguments as well.

Behavior Modification in Prisons. Here the critics were on firmer ground in worrying about built-in elements of repression. Prisons are, after all, institutions for the purpose of repression. Furthermore, they are virtually closed to outside inspection. How repressive should they be allowed to be? Investigators from the National Prison Project were shocked by the conditions in Project START; those experienced in the ways of prisons are likely to shrug and characterize such reactions as naïve responses from people who have no notion of what prison is really like. This argument will not be resolved as long as there is confusion, as discussed above, over whether prisons exist for punishment or for rehabilitation. In the case of behavior modification, this confusion comes close to tragedy. The techniques have demonstrated their effectiveness in benignly changing self-destructive human behavior (control of smoking, overeating, or drinking, for instance, and even in institutional settings such as those for the mentally retarded). But behind bars, the techniques can easily become agents of control or punishment. I am not as convinced as some of the critics that procedural safeguards are impossible here, but they are certainly very difficult, and having them in place would be a necessary precondition to the use of behavior modification techniques in prisons.

The Boston XYY Study. This controversy is by far the most difficult one to adjudicate. The central figures on both sides, by and large, marshaled good arguments and were careful and responsible with them; yet the controversy stirred up so many damaging extraneous events (such as the anonymous telephone calls and the infighting on and about the Harvard committees) that an amazing amount of ill will still remains.

Perhaps some of that ill will is a product of the fact that both sides were partly right, and so it is not possible for any disputant to feel completely vindicated. The critics were right in saying that the informed-consent procedure was inadequate, and the researchers were right in saying that the procedure was no worse than usual for its time, and that it was constantly revised in light of both the criticisms and changing national standards. The critics were right in saying the research would certainly affect the rearing of the boys in the study and could even gravely injure some of them, but Walzer was right in saying that it was immoral to stand by and watch a small child get into trouble if, by intervening, he could mitigate that process.

Aspects of the study are certainly troubling. The fact that the chief investigator and at least some of the parents were not truly blind to the chromosomal makeup of the children renders it something less than scientific. In addition, the notion that expectations could provoke or precipitate the very behavior everyone feared seems—despite the arguments about the validity of the Rosenthal hypothesis—intuitively justified; that possibility needs, at a minimum, to be taken seriously. Nevertheless, I agree with Jonathan Beckwith that, having begun the follow-up studies, the researchers were morally obliged to continue them. With hindsight, I would go further. XYY studies—and there have been several besides the one in Boston—have to a great extent *laid to rest* the idea of a criminal chromosome. On balance XYY men are probably better-off, in terms of stigmatization, that such studies have been done. Indeed, the whole field of behavior genetics is probably better-off, the researchers involved in it having been handed some object lessons in the controversial and socially important nature of the work they do, and the marvelous lability and plasticity of the human genome.

Conclusion

If there is any kind of ultimate lesson here, it appears to me to be threefold. First, if research has even the remote potential to be used for purposes of social control *and* it is also

going on in a time and place where political activists care
about that issue, it will be controversial. XYY projects quite
similar to Walzer's were taking place simultaneously in a half-
dozen North American cities virtually without public notice
and certainly without controversy. Nor do the activists—
conspiracy theorists take note—have to be formally organized. Science for the People's experience at radical critiques
of science, at organizing, and at tactics were extremely important, but defenders of the research who therefore dismissed the critics as a concatenation of Marxist/Luddite ideo-
logues were conveniently ignoring the fact that (particularly
at the outset) the critics comprised a coalition, several of
whom were not associated with Science for the People. What
this probably means is that a vast amount of research into
human behavior is potentially controversial in Boston, California, and a few other places, but would likely be ignored
elsewhere.

Second, scientific controversies are not all bad. These three
have meant that at least some poor research failed to find a
home, research that was both bad science and potentially
socially harmful. The cases also make clear the direct links
between research goals and political climate, something many
scientists still deny. They also can force scientists and their
reviewers to define more carefully their concepts and sharpen
their research design. All these effects have taken place, to
a greater or lesser extent, not just in these three cases but
probably outside them as well, in the professional lives of
some who were simply spectators at the melees but who drew
morals from them.

The last lesson—one that I think is not at all understood
by either side—is that the critics were not, ultimately, as successful as I suspect they believe. True, there is no Violence
Center at UCLA. But the center was never more than an
administrative unit anyway; it never had any thematic co-
herence or overall goal except the getting and disbursing of
funds for a polyglot assortment of unrelated projects—many
of which West has gone on to successfully raise money for

elsewhere. Similarly, the LEAA directive banning behavior modification was regarded as a victory by the critics, but it was written in such a way as to leave loopholes, particularly for projects that could be labeled medical. The fact that so much LEAA money was distributed by individual states made federal directives problematic in any case. Finally, there is the Boston XYY study. Because the initial screening stopped, it was widely assumed that the whole study stopped. Although many of the formal criticisms of the study centered around the consent procedure for the screening, it was really the follow-up study, and its possible harm to the boys, that was most worrisome to many critics. Yet the follow-up continues today.

Researchers who are feeling beleaguered and put upon may draw some comfort from the notion that if they are cautious and persistent, and are careful about the labels they apply to their projects and the part of the country they locate in, they may encounter no problems at all, even over research that is potentially quite volatile. And those who believe sustained and open criticism can bring down research they think is pernicious may want to mull over the thought that an advertised victory may be a bogus one.

PART III
IMPLICATIONS

CHAPTER 4

Science and Social Control

Controversies over Research on Violence

DOROTHY NELKIN and JUDITH P. SWAZEY

INTRODUCTION

Dr. Martin Arrowsmith, the researcher-physician immortalized by Sinclair Lewis, doubtless would feel a stranger in a strange land if he materialized today. The reverential public attitudes toward scientific and medical research, reflected and in part created by earlier twentieth-century fictional works such as *Arrowsmith* and "nonfiction" accounts by writers such as Paul de Kruiff, have changed, and many areas of research

DOROTHY NELKIN ● Program on Science, Technology and Society, Cornell University, Ithaca, New York 14850. JUDITH P. SWAZEY ● Medicine in the Public Interest, Inc., Suite 304, 65 Franklin Street, Boston, Massachusetts 02110.

have come under critical public scrutiny. In fiction, *Arrowsmith's* visions of science and technology are supplanted by images of the *Andromeda Strain*, *The Terminal Man*, and *The China Syndrome*. In real life, research projects are stopped or delayed as groups external to science, and in some cases scientists themselves, question the moral implications of research activities, their immediate impacts, and their long-range social consequences. In the late twentieth-century social assessment of science, questions are raised about the limits of scientific inquiry, and efforts are made to redefine and in some cases to sharply delimit its boundaries.[1] Is some research so threatening to the basic values of certain groups or so potentially risky to human subjects that it should not be done at all? Who are, or ought to be, the "experts" in decisions about the nature and governance of research? Is the traditional freedom of scientists to define and control their own research still reasonable given the expanded possibilities of mdoern science in areas such as human biology and behavior?

For multiple reasons, the very process of carrying out scientific investigation is now suspect. Experiments involving the human fetus threaten the values of right-to-life groups; techniques of recombining DNA molecules, it is feared, may produce new and dangerous forms of infectious microorganisms or lead to an Orwellian future of genetic engineering. Concerns are voiced about the conduct, methods, and objectives of research with human subjects, especially in institutional settings such as prisons or mental hospitals, where concepts such as informed, voluntary consent are particularly difficult to realize.

Some research is challenged because of the potential abuse of the knowledge it may generate. Studies of the relationship between genetics and IQ, research on genetic manipulations, and theories of sociobiology are often attacked on methodological grounds, but the basis of concern is their potential for sociopolitical misuse. Biology, critics claim, is a

---

[1]Limits of Scientific Inquiry, *Daedalus* 107 (Spring 1978).

"social weapon" that provides not only beneficial knowledge and applications but also scientifically accessible means of social control.[2]

Critics of science often evaluate research less in terms of its internal merits than its perceived social implications. Moral concepts of fairness, human dignity, and human rights enter the social assessment of science; and these concepts far outweigh criteria such as "scientific importance," the excellence of design, or the qualifications of investigators—the sorts of parameters by which research is assessed (and funded) within the scientific community.

Given the increasingly critical social assessment of science, it is not surprising that research bearing on the identification, the reduction, and the control of violent behavior, often linked with criminal acts, has been especially vulnerable to critical scrutiny.

THE PROJECTS

The three projects relating to the study of control of violent behavior that we have examined illustrate many of the forces and issues that converge in the social assessment of science. The first project began in May 1970 when Harvard child psychiatrist Stanley Walzer initiated a chromosome screening study of all male newborns at the Boston Hospital for Women, to identify and prospectively study the development of those with an XYY karyotype. Walzer's project grew out of work he had done with Harvard geneticist Park Gerald, including a 1965–1969 chromosome survey of randomly selected, phenotypically normal newborns that was focused chiefly on identifying XXY karyotypes. Criticism of various facets of the XYY study's design and execution began to be voiced early in 1974. In May 1976, although various

[2]Ann Arbor Science for the People Collective, *Biology as a Social Weapon* (Minneapolis: Burgess, 1977).

Harvard review committees continued to approve the study, Walzer stopped the newborn screening phase of the XYY study.

The second project also had its inception in 1972, when the Neuropsychiatric Institute of the University of California at Los Angeles proposed to develop a Center for the Study and Reduction of Violence. This interdisciplinary center was to establish research and demonstration programs to study the causes of pathologically violent behavior, to identify "violent predispositions," and to develop techniques for preventing violence and for treating criminal offenders. The proposed projects included studies of disturbed adolescents and their families, the use of a new drug (cyproterone acetate) for the treatment of rapists, the chromosomal abnormalities related to violent behavior, and the relation between violence and minimal brain damage. The researchers sought funding from the California Department of Mental Hygiene and the federal Law Enforcement Assistance Administration (LEAA). By 1974, after more than a year of protest, both the State of California and the federal government withdrew earlier promises to support the center and plans for its creation were abandoned.

During the same period, several experimental behavior modification programs in prisons, which comprised the third project we studied, also lost their funding from the LEAA. These included the Special Treatment and Rehabilitation Training Project (START) in Missouri, and projects at federal facilities in Butner, North Carolina and Patuxet, Maryland. These prison programs used various behavior modification techniques including group therapy, Synanon-type therapy, electronic techniques of aversive conditioning, and operant conditioning. The prisoners enrolled in the projects had been unable to adjust to regular prison routines because of consistently "maladaptive" and "unmanageable" behavior. The projects were intended to help change the attitudes and behavior of these recalcitrant prisoners so that they could return to regular institutional programs.

The research and demonstration work in these three projects raised sensitive questions about the relationship of genetically mediated characteristics to human behavior, about the morality of modifying behavior by medical or psychological means, about the power of social control offered by new biomedical and behavioral technologies, and about the power relationships inherent in situations and settings where freedom of choice to participate in research cannot be taken for granted.

Biomedical and behavioral research covers a spectrum from "basic" to "applied" and from "experimental" to "therapeutic" research.[3] The three projects can be arrayed, with some overlap, on different loci in the basic–applied and experiment–therapy spectrum. Their location on the spectrum, in turn, helped to shape the nature of the controversy that each project generated.

The XYY study sought to combine basic epidemiologic research in behavioral genetics in the newborn screening portion of the study with a longitudinal follow-up of "experimental" (XYY karyotype) and "control" (normal karyotype) groups that included therapeutic interventions within a research context. The second, multifaceted project, the UCLA Center for the Study and Reduction of Violence, involved various combinations of research and treatment–demonstration projects. The third enterprise, the LEAA-funded behavior modification programs in prisons, primarily involved demonstration projects designed to test the use of various behavior change principles and techniques.

These projects, in their own right and as paradigmatic cases, are open to quite different interpretations depending

---

[3]On distinctions between experimentation and therapy and between basic and applied research see Renée C. Fox and Judith P. Swazey, *The Courage to Fail: A Social View of Organ Transplants and Dialysis*, 2nd rev. ed. (Chicago: University of Chicago Press, 1978), Ch. 3; Judith P. Swazey and K. Reeds, *Today's Medicine, Tomorrow's Science: Essays on Paths of Discovery in the Biomedical Sciences* (Washington, D.C.: DHEW Publication No. [NIH] 78-244, 1978), Ch. 1.

on one's ideological perspective. Is behavior control a way to bring recalcitrant individuals into a less socially deviant and more personally or socially productive life? Or is it a means to better maintain social order at what may be enormous political and personal cost to certain socioeconomic groups? Will research into possible genetic bases for antisocial or criminal behavior enable us to ameliorate or prevent such behavior, or will it only facilitate social control by means of "genetic labeling"? Is a medical-behavioral approach to criminally violent behavior a humane route to reduce the need for punishment, or is it a sinister diversion of attention from the social and environmental factors that help to provoke such behavior?

Underlying all three controversies are different ideological perspectives on the definition of violence and its sources, and on the consequences of the emerging techniques of predicting and manipulating behavior. Thus our analysis of the disputes over these projects focuses on the perceptions of the protagonists, the sources of support and opposition, and the tactics of opposition and defense; our intention is to demonstrate how different ideological and political convictions shape the evaluation and the acceptance or rejection of scientific ideas and their applications.

THE ACTORS

The Researchers

Except in the judgment of the actors themselves, the scenarios of the three projects do not have heroes and villains. In our view, neither researchers nor their critics had pernicious intentions. The researchers for the most part sincerely sought to advance science and to bring what they perceived as the benefits of science to the resolution of social problems, and their opponents, with equal sincerity, sought to expose and stop what they perceived as a misuse or abuse of scientific hypotheses and techniques. In some cases, especially in the XYY study, the scientists identified their study as basic research that should be evaluated by their peers according to norms for judging the intrinsic merit and validity of such research. In addition, they saw practical benefits accruing from their work. It was hoped that if a correlation between the extra Y chromosome and a predisposition to aggressive behavior was established, it would facilitate the development of remedial and therapeutic interventions to prevent antisocial behavior.

At UCLA, investigators sought to develop diagnostic and predictive methods to reduce or prevent criminally violent behavior. They regarded their work as a form of public service that would benefit victims of violence, potential criminals, and society as a whole. Comparably, those involved in the LEAA prison projects perceived their work as a means to enhance institutional order within prisons and to permit alternatives in incarceration; they claimed to be using science to seek humane solutions to problems that usually are handled punitively.

Blinded by long-standing assumptions about the objective, value-free, and apolitical nature of science, the researchers in every case failed to perceive the critical ideological and political questions raised by their work. Moreover, socialized in the tradition of scientific autonomy and professional dominance that characterizes the role of scientists and physicians, they were stunned by the vehemence of the political challenge to their endeavors and responded with moral outrage. The nature of the scientific review system compounded the reluctance with which they acknowledged opposition. Prior to funding, research projects as a rule are reviewed by an institutional board to assure that the risks to subjects are outweighed by potential benefits and that informed consent is obtained by appropriate means. Proposed projects are also reviewed by a funding agency's study section or comparable peer review group to assess scientific design and merit. Such procedures, most researchers feel, are more than adequate controls over the quality and conduct of their work. The fact that the major sources of funding for these three projects came not from the usual sponsors of basic research but instead from such sources as the NIMH's Center for Studies of Crime and Delinquency, the LEAA, the Bureau of Prisons, and the California Commission on Mental Health—agencies that are less concerned with scientific validity than with finding solutions to social problems—did not alert the scientists to the controversial aspects of their work.

Thus, in the XYY study, the researchers defended their project, in part, by citing the multiple reviews that their protocol had undergone within Harvard and the NIMH. They also pointed out that their source of funding—the NIMH's Center for Studies of Crime and Delinquency—was not one to which they had applied directly because they perceived a linkage between their work and the Center's. Instead they had submitted a proposal to the NIMH, and it had been routed to the Center by the NIMH's central grant-processing office, the Division of Research Grants. The source of funding, XYY researcher Park Gerald feels, was misleading. For, he affirms, "at no time has the research that we've been involved in been related to violence." Similarly, Stanley Walzer maintains that "we did not start the study with the assumption that XYY is related to violence, because by the time we began, the literature increasingly was showing that it is not related."

The Critics

Proposals for research funding, and the conduct of research itself, are usually routine and closed matters, handled within their scientific community. But these projects relating to violent behavior produced an extraordinary, indeed a violent response from quite different groups.

The critics of the Boston XYY study were mainly members of Science for the People, a group of scientists socialized during the Vietnam War and sensitive to social and racial inequities and to the potential misuse of scientific knowledge. Their concerns with XYY research grew out of their broader ideological opposition to work in behavioral genetics. They took issue with this specific project on the grounds of its methodological design, the problems of obtaining valid informed consent for research with newborns, and the implications of "labeling" its subjects as chromosomally "abnormal," possibly setting into motion a "self-fulfilling prophecy" about their behavioral development.

At UCLA, the political climate in the early seventies was still charged by the events of the late sixties. Indeed, only several years earlier university research had been a target of student protest because of its links to military objectives. The opposition to research into violence thus grew out of the student movement. But critics of this as well as of the LEAA programs also included the Black Panthers, the NAACP, the United Farm Workers Organizing Committee, the California Prisoners Union, NOW, the Mexican American Political Association, and other groups concerned with ethnic and social equity. Perceiving prisons as a major pillar of institutional racism, such groups often regard inmates as "political prisoners." In this context they regarded the research on violence and the use of behavior modification techniques as efforts to prevent political dissent, to divert attention from unrest among the poor, and to create complacent prisoners for the benefit of guards or complacent children for the benefit of teachers.[4] Despite the diversity of the critics—students, scientists, and political groups concerned with minority rights—they shared similar interpretations of the methodological, moral, and political problems inherent in the research.

THE SOURCES OF OPPOSITION

Critics of the XYY studies at both Harvard and UCLA argued that basic methodological problems distorted the research and precluded the gathering of valid data. On scientific grounds alone, therefore, they held the research to be uneth-

---

[4]Many of them expressed their views in hearings before the California Council on Criminal Justice, July 27, 1973.

ical.[5] Studies of the frequency of the XYY genotype were based on an inaccurate demographic picture of the study population and inadequate control groups. The retrospective studies to identify men with the XYY chromosome used sources such as inadequate military data and often anecdotal records. Prospective studies of the development of the XYY individual violated basic methodological principles by relying on behavioral descriptions of children by parents. How could a researcher assure that information on the chromosomal abnormality would not bias parental attitudes, thereby influencing the very behavior that was being studied? How in such cases can one distinguish the effect of a genetic aberration from the results of parental attitudes?

The Harvard XYY researchers, in retrospect, recognize that they were "frighteningly naïve" about how their work might be perceived. Had they been more attuned to the sociopolitical climate surrounding behavioral genetics in general and XYY research in particular, they might have learned much from the fate of the aborted Maryland screening study of boys in juvenile jails and from underprivileged minority families. That study's design and objectives, its critics held, made it "a parody of clinical research" and a "science of devil's marks"; it was seen as epitomizing "medical totalitarianism" and the use of "fraudulent science" to support sociopolitical views.

Issues of justice and freedom of choice, however, were far more fundamental in shaping the dissent. Each of these projects raised questions about the validity of informed, voluntary consent. The federal guidelines designed to protect participants in human experimentation, based on principles established at the Nuremberg trials, seek to promote and protect the autonomy of subjects and guard them against unto-

---

[5]Critics of the XYY study's design, for example, cited the Nuremberg Code's third provision, which states that "the experiment should be so designed and based on the results of animal experimentation and a knowledge of the natural history of the disease or other problem under study that the anticipated results will justify the performance of the experiment."

ward risk.[6] They require that research using human subjects must make an important contribution to science, that the benefits of the study must outweigh its risks, and that subjects must give their informed, voluntary consent. But what constitutes adequate information? Cannot many subjects be subtly coerced to participate in experiments? Informed consent and voluntary compliance are ideals not easily realized in the coercive environment of a prison, or in other settings where many forms of overt or covert leverage can be placed on potential research subjects or their guardians. The parents of a disturbed or hyperkinetic child who is referred to an experimental program by his school are hardly in a position to give "voluntary" consent.[7] Inmates in a prison, where participation in an experiment may be linked to a system of favors or to existing power relationships, are hardly in a position to avoid coercion. Women given consent forms while in labor are hardly in a situation to assimilate information about a newborn screening program.

Critics of the LEAA behavior modification programs questioned the meaning of procedural guidelines in a setting where discretionary power is held by authorities whose primary goal is maintaining order and cooperative behavior among the prisoners. Indeed, "voluntary participation" in a prison may be compromised by fear of punishment and, above all, by the need to behave in ways that will maximize chances for parole.

Several prisoners described the behavior modification ex-

[6]See George J. Annas, L.H. Glantz, and B.F. Katz, *Informed Consent to Human Experimentation: The Subject's Dilemma* (Cambridge, Mass.: Ballinger, 1977).
[7]Issues of informed consent, as well as of social control, were also central to another research controversy that erupted in Boston in 1972 concerning the effects of psychotropic drugs on learning difficulties and behavioral disorders in children. The coalition of community groups and organizations opposing this project included the Massachusetts Advocacy Center, which also became involved in opposition to the XYY study. See "MBD, Drug Research and the Schools," Special Supplement, *The Hastings Center Report* 6 (June 1976).

periments not as positive reinforcement but as an abuse of their human and constitutional rights, and as cruel and unusual punishment. Some complained of humiliating "token economies" in which routine necessities such as toilet paper had to be earned; others complained of the use of aversive conditioning in which drugs were used to control behavior. One prisoner wrote of "the Nazification of the prison system with the enthusiastic cooptation and cocriminality of the academics . . . prisoners are literally fair game for the mad surgeons, the shrinks, and the social engineers."[8] The conditions of research in a prison, contend its critics, simply preclude rational discourse and independent choice.

Moreover, they argue, the risks of such research far outweigh the usefulness of the knowledge, even assuming that valid results could be obtained. Given the sources of funding and the compelling social pressures to develop rapid technologies for reducing violence, could the projects maintain stringent ethical standards concerning the recruitment of subjects and the conduct of the research? Scientific techniques that promise to reduce or prevent violence have such public appeal that concepts of human dignity or individual rights may be given low priority. Opponents of the research had little faith that scientists could resist such social pressure, for, after all, their own careers were involved.

Critics also feared the long-term implications of research that relates human behavior to genetically mediated characteristics. XYY research brought forth images of eugenics, and fears of generating knowledge that would be used to perpetuate damaging social class and racial biases.[9] Do we really want to know if there is a genetic basis to social behavior? Would not such knowledge affect our belief that individual citizens should be treated with equal respect? Would that not lead to the development of pernicious mechanisms for social

[8]Undated correspondence to Dr. Willard Gaylin, no date.
[9]See George J. Annas, "XYY and the Law," *The Hastings Center Report* 2 (April 1972); Richard Roblin, "The Boston XYY Case," *The Hastings Center Report* 5 (August 1975): 5–8.

control, particularly of racial minorities and the poor? In the case of UCLA's proposed center, critics did not miss the fact that the Los Angeles schools to be used for the study of troubled adolescents were in black and Chicano areas. Similarly, those who drew critical attention to the proposed 1970 Maryland XYY chromosome screening study pointed out that half of the test groups consisted of children from predominantly poor, black families enrolled in a free medical program at Johns Hopkins, from whom the researchers had not planned to obtain consent. Studies of the families of aggressive children, the critics observed, mainly focus on the poor, if only because the middle class is better able to conceal its problems. Assessing the research in such political terms, critics attacked it through political action—demonstrations, petitions, referenda, and various "media events."

THE TACTICS OF OPPOSITION AND DEFENSE

> We're here to cure your troubles and fill your life with hope.
> We'll treat your criminal tendencies with lobotomies and dope.
> Dope to make you feel you're drowning, dope to give you pain.
> Dope to keep you quiet while we're cutting out your brain.[10]

In the UCLA and LEAA projects, the critics saw scientists as "collaborators" with prison officials, and their rhetoric left little to the imagination. They called researchers "racists" and "Nazi butchers," and related the research on violence to "fascism," "eugenics," and "genocide." The scientists were accused of "sprinkling the perfume of scientific legitimacy over the stench of experimentation on prisoners." (One cartoon shows a fiendish scientist at UCLA converting prisoners into robots by running electric wires through their heads.)

They attacked the political backing of the projects, the sources of funding, and, at UCLA, the support of Ronald

[10]*Daily Bruin* (UCLA student newspaper), January 11, 1974. Much of the diatribe against the project appeared in this newspaper throughout 1973 and 1974, and in petitions and other ephemera.

Reagan and other conservative California politicians. They searched for vulnerable points—especially the aura of secrecy that seemed to envelop the projects. The UCLA center proposed at one point to locate some of its experimental programs at a Nike missile base that had been abandoned by the Army. This isolated site was far away from residential neighborhoods, and was selected in order to avoid community opposition to the experiments. But the plan backfired as critics saw this choice of location as a means to maintain secrecy: Just what would be done at this isolated laboratory? Suspicions were reinforced when investigators hesitated to distribute information on controversial aspects of the program. At first, this reluctance was probably out of habit; scientists, after all, regard their work as technical and not for public distribution. Later materials, however, were withheld out of self-defense. Critics interpreted this inaction as an effort to avoid criticism, and when material was distributed, they then publicly accused scientists of "sanitizing" it in response to criticism.

They also seized on the vague nature of the research guidelines. How would prisoners be selected? What were the research protocols? Scientists may leave such specifics open for several reasons. The UCLA center was conceived as a coordinating base for existing research and there was little point in limiting the research to be included prior to funding. Moreover, flexibility and lack of early specification about research is advantageous, allowing autonomy and flexibility in its actual implementation. For critics, however, the open-end nature of the proposal allowed the possibility of psychosurgery, brainwashing, and other unethical activities. And lack of specification reduced public accountability. Indeed, the UCLA plan resembled the loosely structured university research centers that had so easily adapted to military research during the Vietnam War.

The point of the critics' dramatic frontal attacks on the projects was to arouse public concern and thereby to indirectly apply pressure on public agencies and scientific institutions.

The critics of science see no direct way to implement their views through legitimate institutional channels. The peer review panels, the university committees, and even the institutional review boards are perceived as mechanisms to foster the interests of the professional community. And this perception is often reinforced, as in the case of the critics of the XYY project who first, unsuccessfully, tried to work through Harvard's review committees. Accordingly, tactics of public protest are seen as more effective. And indeed they worked. There were, however, costs.

In many protests, "storm troopers" appear who take up the cause, extending the tactics to a point that is often embarrassing to the leadership of the opposition. The personal harrassment of Stanley Walzer, the principal investigator of the Harvard XYY research, and his family was not intended by those who initiated the criticism of the project. Walzer, in turn, felt defenseless against the storm-trooper tactics of personalized attacks, and was profoundly relieved when, in May 1976, he halted newborn screening.

> If someone has set out to destroy you and would use any means to do so, in their belief that you are inherently evil and must be stopped, you will be destroyed. There is no defense against an assault in which any means will justify the end.

Even for those scientists who were not subjected to personal harassment, public criticism of their work was hard to accept, and they responded by hardening their opposition to the "intrusion" of those who raised difficult questions.

The scientists felt vilified by the attacks and retaliated by characterizing their critics as "professional character assassins," "irrational" and "hysterical" people, a "small number of self-interested, politically motivated people who wish to see the prison system of this country destroyed." They accused their critics of spreading "false propagandistic horror stories"; they felt harassed and intimidated by "witch-hunters." To defend their autonomy they invoked the norms of science as an apolitical, value-free activity, even where their

research was clearly more applied than basic, more therapeutic or corrective than experimental. And they rallied the
support of their peers, pointing to the fact that the research
had been reviewed and approved, although by those very
institutions rejected by critics as totally inadequate to assess
it.

THE CONTEXT OF MISTRUST

What was it about these projects that aroused such often
volatile controversy? The research sought ways to predict and
control antisocial behavior, but the disputes framed basic
problems in the very definition of antisocial behavior, in the
assumptions concerning the cause of violence, and in the
selection of appropriate solutions. What, in fact, constitutes
violent behavior? Sometimes the answer is clear-cut; but the
propriety of some forms of behavior may rest entirely on
debatable social norms and value judgments. Behavior may
be defined as violent because it threatens existing power relationships; "incorrigibles" and "radicals" are often grouped
together as "troublemakers." People who fight against dehu-
manizing conditions, or who organize political or religious
groups that threaten the power structure of a prison, may be
defined as "maladapted." Similarly, children who respond to
chaotic conditions in disorganized classrooms or to overly
controlled situations by hyperactive behavior may be defined
as maladapted or even "brain damaged."

Explanations of the sources of violence also vary: Is violent behavior primarily a problem of the individual offender,
or a social problem that can be attributed to injustice, repression, or exploitation? Quite different perspectives divided the
scientists from their critics. Investigations of genetic mediators
of violent behavior or the use of behavior modification by definition focus on the individual as a present or potential offender. They define violence as a problem of deviance and seek
to adapt the individual to the social system. Opponents of

this research focus their attention on the social environment that produces violence:

> Violence is primarily a social reaction to situations in which individuals believe no other means can remove intolerable conditions. In the United States the most oppressed groups are the ones most likely to react violently. . . . To provide the government with a medical tool for combatting violent behavior offers yet another possible weapon for repression without dealing with the root causes of violence.[11]

By dwelling on the individual offender, contend the critics, scientists divert attention from the social injustice, the poverty, and the many other problems responsible for violence. Science thus legitimates the prevailing neglect of social problems, allowing those in power to deny their share of responsibility and to avoid searching for social solutions. Holding such views, critics regarded research on violence as a political activity, a biomedically grounded technological means to manage socially disruptive behavior in order to maintain social control. Such differences in perceptions of violence and its sources are not just academic; they have operational consequences, and it is these consequences for the prison system, for offenders, and indeed for scientists that contributed to the intensity of the dispute.

For the scientists the fundamental question raised by these disputes was, who controls and evaluates research? There is no consensual basis to measure the effectiveness of medical or psychiatric techniques for resolving problems of criminal violence. Professional evaluations or research in this area can easily be discredited. Acceptance must rest on trust in professionals and acceptance of the social relationships involved in the research process. In these projects trust clearly did not exist.

In part the declining trust in science and its governing authorities to represent public values is part of a larger syndrome. A Harris poll, for example, found that from 1966 to

---

[11]*Daily Bruin*, February 25, 1974.

1973 the proportion of the public expressing a great deal of confidence in the leadership of institutions declined as follows: federal executives, 41 to 19 percent; Congress, 42 to 29 percent; major companies, 55 to 29 percent; higher education, 61 to 44 percent; medicine, 72 to 57 percent. Antiprofessional attitudes are widely expressed in the demands for greater accountability and participatory control; deception, manipulation, loss of autonomy, and lack of choice are ubiquitous complaints.[12] It is in this social climate that the disputes over violence research took place—a climate in which the policies and procedures governing science increasingly are subject to a democratic process that includes active political debate.

Historically, the social applications of science have often been legitimated by their association with basic research, and basic research is often justified by appeal to its potential social utility. More recently, in many areas of science there is little to distinguish what is labeled "research" from other activities normally subject to the political process.[13] In these three projects, for example, only the XYY study could appropriately be labeled "basic" research; the others, although referred to as research, involved active interventions or social policy. Their sources of funding, the compelling pressures for quick solutions to the problem of violence, and the entrepreneurial character of the project leadership all indicate their policy orientation. These linkages between science and its social applications, coupled with distrust in institutes and "experts," contribute to present demands for a renegotiation of society's contract with scientists that involves more democratic governance procedures.

In this context it is hard to believe that the scientists were entirely taken by surprise. The campus protests of the late sixties had just abated. And the rhetoric of rights—women's

---

[12]Dorothy Nelkin, ed., *Controversy: Politics of Technical Decisions* (Beverly Hills, Calif.: Sage, 1978).
[13]See the discussion by H. Green in "Law and Genetic Control: Public Policy Questions," *Annals of the New York Academy of Sciences* 265 (1976).

rights, patients' rights, consumers' rights, and indeed prisoners' rights—was in the air. Yet the reaction of scientists was one of moral outrage and defense as they sought to maintain their autonomy and avoid political engagement.

As conflicts bring science and technology into the realm of pluralist politics, subject to the claims of diverse moral views and political interests, key questions about the control of research and its applications are being addressed, revolving around the issue of "Who should control?" If there is conflict between scientific goals and public values, can one rely on researchers to assess the implications of their own work? Given the professional norms of science, the general political inexperience of researchers, and their distaste for political involvement, can they be trusted to perceive the political and social implications of research? And will they publicly surface problems that might jeopardize their own careers, particularly if they feel that they or their colleagues have been or will be harmed by the controversy that "going public" can entail? "When things begin to get too hot," one such researcher has declared, "the academic context probably is not the place to look for many profiles of courage." The actions of scientists most closely involved with recombinant DNA research in drawing public attention to the potential risks of their work shows that scientists can engage in and act on a social assessment of science; but the "going public" of the recombinant DNA researchers was a relatively rare event, as was their decision to call for a moratorium on their field of research.[14]

Without the discomforting actions of opposition groups, then, who will raise questions about research? For a variety of reasons, as we have suggested, researchers and their peer reviewers are unlikely to voice social assessment types of concerns, and indeed often fail to deal adequately with questions about the intrinsic validity of research proposals. If not the critics, who will raise these questions, and in part speak

---

[14]See "Biotechnology and the Law: Recombinant DNA and the Control of Scientific Research," *Southern California Law Review* 51 (September 1978).

for the usually "voiceless" subjects of research? In these three projects, not atypically, the development and evaluation of proposals never involved the subjects or consumers of the studies—the prospective parents, minorities, the poor, or prisoners.

These questions about the governance of research are addressed by these three controversies over projects on the prevention and control of violent behavior. In retrospect, and, we would argue, prospectively, the projects had certain characteristic features that made them potentially volatile undertakings. The controversies that did in fact erupt may be interpreted as essentially a struggle for power over new techniques of social control that are opened up by scientific research.[15] The idea that research projects such as these should be stopped or, at the very least, scrutinized and controlled by groups outside the scientific community illustrates the growing awareness of the political power inherent in the control of science and technology.

[15]Stephen Chorover, "The Pacification of the Brain: From Phrenology to Psychosurgery," in *Current Controversies in Neurosurgery*, ed. T.P. Morely (Philadelphia: W. B. Saunders, 1976), p. 758.

CHAPTER 5

Embattled Research

Psychiatry, Politics, and the Study of Violent Behavior

RONALD BAYER

VISIONS OF A PSYCHIATRIC CRIMINOLOGY

To those concerned with crime and violence the social and behavioral sciences have held out the promise of providing insight into the social and psychological roots of such threatening behavior. Armed with the scientific understanding of crime, it would then be possible to devise the forms of social intervention necessary for the suppression of disorder. To those appalled by the waste and suffering that followed from prescientific social practices founded on the principles of retribution and characterized by the seemingly primitive expres-

---

RONALD BAYER ● Institute of Society, Ethics, and the Life Sciences, The Hastings Center, 360 Broadway, Hastings-on-Hudson, New York 10706.

sion of social vengeance, the behavioral sciences have held
out the possibility of fashioning instruments of social control
and defense designed to rehabilitate, educate, and treat the
character of the transgressor.

Aligned with the behavioral scientists were those who,
for a variety of ideological reasons, saw in the modernist
attempt to transform the social response to criminality a natural expression of their own reformist tendencies with regard
to society at large. Among the forces supporting a greater role
for the behavioral sciences, but especially for psychiatry and
the allied therapeutic professions, have been humanitarians
opposed in principle to punishment and those of the professional and social strata concerned with the rationalization of
all social processes. In the United States for the greater part
of this century it has been those identified with the reformist
and liberal political traditions who most notably aligned themselves with the effort to enhance the role of the behavioral
sciences in the understanding of crime and of psychiatry in
its treatment.

In the twentieth century, the vision of a psychiatric criminology found early and self-confident expression in the work
of William Alanson White. Brushing aside the traditional dis-
putations regarding the insanity defense, he argued in *Insanity
and the Criminal Law* that the sole purpose of a jury trial should
be to determine whether or not the defendant in fact committed the crime with which he was charged. *Mens Rea* was
an irrelevant consideration.

> If he is found guilty then it should be the right of the state to
> prescribe the *treatment* which . . . seems calculated to effect the
> best results in the end.[1]

The nature of the therapeutic interventions as well as their
duration would be determined not by law but by therapeutic
need. Release from secure detention, like release from any

---

[1]William Alanson White, *Insanity and the Criminal Law* (New York: Macmillan,
1923), pp. 151–152.

therapeutic setting, would be determined by the expert's pronouncement of a "cure."[2]

During the interwar period that view of the legal process was shared by other critics who, like Sheldon Glueck,[3] sought a thoroughgoing transformation of the legal process. The goal was aptly captured by Albert Deutsch:

> The criminal court [should be] a clinic dedicated to the scientific solution of problems of maladjustment replacing its present function as a blind, retributive tribunal.[4]

The enthusiasm and promise of psychiatry with regard to the control of crime in the period immediately following World War II is clearly indicated in Franz Alexander's 1948 epilogue to the early and seminal psychoanalytic study of the criminal justice system that he and Hugo Staub had written years earlier.

> I see one of the most important contributions of psychiatry to the prevention of crime in transforming our prisons into institutions in which the offender against the law has the opportunity for reform and rehabilitation. Psychiatry in the last 40 years has developed systematic procedures by which personality traits can be methodically influenced and changed. The application of these methods to the rehabilitation of the criminal personality is perhaps one of the most important social functions of psychiatry.[5]

While psychiatry pressed its vision of a reformed scientific criminology with increasing vigor, many within the legal profession resisted the pressure as an unwarranted encroachment. The law, it was argued, had developed its own mode of fact finding and its own common-sense understanding of

[2]Ibid., p. 276.

[3]Sheldon Glueck, *Mental Disorder and the Criminal Law* (Millwood; N.Y.: Kraus Reprint, 1925).

[4]Albert Deutsch, *The Mentally Ill in America* (New York: Columbia University Press, 1967), p. 417.

[5]Franz Alexander and Hugo Staub, *The Criminal, the Judge and the Public* (Glencoe, Ill.: Free Press, 1956), p. 234.

human motivation and behavior. It had a vitality and flexibility tested by the experience of centuries. Psychiatric criminology was thus perceived as presumptuous, ill equipped to comprehend the complex interaction between criminal behavior and the requirements of the rule of law.

It was to bridge the increasingly distressing gap between the legal and psychiatric perspectives on crime that the American Psychiatric Association established the Isaac Ray Award Lectures in 1951.[6] A vision of collaboration and mutual respect underlay this step. But it was a vision that drew its inspiration from the anticipation of a future in which the law would come to recognize the hard-won insights of psychiatry. The former's concern with social order would complement the tendency toward a focus upon the individual in the latter. It was psychiatric "science," however, that would replace the common sense of the law.

The powerful impact of White and those who followed him is strikingly apparent in the arguments made by those honored with the Isaac Ray Award in the 1950s and early 1960s. Many of those recognized for their contribution to the rapprochement between law and psychiatry stressed the psychopathological basis for *all* criminal behavior. Among those who took this position in a forthright manner were Alistair Macleod and Philip Roche. Referring to criminal recidivism as a "deficiency disease," Macleod went on to argue:

> Just as the lack of essential food elements in the physical diet can cause deficiency diseases such as scurvy and pellagra, may it not be possible that the lack of essential ingredients in the emotional diet causes deficits in personality development?[7]

For Roche, the criminal law revealed its prescientific roots in its stress upon "responsibility":

---

[6]The award was named after Dr. Isaac Ray, author of *A Treatise on the Medical Jurisprudence of Insanity,* published in 1838. It was reissued by Harvard University Press in 1962.

[7]Alistair Macleod, *Recidivism: A Deficiency Disease* (Philadelphia: University of Pennsylvania Press, 1965), p. 40.

> If the law should find a way to abandon its untenable concept
> of criminal responsibility as it pertains to the subjective element
> in crime and come to the view that all felons are mental cases,
> there would be a reformation in penology.[8]

For those who could not accept the thoroughgoing equation of criminality and psychopathology, the need for a preeminent role for psychiatry and other clinical disciplines was dictated by the expertise they possessed with regard to the evaluation (diagnosis) and handling (treatment) of the criminal. Winfred Overholser, superintendent of St. Elizabeth's Hospital in Washington, D.C. and the recipient of the first award in 1952, thus stated:

> The day of the predetermined fixed sentence a la Beccaria, or
> indeed the setting of a term of imprisonment by a single judge
> appears to be drawing to a close, to be succeeded by a true
> individualization of correctional and penal treatment based
> largely upon social and psychiatric explanation.[9]

Karl Menninger, recipient of the 1962 award, reiterated this position in characteristic fashion, stressing instrumental therapeutic control while dismissing traditional legal values:

> The very word justice irritates the scientist. No surgeon expects
> to be asked if an operation for cancer is just or not. Behavioral
> scientists regard it as . . . absurd to invoke the question of
> justice in deciding what to do with a woman who cannot resist
> her propensity to shoplift . . . This sort of behavior has to be
> controlled; . . . This to the scientist is a matter of public safety
> and amicable coexistence.[10]

Not only in America but in Western Europe as well, there was a strong interest in the merging of the law enforcement process with the psychiatric-therapeutic orientation. No more

[8]Philip Q. Roche, *The Criminal Mind: A Study of Communication between the Criminal Law and Psychiatry* (New York: Farrar, Straus & Cudahy, 1958), p. 241.

[9]Winfred Overholser, *The Psychiatrist and the Law* (New York: Harcourt, Brace, 1953), p. 50.

[10]Karl Menninger, *The Crime of Punishment* (New York: Viking Press, 1969), p. 17.

notable example can be cited than that of Barbara Wooton,[11] whose arguments in favor of a purely forward-looking, therapeutic criminal law have provoked attention and argument for more than two decades.

LIBERALISM AND PSYCHIATRIC CRIMINOLOGY

In the United States liberal social thought with regard to crime and delinquency has been characterized until quite recently by a restless search for deterministic explanations. Perceiving modern science as the source of an understanding of all lawful processes, natural as well as behavioral, it was assumed that the moral categories resting on premises of willful antisocial behavior were part of a premodern religious tradition. Hence the search for explanations of criminality was characterized by a concomitant interest in exculpatory formulations.[12]

Especially with regard to the criminality of the lower classes, the search for explanations tended to focus on conditions of social deprivation. Sociological analyses thus provided the evidence needed to lift the burden of guilt from the criminal while providing added support for the demands for social reconstruction within the framework of a reformed capitalist society. This social view coexisted, sometimes with greater and sometimes with lesser ease, with psychodynamic

[11]Barbara Wooton, *Crime and the Criminal Law* (London: Stevens & Sons, 1963) and *Social Science and Social Pathology* (London: George Allen & Unwin, 1959). For typical critiques see, for example, Francis A. Allen, *The Borderland of Criminal Justice* (Chicago: University of Chicago Press, 1964), Sanford Kadish, "The Decline of Innocence," *Cambridge Law Journal* 26 (1968): 273–290.

[12]See generally Leon Radzinowicz, *Ideology and Crime* (London: Heinemann, 1966); Thorsten Sellin, "Corrections in Historical Perspective," *Law and Contemporary Social Problems* 4 (1958): 585–593; Marc Ancel, *Social Defense* (New York: Schocken Books, 1966). I have discussed this issue in"Crime, Punishment and the Decline of Liberal Optimism," *Crime and Delinquency* (April, 1981).

explanations of criminal behavior, with their almost exclusive focus on individual psychopathology. The effort to merge the apparently conflicting perspectives often rested on the attempt to suggest that the personal pathology of the criminal was linked to socially structured environmental factors.[13] Especially in those instances that involved sexual assault and gratuitous violence, psychological explanations seemed to provide a key to the understanding of the apparently senseless—a demystification of the hideous. With such understanding came the prospect for control and ultimately of safety. Yet even in the period of its greatest popularity, the psychiatric perspective did not really rival the socioeconomic. Nothing more clearly reflects this fact than the extreme reluctance to embrace formulations such as those of Benjamin Karpman, who attempted to provide a fully developed theory of criminal psychodynamics.[14]

More than the explanatory force of psychodynamic formulations, it was the promise of achieving correctional ends without recourse to punishment that created a strong affinity between psychiatry and American liberals. Intense commitment to rehabilitation thus turned liberals to psychiatrists and those in the allied clinical professions of psychology and social work who, it was hoped, could provide the manpower necessary to advance penology beyond "blind retribution." It

[13]A clear example of this effort is to be found in the liberal discussions of drug addiction. I have discussed this aspect of the problem in "Heroin Addiction, Criminal Culpability and the Penal Sanction: A Perspective on the Liberal Response to Repressive Social Policy," *Crime and Delinquency* (March 1978).

[14]Karpman had written, "Basically criminality is but a symptom of insanity using the term in its widest sense to express unacceptable social behavior based on unconscious motivation flowing from a disturbed intimate and emotional life whether this appears in frank psychoses or in less obvious form in neuroses and unrecognized psychoses." See "Criminal Psychodynamics: A Platform," *Journal of Criminal Law, Criminology and Police Science* 47 (1956): 8–17. For a critique of this position see Walter Goodman's three-part series, "Lawyers, Psychiatrists and Crime," *New Republic*, August 1, 1955, pp. 13–16; August 8, 1955, pp. 14–17; August 15, 1955, pp. 12–15.

must be emphasized, however, that even during the period of liberal faith in rehabilitation there was never a willingness to jettison traditional legal values, to adopt a purely therapeutic model of justice. Too deep a distrust for the agencies of authority permeated even the ideology of welfare liberalism. Thus the line of thinking that ran from White to Menninger was never fully embraced by American liberals.[15]

If ambivalence characterized the liberal attitude to psychiatric criminology and penology, no such uncertainty was to be found among liberals, especially in their journals of opinion, in the response to the efforts to apply the techniques of behavior modification to criminals and delinquents. These techniques, unlike the more traditional verbal therapies, were perceived as short-circuiting the autonomy of the prisoner and thus appeared to be a threat to the very dignity that rehabilitation was, in contrast to punishment, supposed to enhance.[16]

PSYCHIATRIC CRIMINOLOGY UNDER ATTACK

Most typically, in the period following World War II, criticism of psychiatric legal thought came from those who, like legal theorist Jerome Hall,[17] saw in this perspective a disquieting challenge to principles of the criminal law. Other significant early opponents of the advance of psychiatry included Michael Hakeem[18] who, in the wake of David Bazelon's *Durham* decision,[19] argued that psychiatry had neither

[15]See, for example, Goodman; Victor Ferkiss, "A Life for a Life," *Commonweal,* October 7, 1955, p. 12; William Ryan, "The Crime of Punishment," *Commonweal,* January 24, 1969, p. 533; Christopher D. Stone, "Crises and Criminality," *The Nation,* April 21, 1969, pp. 510–515.

[16]"Talking Pillows," *Commonweal,* December 17, 1957, p. 327; "Hypnopaedia," *The Nation,* January 25, 1958, p. 62.

[17]Jerome Hall, "Psychiatry and Criminal Responsibility," *Yale Law Journal* 65 (1956): 761.

[18]Michael Hakeem, "A Critique of the Psychiatric Approach to Crime and Corrections," *Law and Contemporary Social Problems* 23 (1958): 650–682.

[19]*Durham* v. *United States,* 214 F. 2d 862 (D.C. Cir. 1954).

the capacity to diagnose, predict, nor cure criminal behavior, and, of course, the heterodox Thomas Szasz,[20] whose precocious attacks on his psychiatric colleagues were just beginning.

It is thus rather striking that, as concern about crime, violence, and social disorder began to mount in the mid-1960s, and as psychiatry and the allied therapeutic professions appeared to be gaining an increasingly important role in the effort to control social deviance, the political foundations of that expanded influence began to crumble. Although psychiatrists had always endured the criticism of those associated with conservative social forces, it was a dramatic reversal to be subject to liberal criticism. Psychiatrists, who had been perceived (and who had perceived themselves) as the cutting edge of the critique of retribution and punishment, were increasingly classed among the forces of repression. Repeatedly and with ever-intensifying shrillness, the very liberal journals that had called for a greater role for psychiatry in the legal process attacked the practices of psychiatrists in prisons. Institutional psychiatry was depicted as posing a threat to the dignity of those whom it attempted to treat and control. It was a particularly insidious threat since it masked its role through the appropriation of the symbols of the rehabilitative ideology that, for liberals, had provided the starting point for a critical analysis of prisons.[21]

A number of factors contributed to the change in liberal attitudes toward correctional psychiatry. Increasingly, experimentation, both inside and outside of prisons, had come to rely on suspect nonverbal therapies. Both the use of psychotropic substances and the behaviorist manipulation of environmental factors were perceived, by those concerned with limiting the invasiveness of state power, as posing grave dangers. For institutionalized populations, such dangers raised

[20]Thomas Szasz, *Law, Liberty and Psychiatry* (New York: Macmillan, 1963).
[21]See, for example, Clay Steinman, "Behavior Modification: The Case of the Frightened Convict," *The Nation*, December 3, 1973, pp. 590–593; Bernard Weiner, "Prison Psychiatry: The Clockwork Cure," *The Nation*, April 3, 1972, pp. 433–436.

profoundly vexing issues. Second, the liberal commitment to rehabilitative penology had yielded at first to skepticism and then to hostility. That shift was of course linked to an erosion of liberal optimism and a decline in the strength of liberal commitment to social engineering. With deterrence and "just deserts" replacing rehabilitation as central elements of liberal social thought, psychiatrists could no longer have an important role to play in the social control of prisoners. Finally, the changed status of psychiatry itself—a change that was brought about at least in part through the efforts of liberals—created a highly charged situation. As long as psychiatric thought and programmatic proposals could provide the scientific basis for a critique of the practices in penal institutions, psychiatrists could remain untainted. To the extent that it began to take on increasing importance in prisons and in the control of deviant behavior, psychiatry became subject to the criticism of liberals who characteristically assumed a posture of suspicion toward the social agencies whose primary function was the maintenance of law and order.

It is worth noting here that in Scandinavia, where the influence of psychiatric thought and practice on penology is very advanced, a similar process of disenchantment has occurred. Thus Inkeri Anttila of Finland has commented:

> Treatment ideolog[y's] equating of criminals and the sick was, in the beginning when the ideology was still weak, often devoted to humanizing actual criminal care. But, as treatment ideology has increasingly dominated the system and as treatment personnel have gained increasing power, the negative side of the ideology has become more evident and the criticism against treatment ideology has grown sharper.[22]

The critique of psychiatric thought and practice in liberal political circles was mirrored within the psychiatric profession itself. No longer was Szasz alone. So careful an observer of the relationship between psychiatry and the law as Dr. Bernard Diamond noted in 1973:

[22]Inkeri Anttila, "Conservative and Radical Criminal Policy in the Nordic Countries," *Scandinavian Studies in Criminology* 3 (1971): 14–15.

The day is long gone when the public saw psychiatry as the panacea for whatever ails the individual and society. The medical model of treatment has serious limitations when applied to social problems and whatever may be the future solutions to problems of crime and control, I do not expect the psychiatrist to play the dominant role.[23]

In 1965 Willard Gaylin could argue, like others in the tradition of William Alanson White, that psychiatry and behavioral science had an important role to play in the determination of the appropriate treatment of the offender.[24] Nine years later he would write:

The therapeutic model is a complicated one; but worse, the therapeutic experiment has not worked out: Prisons are not more effective, not more rehabilitative.[25]

Although Gaylin's criticism here focuses on the question of efficacy, he and other psychiatrists have increasingly stressed the potential for the abuse of psychiatric authority in the criminal justice system. As the ideological conflict has intensified, professional relations have taken on partisan features with scientific arguments being marshaled by psychiatrists in defense of political positions.

In an earlier era, concern for the potential abuses of behavioral technology was reflected in references to *1984* and *Brave New World*. More recently the imagery has been drawn from *A Clockwork Orange*. The difference between the earlier and later works is of some significance. In the work of Orwell and Huxley, we are concerned for those caught in a repressive universe where any striving for freedom and autonomy provokes a coercive response designed to impose conformity. In the Burgess–Kubrick work, behavioral scientists attempt to transform the character of a vicious criminal. Yet he is our

[23]Bernard L. Diamond, "From Durham to Brown, a Futile Journey," *Washington University Law Quarterly* (1973): 118.

[24]Willard Gaylin, "Psychiatry and the Law: Partners in Crime," *Columbia Forum* 8 (1965): 25–27.

[25]Willard Gaylin, *Partial Justice: A Study of Bias in Sentencing* (New York: Alfred A. Knopf, 1974), p. 23.

hero. It is his confrontation with behavioral technology that is designed to evoke our concern. So widespread had become the hostility toward psychiatry that his struggle had become not only understandable but capable of evoking the sympathy of a mass audience.

It is in the context of this situation—characterized by the withering of liberal support for psychiatric criminology, intraprofessional dissension, and widespread popular suspicion regarding the role of psychiatrists—that the abortive efforts to establish a Center for the Study and Reduction of Violence at UCLA and the jettisoning of the behavior modification program at the federal prisons can best be understood. Because the Boston XYY controversy raised (for some) the specter of genetic determinism, it involves some different issues and can best be discussed by way of contrast.

EMBATTLED PSYCHIATRY AND THE STUDY OF VIOLENCE

The psychiatrists and behavioral scientists willing to cooperate with prison authorities in creating programs for the control of disruptive inmates accepted both the necessity and legitimacy of maintaining prison discipline. The political function of those who cooperated in such an enterprise could, however, be expressed in professional-instrumental terms. That is not to suggest that psychiatrists and behavioral scientists functioning in such capacities were unconcerned about obviously brutal aspects of prison life, but rather that they accepted the primacy of the prison authorities' right to elicit cooperative behavior on the part of inmates. If the extent to which it was necessary to rely on force to impose prison discipline could be reduced by reliance on assumedly scientific and therefore more measured, reasonable forms of intervention, then both the prison and the prisoner would have been benefited. In speaking about START, one prison official asserted that it was "a humanitarian obligation of ours."[26] Such a perspective allowed for the assumption of a single overriding interest among prison authorities, behavioral scientists, and inmates. In explaining the basis on which prisoners would be selected for transfer to Butner, Ray Gerrard of the Bureau of Prisons could thus cite *"treatment needs."*[27]

Unlike those willing to cooperate in the process of prison management, those who opposed the increasing utilization of behavioral technologies were perforce obligated to bring into question the very givens of the situation. Thus in an extended critique of prison psychiatry in California, Bernard Weiner wrote in *The Nation:*

> The Department of Corrections tends to see prison violence and mental disturbance either as organic malfunction or as a result of some outside conspiracy. Like prison administrations everywhere, it will scarcely acknowledge that the prison system itself produces the violence.[28]

With the prison seen as a brutalizing and crushing institution, with disruption and unruliness seen as manifestations of protest, the effort to restore order—through traditional displays of force or psychiatric-behavioral technologies—could thus be termed repressive. In an attack on the Contingency Management Program in the Virginia prison, a spokesperson for the ACLU's National Prison Project asserted:

> While the director of the program seems to have an idealistic notion that his program is going to make prisoners better people, all he is doing is helping the prison make them more docile.[29]

With the goal of adjusting inmates to prison life itself suspect, it is not surprising that research and experimental programs

[26]Steinman, p. 591.
[27]Hastings Center Files (hereafter HCF).
[28]Weiner, p. 434.
[29]HCF.

characterized by deprivations and suffering, which would not have been tolerated under the color of more acceptable ends, became the target of political challenge.

Given the revelations regarding the abuse of prisoners in such experimental settings as Springfield, Missouri and Vacaville in California, there was little that the proponents of behavior modification programs could do to assuage the suspicion of those who opposed such undertakings. At the very moment when START was under court challenge for allegedly brutal deprivations, the Bureau of Prisons was attempting to justify all of its programs by stating that it countenanced *no* such deprivations in *any* of its prisons.[30] Under such circumstances opponents of Butner could only imagine the "chamber of horrors" that Dr. Groder might have created. In an article reflective of this profound distrust, Mark Pinsky wrote in *The Nation:*

> At this point, it appears that Butner will not become the chamber of physical horrors it was once advertised to be. It is uncertain whether that concept was ever part of the original plan at all, or whether the mobilization of public concern forced its modification but the latter is quite probable.[31]

In an atmosphere so charged, ambiguities regarding research design and programming were readily transformed into "evasions" by those who expected the worst from officials responsible for the functioning of the prisons. Reacting to this situation the medical director of Vacaville expressed his dismay: "There is no trust in us. What's happened to trust in this country?"[32]

The controversy that surrounded the UCLA Violence Center presents a more complex situation. Both proponents and opponents of the center acknowledged that clearly identifiable forms of individual violence were of legitimate concern.

[30]HCF.
[31]Mark Pinsky, "Who Is Dr. Groder: Alarms in the Prison Grapevine," *The Nation,* October 5, 1975, p. 294–297.
[32]Weiner, p. 436.

Although Genet-like celebrations of violence may have surfaced during the debates, in large measure all parties concerned recognized in rape, sexual assault, child beating, the battery of women, and gratuitous mass violence appropriate targets for research and ultimately control.[33] Thus an explanation of the intense hostility directed at the Violence Center as a research enterprise cannot be attributed to the same questioning of ends noted in the preceding discussion.

Dr. West has acknowledged that in large measure his ability to interest the conservative state government of Ronald Reagan in his center was the consequence of general public alarm over crime and violence. Indeed, supporters of the center in often hyperbolic fashion asserted that the people of California could expect a reduction in the level of violence and disorder within several years after its opening.[34] Designed to enhance public support, such remarks succeeded in antagonizing those who were suspicious of the undertaking.

On an ideological level, those who saw in violence and crime a social problem requiring social analyses and social solutions were highly critical of the project. In a handbill circulated by Dr. Isidore Ziferstein and his colleagues at the 1973 American Psychiatric Association meetings in Honolulu it was charged:

> The main problem with such a Center is that violence as a social phenomenon, even if lip service is paid to this concept, is pushed to backstage while the biology or psychology of certain individuals is limelighted.[35]

Far more serious to those who opposed the center, however, were the concerns generated by the research projects themselves and the fears regarding the use to which the knowledge obtained from them would be put. There is no need to re-

---

[33]Transcript of a meeting on the Violence Center at The Hastings Center, February 2–3, 1978 (hereafter Transcript).
[34]HCF.
[35]HCF.

hearse here the extent to which opponents were worried about the status of Dr. Ervin, the possibility of psychosurgery, and the potential for the abuse of experimental subjects, especially those in prisons and mental hospitals. It is more important for our purposes to note the degree to which each assurance on the part of West and his colleagues was met by disbelief. Thus the Committee Opposing the Psychiatric Abuse of Prisoners could charge:

> The Center is, in short, a laboratory for the Department of Corrections and law enforcement officials with the diaphanous veneer of UCLA used to make it appear to be a respectable university research facility.[36]

In an advertisement appearing in the *San Francisco Chronicle*, it was charged: "This proposed Center will be . . . a chamber of horrors."[37] Finally, there is no greater indication of the extent to which suspicion had begun to affect intraprofessional relations than the fact that the Northern California District Branch of the American Psychiatric Association[38] had raised objections to the center and the Southern California District Branch had even recommended against its funding.[39]

West himself acknowledged the extent to which the atmosphere surrounding his project was poisoned by the revelations of political corruption, venality, and abuse of power in the Nixon administration, the exposés regarding Vacaville, the role of Governor Reagan in announcing the project, the status of Dr. Ervin, and the fear generated by the film *A Clockwork Orange*.[40] He insisted, however, to the very end, that these factors were "irrelevant to the scientific and public interest"[41] aspects of the project. Even those who did not charge

[36]HCF.
[37]HCF.
[38]HCF.
[39]HCF.
[40]Transcript.
[41]Ibid.

West with prevarication could not accept his assurances. For them, there was every reason to suspect that a project that sought to generate a technology for the prediction of violent behavior would involve research procedures and findings inimical to privacy and freedom from unwarranted governmental surveillance.

In both cases under review, behavioral scientists and psychiatrists sought to put themselves at the service of what they considered the overriding social interest in the reduction of violence. In both instances, liberals who most typically had supported psychiatric and behavioral research withdrew their support because of profound suspicions regarding the potential abuse of research subjects and concern about the ultimate ends to which the new knowledge would be put. Thus the crisis of institutional life in the United States severely constrained the extent to which scientific research could be pursued.

In his account of the rise of the disciplinary authority of the modern penitentiary, Michel Foucault has noted that, although the recognition of the inner man had at one point served to limit the torture of transgressors, that same discovery attracted the attention and interest of modern penologists who sought to transform the character of the malefactor.[42] In both the UCLA case and that of the federal prison behavior modification programs, it appears that in large measure the awareness of the existence of the inner man has again begun to serve the function of a limitation on research and experimentation. Underlying the opposition in both instances was a suspicion that the knowledge that was sought could only be gained through unacceptable procedures, which of necessity would have to violate a rediscovered inviolable space. Unlike the period preceding the advent of a scientific technology capable of the deepest intrusions, it was neither ignorance nor ineptitude that could act as a limiting factor in the 1970s,

[42]Michel Foucault, *Discipline and Punish* (New York: Pantheon Books, 1977).

but rather conscious political and moral decisions regarding the deployment of scientific power.

With liberals expressing increasing concern about the abuses of even putatively benevolent state power and with their interest turning toward a criminal justice system characterized by severely restricted discretionary authority, psychiatric criminology and penology could no longer rely on their traditional sources of political support.[43]

To argue that these projects were aborted primarily because the historical alliance between a liberal constituency and psychiatry had been ruptured would, however, be a mistake. Although the loss of its seemingly natural political ally was a matter of great significance for psychiatry, these projects might well have survived had other political and institutional forces seen in them a vital element in the effort to establish order in the prisons or social peace in the community. Such was clearly not the case. The psychiatric explanation of crime in general and violence more specifically had always been suspect among more conservative social forces where the personal responsibility of the criminal was considered the starting point for the attribution of guilt and the justification for punishment. Both Dr. West and Dr. Groder, stunned by the liberal desertion, understood this point well. Commenting on the success of his opponents, West stated:

> With friends like Ziferstein and Hiestand the prisoners and the ghetto dwellers don't need enemies because in the long run society is going to be harder on them than if it could find alternative solutions like the ones we were seeking.[44]

Groder, noting the decline in rehabilitative programs, argued:

---

[43]See, for example, Willard Gaylin, et al. ed., *Doing Good: The Limits of Benevolence* (New York: Pantheon Books, 1978); Andrew von Hirsch, *Doing Justice: The Choice of Punishments* (New York: Hill & Wang, 1976); Twentieth Century Fund Task Force on Criminal Sentencing, *Fair and Certain Punishment* (New York: McGraw-Hill, 1976); James Q. Wilson, "The Political Feasibility of Punishment," in *Justice and Punishment*, eds. J. Cederbloom and William Blizek (Cambridge, Mass.: Ballinger, 1977).
[44]HCF.

"Policy makers want to buy the idea that nothing works so they can get on with the grand old business of repression."[45]

Finally, despite the apparent advances of psychiatry in the post–World War II period, it remained in the early 1970s a rather marginal element in the overall law enforcement apparatus in the United States. It required little in the way of excision for the officials concerned with the functioning of the prison and the criminal justice system to reduce that role even further. Psychiatrists and behavioral scientists simply did not have the organizational capacity to weather the turmoil that surrounded their projects. With bureaucratic interests concerned with the maintenance of efficient organizational functioning, it made good sense to cut losses by eliminating these sources of conflict.

The controversy surrounding the effort to determine the extent to which the XYY chromosomal anomaly could be linked to aggressive behavior differed from the two cases discussed to this point in large measure because of the very different history of liberal attitudes toward the effort to find a psychosocial—as contrasted with a genetic-biological—explanation for human behavior. All three enterprises involved the search for causal and hence exculpatory factors in antisocial behavior. On that level they were all compatible with the effort to develop a scientific perspective on deviance, a perspective that could have little appeal to those who considered the establishment of culpability a matter of primary social and moral importance. Yet whereas the search for psychosocial determinants of behavior was at least theoretically compatible with a rehabilitative posture, genetic explanations suggested an immutability that was anathema to the liberal belief in the malleability of both the environment and human nature. More importantly, the search for genetic explanations bore too close a connection to the eugenics movements and their racist dimensions. Whereas the controversy at UCLA and the federal prisons took place against a backdrop of a

[45]HCF.

profound reversal in liberal attitudes toward psychiatric criminology, no recent history of liberal support for genetic explanations of crime existed.[46]

In the Boston XYY controversy, much of the debate focused on the adequacy of the research design and the extremely complicated issue of informed consent with newborn screening. On that level those who were critical of the research, especially those in Science for the People, were able to elicit a succession of modifications designed to meet their objections. As important as those issues were, however—and they seemed to occupy an extraordinary amount of energy and time on both sides of the controversy—they were really secondary to the question of whether the search for a genetic determinant of aggressive behavior was a legitimate scientific enterprise.

Thus Jonathan King, a leader of the opposition, stated:

> I have never seen . . . a study on the alleged genetic determinant of human behavior that I considered a beneficial, scientifically valuable, informative, enlightening or [which] had any kind of positive value. The whole history of it has been used by one group of people to justify a particular set of social relations.[47]

To King and his associates in Science for the People, the search was designed, in addition, to divert attention from what they, as had Dr. Isidore Ziferstein, believed were the social roots of crime and violence. At a time of increasing social unrest, they saw such an effort as inherently politically regressive.

Although the primary antagonists to the research in Boston were to the left of American liberals, their capacity to elicit support, both tacit and active, for their opposition can only be understood in the context of the liberals' historical attitude to such work. With the freedom to conduct research under

---

[46]For a discussion of the relationship between genetics and political ideology, see Loren R. Graham, "Political Ideology and Genetic Theory: Russia and Germany in the 1920's," *The Hastings Center Report* 7 (October 1977): 30–39.

[47]Transcript of a Meeting on the XYY Controversy at the Hastings Center February 9–10, 1979.

challenge, the reluctance of the liberal community to forcefully support an academic investigation is a potent expression of that mood. Focusing on the details of the project provided critics with a seemingly less value-laden justification for inaction in the face of yet another instance of embattled research.

The three unsuccessful research efforts examined here do not of course signify an end to psychiatric, behavioral, or genetic research into violence. Scientific and professional orientations have their own dynamics and there is no reason to believe that the focus on the biological-psychiatric roots of violence has exhausted itself. Instead what is suggested is that at the time these projects were proposed, the political climate was such as to make them particularly vulnerable. It is the nature of that vulnerability that I have attempted to explore.

CHAPTER 6

Fragile Knowledge and Stubborn Ignorance

Agenda for the Study of Violence

JOHN P. CONRAD

Why should violence be a subject for research? Only during the last century has it inspired the application of the scientific method. For all the preceding millennia, violence has punctuated human existence without being considered a topic for empirical study. It was extolled by epic poets as the ultimate test of masculine virtue, it was denounced by prophets and moralists, it was endured by ordinary people as a natural risk in the human condition. All these responses to the infliction of physical harm by men upon each other persist to the present time. Until the angry stay their hands, the brave will be

JOHN P. CONRAD • The American Justice Institute, 1007 Seventh Street, Sacramento, California 95814.

praised, the cowards will be scorned, and the brutes will be hated.

What is new is the notion that the means for reducing violence might be discovered by social science. It is a plausible position that if we understood the causes of violence we might prevent some of it and deal more effectively with those who threaten or inflict it. The success of this approach remains to be seen. So far, the results are unpromising.

Science is done by men and women who perceive puzzles to be solved in their environment. Sometimes scientists gratify us all, as when a disease is conquered. Sometimes their achievements arouse new and troubling anxieties, as in the conquest of the atom. Many social scientists have accepted the abatement of criminal violence as a proper challenge to the scientific method. It is a topic in which many elusive puzzles are embedded. Humanity cannot fail to benefit from their solution and the application of those solutions to public policy and private behavior.

Certainly our culture is permeated with our fear of each other, whether such fear is justified or not. It is generally believed that our cities have always been dangerous to their inhabitants, and that there is no evidence that the danger has increased over the centuries of Western urban life. That interpretation is beside the point. Americans have been conditioned to expect benefits from the scientific method; they find it credible that knowledge gained from the scientific study of violence will reduce it. Criminologists have shared that belief. Those who profess that they can add to our knowledge and understanding of the physical risks in human association by using methods similar to those that have unlocked the secrets of nature will be given the means to try.

Riots, assassinations, and routine street crimes have different causes and different consequences. Their common denominator is the exercise of unlawful physical force. Public alarm has inspired the governments of several countries, the United States foremost among them, to support criminology and its associated disciplines as never before. During the last fifteen years four national commissions have been appointed to explore violence and to recommend action to prevent it.[1] The Law Enforcement Assistance Administration, the prime source of support for criminological research, owes its existence to the national fear of rapists and muggers.

So far this campaign to discover rational means for the prevention and control of irrational behavior has moved slowly. It has become evident that the criminal justice system cannot reach the causes of most of the violence that citizens fear, even though the opinion still prevails that the control of crime is the primary function of the criminal courts. Despite the meager benefits of criminological research, a fearful public continues to support it. The opinion that the reduction of violence depends on successful research is by no means unanimous, but it is shared by enough persons of influence to assure its continuity in institutes and graduate schools.

Robbery and rape, along with the long list of other crimes, violent and nonviolent, continue to increase in incidence and

---

[1]First came the President's Commission on Law Enforcement and the Administration of Justice, which in 1967 published *The Challenge of Crime in a Free Society*, followed in rapid succession by no less than nine task force reports and a fine crop of consultants' papers. For a perspective on crime problems of every description, these reports still stand as an invaluable source of ideas and information, marred, I think, by series of bland and sometimes banal recommendations. The second national commission was directed by Judge Otto Kerner and was addressed to the prevention of riots such as the nation experienced in the midsixties: The National Advisory Commission on Civil Disorders, which in 1969 published a report usually designated as the Kerner report, along with numerous articles, papers, and supplementary studies. The Kerner report is perhaps most notable for its vigorous warning to the nation that the races could not continue to drift into separate communities without damage to the whole. In 1969, the National Commission on the Causes and Prevention of Violence published thirteen volumes of learned reports, directed by Professors James J. Short and Marvin E. Wolfgang. This commission was inspired by the assassinations of Senator Robert F. Kennedy and the Reverend Martin Luther King; it was chaired by Dr. Milton Eisenhower, then president of Johns Hopkins University. In sheer volume its reports surpass them all, but the level of erudition is lofty and less accessible to the media and the general public than were the works of the preceding

rate despite the allocations of federal funds to research and development. Nevertheless, although the statistics do not reflect success in the reduction of crime, the outcome of the research inspired by fear is not inconsequential. The statistics of crimes of all kinds have vastly improved in comprehensiveness and reliability, thereby making possible a realistic discourse about what is needed for effective social control. The distribution of violent behavior has been mapped, and the careers of violent criminals have been traced and classified. We can estimate the economic and human costs of the limited measures available to the criminal justice system for the protection of civic life from disruption by violent men, women, and children. These achievements are not to be dismissed as trifling feats of primary interest to professors and bureaucrats. But the promise of societal or personal intervention to diminish the incidence of violent crime is far from fulfillment.

During the Behavioral Studies Research Group's investigation of the ethical and political obstacles to research on

---

commissions. A fourth commission, the National Advisory Commission on Criminal Justice Standards and Goals, was appointed during the Nixon administration, and in 1973 published its report, *A National Strategy to Reduce Crime,* followed by five task force reports. This commission was more normative than investigative; its recommendations were intended to become the basis for the program of the Law Enforcement Assistance Administration (LEAA) and the various state planning agencies for local criminal justice assistance. The "standards and goals" enunciated received a good deal of attention in the state and municipal planning groups, but it is doubtful that they guided the subsequent course of criminal justice. In spite of the commission's published standards, the volume of crime has not been reduced by a sufficient amount to indicate that there will be 50 percent less of it in 1983 than there was in 1973, as projected by the commission. The commission also projected the elimination of plea bargaining, a forgotten goal, and recommended against the building of new prisons, a proscription that has been disregarded. What we seem to learn from these four commissions is that they all begin with high hopes, disperse into task forces charged with carrying out months of excited drudgery to meet deadlines, followed by recommendations that are disputed within the commission itself, and end in reports with a long half-life as source material for graduate students.

violence, my colleagues and I have seen that there is wide disagreement as to the boundaries of legitimate inquiry. I shall leave a review of that debate to other contributors. This essay will be limited to a review of what we know—or think we know—and will then proceed to the formulation of the major questions that might lead to useful answers. I shall discuss the institutional apparatus needed for the conduct of successful and responsible research addressed to the reduction of violence. Researchers in these fields of inquiry have stumbled over some troublesome ethical issues, some of which do not seem to provoke much public concern. I shall identify them, not expecting to resolve them, but rather to report the perspective of a researcher on the dilemmas he confronts.

The little knowledge we have compiled is fragile. We are unsure of its eventual usefulness for relieving society of its fears. Epistemological problems abound. What we think we know is cluttered with uncertainties, beginning with the impenetrable uncertainty about the true volume of crime and the numbers of criminals who are not caught, or caught too late, after the commission of a sequence of offenses for which they had never been suspected.

Confidence in the very foundations of criminal justice has been shaken by empirical studies. For centuries it has been an article of belief that certainty of arrest and severity of punishment deter potential criminals from the commission of offenses in sufficient numbers to affect the crime rates. We are no longer so sure.[2] The hopeful belief that the rehabilitation of offenders would reduce the crime rate by reducing recidivism has been called into serious question. The evidence of two decades of uneven research accumulates in one direction:

[2]Alfred Blumstein, Jacqueline Cohen, and Daniel Nagin, eds., *Deterrence and Incapacitation: Estimating the Effects of Criminal Justice Sanctions on Crime Rates* (Washington, D.C.: National Academy of Sciences, 1978). See especially the chapter by Nagin, "General Deterrence: A Review of the Empirical Evidence," pp. 95–139.

the rehabilitative ideal will never be realized in a system of treatment.[3]

And ignorance is stubborn. In the natural sciences the power of prediction confirms success in the pursuit of knowledge. But there is little that criminologists can predict with confidence. Decades of effort have gone into attempts to create a predictive method that would enable us to predict the likelihood of the commission of a violent crime, but it is now generally conceded that such a method is a will-o'-the-wisp that will forever elude us. We have yet to approach the predictive power of a flip of the coin, and there are good reasons to suppose that we never will.

Uncertainty and ignorance are the lot of man as he confronts the social world. In a summary of the philosophical contributions of Karl Popper, Bryan Magee wrote:

> [Popper's philosophy] condemns as "scientism" the notion that science gives us certain knowledge and might even one day be able to give us settled answers to all our legitimate questions. A great deal of disillusionment with science and reason which is so widespread in our age is based on precisely such mistaken notions of what science and reason are.[4]

Nowhere is the tentative nature of knowledge more evident than in the social sciences, and nowhere is the quest for certainty more scientistic than in the study of crime. What is conjectural knowledge, to use Popper's term, crumbles into refuted propositions. Nineteenth-century reformers *knew* that delinquent boys and girls could be reformed in residential institutions that they called "reform schools." We know bet-

---

[3]See Douglas Lipton, Robert Martinson, and Judith Wilks, *The Effectiveness of Correctional Treatment* (New York: Praeger, 1975). This compendium of research reports must be handled with caution. It has been widely interpreted as proof that rehabilitation does not "work," and that is an exaggeration disclaimed by its authors. What it shows, along with most studies of rehabilitative systems in criminal justice, is that there does not seem to be any prospect of making a *system* out of the occasional and sometimes frequent successes in redirecting criminals into less destructive careers.
[4]Bryan Magee, *Popper* (London: Fontana/Collins, 1973), p. 68.

ter, now, after countless studies have shown that these "schools" are futile at best and often barbarous. We still have them because no one has thought of an alternative method for controlling the youths of whom we are most afraid. We can reasonably hope that the continued interaction of imagination and increasing knowledge will produce new and more satisfactory conjectures. It may be a long wait before such conjectures are translated into change of law, policy, and care of young delinquents. Understanding comes slowly and leads only to a better approximation of justice for the time being. Our knowledge of our society and ourselves is never immutable.

THE STATE OF KNOWLEDGE

What we know about violent crime consists of a modest fund of knowledge left over after the explosion of various convenient beliefs. To project the course of desirable future research, a rough assessment of what we tentatively know is needed as a baseline; I shall proceed with an inventory of sorts, not trying for an exhaustive survey within the limits of my space, but hoping that a sketch of the boundaries of present knowledge may be useful for an understanding of future needs.

Biology and Violence

The origins of empirical criminology are to be found in the effort to identify some physical characteristic common to criminals and less common among the law-abiding. The famous Italian criminological anthropologist, Cesare Lombroso, offered the crude but comforting theory that criminals were atavistic mutants representing an older and lower level of human evolution. That theory has been discarded for good, and along with it the various speculations about the physiognomic signs of criminality. Likewise, no one talks now of the Jukes and the Kallikaks in support of notions that there are heritable strains of criminal traits. If there is a biological basis for aggressive behavior, it will not be found by collating the facial stigmata of murderers and rapists or by tracing brutes and scoundrels on family trees.

But the biological substrates of criminal violence continue to receive attention, partly because some criminals are seemingly affected by physical or psychological conditions that differentiate them from ordinary people, and partly because of a lingering hope that medical or psychiatric interventions will assist in control of these conditions or provide remedies for disorders yet to be defined. The connection between psychosis and crime is of little significance for the control and management of criminals, even though on infrequent occasions these conditions combine to culminate in terrifying events. Most criminals are without mental illness, even though it has been argued that their lack of symptoms constitutes no more than a mask of sanity.

The diagnosis usually applied to persistent offenders used to be "psychopathy," a term that has deservedly fallen into psychiatric disfavor. But for generations theories accounted for the condition by tracing its origins to defective relationships with one or both parents in early childhood, or to early lack of discipline, or to the "culture of poverty," in each case inevitably leading to circular reasoning without accounting for all the individuals who somehow escaped a life of crime but were subjected to similar influences.

Other terminology has been adopted. Now we hear of character disorders, antisocial personalities, and various other designations that still seem to be characterized by the same circularity of definition. What seems common to most of those who are so diagnosed is a willingness to endure a condition with which they are not dissatisfied.

That there are forms of brain damage that increase aggressivity and lead to violence is generally accepted, although these conditions are rare. A good beginning has been made toward an understanding of the processes that impair control is such cases, but much more work remains to be done before safe and reliable treatment can be prescribed. Various remedies have been proposed, but none of them is without risk of irreversible damage. The early promise of prefrontal lobotomies was tragically gutted by the horrifying incidence of vegetabilization; since that time the courts and medical policy makers have been understandably conservative in authorizing surgical or other mechanical interventions with the functioning of the brain. Until the grave ethical problems arising from this history of surgical harm are satisfactorily resolved, treatment for the relief of these conditions will lag. For the few who suffer from this kind of impaired control, the dilemma is real, but its resolution is in the hands of courts and officials who cannot act. Numerically it is not an important problem; although the crimes involved may be of the gravest kind, their infrequency limits the significance of research from the standpoint of the control of violence.

The inability of medical and psychiatric research to explain violent crime after a century of trying—except for the unusual situations of the psychotic or brain-damaged offender—suggests that the prospects are not bright that progress will be made toward successful medical treatment of violent offenders not afflicted with mental illness of injury. The interventions to which this research might lead—the use of electric stimulation of the brain, powerful psychoactive drugs, and surgery—run counter to prevailing public attitudes toward these kinds of treatment. Response of the offender without psychosis or cerebral malfunction to psychotherapy has been uniformly disappointing, and not much innovative research is now under way to improve the effectiveness of treatment. No one can predict how long this impasse will continue, but indications of change are not on the professional or cultural horizons.

Age and Violence

The young commit the greatest amount of violent crime. Cohort studies of young offenders, followed longitudinally into adult years, show that the typical career of violent crime erupts in midadolescence. The modal age of onset of such careers is fourteen or fifteen. But the same research also shows that about a third of those who commit their first violent crime during adolescence will desist after arrest and their first court appearance. We do not know how to differentiate these desistors from youths who continue committing offenses. Many of these recidivists will continue a criminal career until they are thirty to thirty-five years old, mixing violent and nonviolent crimes. Once past the twenties, these careers of violence terminate in a process of extinction that has not been sufficiently studied.[5]

A cohort study recently completed by some of my colleagues shows that violent offenses may begin long before adolescence; we noted some arrests as early as eight years old. There does not seem to be any special significance to such early onset, nor is the violence committed very serious. Really grave violent offenses do not begin until age twelve or thirteen, but aggression at this age usually presages a long and reckless career.[6]

Offenders who commit violent crimes seldom limit themselves to those categories. Most cohort studies show that violent criminals are "generalists"; especially in their younger years they will commit crimes of opportunity. It is not uncommon to find a criminal history listing a half-dozen different kinds of offenses, violent and nonviolent. It seems to be true, however, that the more offenses a youth commits the more serious they will be. The well-known study by Wolfgang, Figlio, and Sellin[7] found that in a cohort of nearly 10,000 Philadelphia boys, delinquent and nondelinquent, about eighteen percent of the delinquents had been arrested five or more times between the ages of ten and eighteen. They were

[5]Simon Dinitz, Stuart Miller, and John P. Conrad, *The Career of Violence* (Lexington, Mass.: Lexington Books, 1982), (in preparation).
[6]Donna Martin Hamparian *et al. The Violent Few* (Lexington, Mass.: Lexington Books, 1978), pp. 56–68.
[7]Marvin E. Wolfgang, Robert M. Figlio, and Thorsten Sellin, *Delinquency in a Birth Cohort* (Chicago: University of Chicago Press, 1972), pp. 130–150.

designated as "chronic recidivists," and further investigation showed that they were responsible for more than two-thirds of the serious crimes committed by the entire cohort. This finding has been replicated in the study of violent youth in Columbus, Ohio recently completed by my research group.[8]

The connections between youth and violent crime can be established readily enough, and some writers have seized on the empirical verification of what seems to many as common knowledge to recommend that severe measures should be taken with violent young delinquents once they have recidivated to a level that can be described as chronicity.[9] Although research findings of this kind appear to justify a severe new policy of this nature, they do not take us any farther. We are not nearer to an understanding of the chronic offender when we apply that label, nor do we know what to do with him in the course of the severe sentence that we are told we should administer to him. Eventually he must be released from custody and other controls; what happens to him in most kinds of juvenile incarceration seems to accelerate his return to crime after release rather than promote law-abiding conduct. Our statistics express the results of our efforts at control, but they do not lead to *verstehen*. The puzzle is still there, awaiting more heuristic inquiry than mathematical criminology can contribute.

Race, Poverty, and Violence

Although there are statistical links between violent crime and racial identity, manifested by the high incidence of violent crimes committed by blacks, the most obvious explanation of this correlation is to be found in the overrepresentation of blacks in the lowest economic strata. All studies of the epi-

[8]Hamparian et al., pp. 69–71.
[9]James Q. Wilson, *Thinking about crime* (New York: Basic Books, 1974), pp. 208–209). See also Ernest van den Haag, *Punishing Criminals: Concerning an Old and Painful Subject* (New York: Basic Books, 1975), pp. 248–249.

demiology of criminal violence, wherever they have been conducted, have consistently found that the poor commit by far the most violent crimes and are by far the most frequent victims.

This conclusion is unpopular with those who prefer to believe that nothing can be done about poverty except to keep the poor under firmer control. Those whose thought moves in this direction argue that poverty cannot account for the high incidence of crime because so many poor people commit no crimes at all. From this undeniable truth it is reasoned that we must look elsewhere for some as yet unidentified influence that disposes some poor people to aggression as a way out of their predicament, whereas most others are passive. This argument is an irrelevance. Street crime cannot be understood without a recognition that it is the poor who commit it. To point to the high incidence of crime and delinquency among the rich (and some of the offenses committed by the affluent are far more reprehensible than those that a poor person can possibly commit) is to obscure the issue of violence. The overwhelming majority of street crimes have always been committed by poor young men.

In the United States, they are predominantly poor young black men. In his recent survey of criminal justice, Silberman has shown that the rate of violence among the black poor in our major cities exceeds by far the rates for the same offenses committed by Hispanic young men, who are at least as poor as the blacks.[10] The notoriously high unemployment rate for young black males is a statistically verifiable correlate of black violence, understated because so many young blacks never enter the conventional labor market. At this point the statistician must be silent. No survey can be devised to put statistical values on the conviction that prevails among blacks that their poverty is the result of a history of oppression that began in slavery.

[10]Charles E. Silberman, *Criminal Justice, Criminal Violence* (New York: Random House, 1978), p. 120.

All these facts are familiar enough to the comfortable and the poor alike. They have been presented in immeasurably greater detail by the macrosociologists of crime and by statisticians working with whatever data they can assemble. The situation worsens with economic adversity, but there are still criminologists who hope they can discover "root causes" that can be addressed without dealing with poverty and racial discrimination.

To face these intractable conditions is to recognize that the reduction of criminal violence is a distant goal. Prevention of crime in the black inner city and "rehabilitation" of the black offender depend in almost every respect on conditions that the criminal justice system cannot reach. The elevated rate of black violence is a signal that corrective measures must be taken. That none is in sight assures that not merely crime but all the other unfavorable consequences of racial discrimination and poverty will persist and increase in malignancy.

The Uncaught Thug

For the criminologist and the police, it is a disturbing frustration that only a minority of even the more serious offenses—except for murder—are ever cleared. An example from the well-policed city of Columbus demonstrates the statistical gap between crimes known to the police and those for which arrests were made.[11] In a study of the restraints imposed on violent recidivists, our group traced the disposition of 2,892 violent crimes known to the police in 1973. Of this number, only 792 were cleared by arrest. There were 65 homicides of which 64 were cleared, a typically high rate of clearance for that crime. But of 326 violent sex offenses, only 161 were cleared, slightly less than half. Of 1,554 robberies 435 were cleared, about 28 percent. Of 847 reported assaults 132 were cleared by arrest, about 14 percent. Although it is true

[11]Stephan Van Dine, John P. Conrad, and Simon Dinitz, *Restraining the Wicked* (Lexington, Mass.: Lexington Books, 1979).

that the police were able to clear many of the assault charges by investigation but were unable to persuade the victims to file charges, it is still true that the majority of crimes known to the police are not cleared either by arrest or a completed investigation. Some of the offenders who were arrested for these crimes were also responsible for uncleared crimes; no one can be sure how many. Along with many others who have engaged in such studies, we believe that few criminals escape apprehension; there is no cadre of master criminals so proficient at their trade that they are never caught.[12] Self-report studies suggest that some offenders are guilty of hundreds of crimes committed every year for which they are not apprehended. The majority of these crimes cannot have been violent, but it is likely that a substantial number were robberies. A topic of frequent but inconclusive discussion is the number of crimes per year that are prevented by the incarceration of one criminal for one year. No one can be sure of the answer; one of the curses of criminology is the necessity of mixing facts with speculation.

The Limits of Knowledge

It may be that the last few decades of intensive research have been most significant in that they have established some probable limits to what can be known about these common crimes, as common now as they were in antiquity. Whatever we know or suppose we know about the correlates of violence, we have learned little that gives us a basis for preventing it. The most significant generalization that we can make could be inferred by the thoughtful reader of the daily crime news: unemployed, young black males commit crimes against the person at a rate that exceeds that of any other identified group, and many such young men are repetitively violent, committing offenses of the utmost gravity. But this kind of knowledge only illustrates the stubbornness of the problem.

[12]Ibid., p. 120.

We do not have a solution to the unemployment of black youth, and there is reason to believe that the situation is worsening while the economy stagnates.

The stubbornness and ignorance are also illustrated by the meager and unimpressive results so far obtained from the study of collective violence. Riots in prisons and in inner cities periodically sweep across the country. It is easy enough to attribute the rapid succession of such disturbances in widely separated cities to a process of emulation by large numbers of poor people with little to lose. So far this explanation has not accomplished more than to alert the police to the imminence of danger; the prevention of such disturbances depends on measures to improve the quality of life of the participants. Whether social science has anything to contribute to the prevention of civic disorders remains to be seen. Further knowledge will increase understanding of the causes and consequences, but until we can remedy the conditions in which the black poor live our cities will continue to be in danger.

The search for facts about violence and those who commit it has been fruitful for administrators and planners—or would be if the data were presented with interpretations useful for their purposes. The theoretical explanations that emerge from the data are little better than platitudes. Research offering deeper insights is uncommon and not much of it is under way. What criminology has to tell the world describes the underlying pathology of a society enduring many miseries besides crime with little hope of a cure. Violent crime is one of the most serious symptoms. Its incidence is related to conflicts and inequities for which no resolution is in sight.

The Cure of Violence

Once a criminal has been convicted, society imposes on him a punitive action that is supposed to serve the combined purposes of incapacitating him from the commission of further offenses, intimidating him sufficiently so that he will prefer not to commit another crime when released, and rehabilitating him so that he will not have an economic or a psychological need to offend again. All these measures are effective with some offenders, but their effectiveness does not greatly affect the crime rate as a whole. The incapacitation of violent offenders will marginally affect the rates of violent crime—perhaps by two or three percent, depending on the length of the sentence. The effectiveness of intimidation is mixed. About half the men and women released from prison manage to abstain from further criminal conduct over fairly long follow-up periods. The most plausible reason for their compliance with the law is the wretchedly unpleasant experience of incarceration; it is unlikely that the rehabilitative programs to which they were exposed substantially contributed to their changed ways. The rest are recidivists. When young, they spend less time at liberty after each period of restraint. As they age, they eventually desist from violent crimes, though not necessarily to become lawabiding citizens. Unquestionably intimidation "works" for a large number of first offenders who are sent to prison; just as unquestionably the substantial population of recidivists in prison represent the extent to which this form of deterrence does not work. Although there are no studies specifically addressed to the effectiveness of "special" deterrence, there is no reason to believe that the marginal increases that are conceivable by making prisons even more intimidating would perceptibly affect the crime rate.

It is fashionable to assert that attempts to rehabilitate offenders are futile. I do not contest the general opinion that little is to be gained from the meager and mostly incompetent programs to be found in most American prisons today. But, poor as they are, some prisoners do get some benefit from some of them. Illiterates learn to read. Men and women who had been previously limited to unskilled labor have acquired skills that have made them employable at honest livings. These achievements are verifiable. Although their effect on the subsequent criminality of prisoners is uncertain, they must be counted as substantial benefits.

Less certain are the benefits of psychological treatment. In any clinical setting the statistical demonstration of the success of psychotherapy has always been elusive. Nowhere has this difficulty been more intractable than in the treatment of offenders. Because it has been impossible to show that any kind of psychological treatment has any effect on the recidivism of those exposed to it, many penological critics have seized on this default as proof of the futility of any kind of counseling or psychotherapy. This position is extreme. Most of the research that leads to it consists of the testing of poorly defined independent variables (e.g., "group counseling" at weekly intervals for a period of a year or more) by their impact on the remote variable or recidivism months or years after the termination of treatment. It is little wonder that nothing significant has emerged from such slovenly research. The real wonder is that anyone supposed that positive findings could be expected.

Most social scientists as well as most of the educators, psychologists, and social workers employed in the corrections field find the pessimism about rehabilitation hard to accept. After all, illiterates learn to read in prison, unskilled laborers become artisans, and many a confirmed drunk has found Alcoholics Anonymous a route to an orderly and law-abiding life. Psychotherapists can point to their victories anecdotally if not statistically. Do these achievements mean nothing in the face of the statistics of ineffectuality?

Again, the statistician must be silent. So far as it goes, the contention that "nothing works" rests on an impressive array of program evaluations that arrived at inconclusive results. Probably that general picture will not be shaken by data to come. What has been proved is that there is no way to make a system out of the good luck that can sometimes befall the previously unlucky. What the positive anecdotes of the various correctional professional persons show is that the opportunities they provide must continue to be available.

There remain to be considered various interventions that do belong in the correctional repertoire. For the purposes of this discussion we can disregard the arguments in favor of fines, restitution, and community service; there are few who advocate this kind of sanction for the violent offender, nor is there much experience with the administration of such sanctions for crimes of violence.

Capital punishment, however, has a large number of insistent advocates. They are not to be satisfied of its ineffectiveness in deterring potential killers from killing despite the inability of most analysts to prove the deterrent effect of the gallows or the electric chair.[13] What is evident from the data is that persons convicted of homicide and committed to life sentences rarely recidivate. Paroled "lifers" who kill on second occasions are exceptional. It is not at all evident that the execution of a murderer prevents a crime that he might commit if permitted to live, or that anyone inclined to homicide is significantly more deterred by the threat of the death cell than he would be by the prospect of a lifetime in prison. Further research on the usefulness of capital punishment as a deterrent is unlikely to be productive.

The debate between the true believers on both sides must be settled on the grounds of desert rather than deterrence. Although the empirical position is unfavorable to those who would retain capital punishment, it must be doubted that many of these persons hold to their position in the belief that homicide is really deterred, all rhetoric to the contrary notwithstanding. Like Kant,[14] they adhere to the *lex talionis*, firmly believing that nothing less than death is a sufficient pen-

---

[13]For a definitive review of the research done on capital punishment, see Blumstein, Cohen, and Nagin, pp. 59–63.

[14]Immanuel Kant, "The General Theory of Justice." In *The Metaphysical Elements of Justice*, trans. John Ladd (New York: Bobbs-Merrill, 1965), pp. 102–107. Although most readers are repelled by Kant's vigorously uncompromising advocacy of capital punishment for murder, his exposition of the logic of retributivism is still a lucid and uncluttered analysis and deserves to be considered as a line of reasoning opposed to the utilitarianism that was developing at that time and of which Kant scathingly disapproved.

alty for murder. There is nothing that research can contribute to this kind of debate.

Whether it is squeamishness or a collective intuition as to its ineffectiveness, the American public, so much inclined to favor capital punishment, has never shown a disposition to the legal administration of corporal punishment. Only Delaware among the states has consistently kept such legislation alive; its use has been infrequent. Only one study is to be found concerning its effectiveness, and the results were negative.[15]

Castration for rape and some other sex offenses has been more frequently advocated and, for a number of years, was popular in Denmark as an option by which a sex offender could avoid lengthy incarceration. Although its incapacitative effect was beyond question, it has been abandoned, perhaps because of the revulsion of the Danish people for so drastic an intervention, perhaps because the data have never been convincing that a reasonable term of incarceration would not have served as well in reducing recidivism and deterring potential offenders.

The use of psychoactive drugs to regulate the behavior of destructive and ungovernable prisoners and mental patients has been accepted practice for many years. Its undeniable success in converting bedlam into a semblance of tranquility has suggested to many clinicians and lay administrators that there may be other drugs that could be used for long-range intervention that would be less drastic, less costly, and perhaps more successful than incarceration. Experimentation has been cautious, and the constraints of informed consent have all but ended the few explorations that have been attempted with prisoner populations. From the little that has been done there is some evidence that violent behavior can be moderated by some kinds of drugs, but with

[15]Robert Graham Caldwell, *Red Hannah, Delaware's Whipping Post* (Philadelphia: University of Pennsylvania Press, 1974).

what degree of effectiveness, with what side effects, and for how long a period of time nobody can say.[16]

The position is about the same with respect to psychosurgery, once thought to be a panacea for violence during the heyday of prefrontal lobotomies. Advocates of psychosurgery argue that their methods have vastly improved since the early disasters that discredited these procedures. With increased precision, they assert, relief from brain conditions predisposing offenders to violence can be obtained without vegetablizing the patient. Proof of this contention is not at hand so far as criminals in custody are concerned, nor is it likely to become available soon in American practice given the prevailing judicial interpretations of the rules of informed consent.

Effective intervention with violent offenders is not likely to emerge from the research completed or now under way. No one doubts that the persistent violent recidivist must be locked up, but doing so can deter few others and will not noticeably affect the rate of violent crime. No treatment is predictably effective, but some treatment unpredictably works with some people. Various medical interventions have been tried but the risks are so great that whatever their promise responsible courts have been unwilling to authorize them. Although it is clear that a large number of violent first offenders do not recidivate and may be presumed to have been intimidated by the system, it is also true that there are many chronic violent offenders who are insufficiently intimidated by their experience of incarceration. Eventually age slows them down, but no one knows how to accelerate the process that finally

---

[16]See, for example, Harry Allen *et al.*, "Sociopathy: An Experiment in Internal Environmental Control," *American Behavioral Scientist* 11 (1976): 215–226. In this article the authors report an attempt to modify sociopathic behavior in forty-one prisoners in the Ohio correctional system by the administration of imipramine. The experiment was aborted on advice of counsel after court decisions specified minimum conditions for informed consent that could not be met in a project using prisoner subjects. The preliminary results indicated that sociopathic subjects benefited from the drug regime whereas the non-sociopaths did not.

extinguishes the career of violence. It must be conceded that research so far has turned up little of value for improving the effectiveness of the system in intervening with dangerous criminals.

Prediction

The power to predict the future behavior of phenomena studied is the goal of most scientific work and the evidence of its success. Much effort has gone into the prediction of criminal behavior, partly because social scientists have thought that a method of prediction might be useful and partly because they hoped thereby to demonstrate the validity of their explanations.

As for crime in general, the statistician is now able to predict the recidivism of offenders in an actuarial sense. Like an insurance actuary, he can classify offenders into groups according to the percentage who can be expected to commit new crimes. Some groups are composed of individuals who will not commit another crime; such groups rarely produce an exception. At the other end of a long continuum, groups can be identified in which all members will certainly commit additional crimes when they get the chance. In between these extremes is the bulk of the offender population, for whom the chances are more nearly even; a considerable percentage will recidivate and a complementary percentage will not. Judges and parole boards have not found this kind of prediction very useful, although it does have some value in research methodology in comparing the effects of independent variables.

The position is even more unsatisfactory as to the prediction of a violent offense. Although chronic offenders, defined as persons who commit five or more felonies, will commit more violent offenses than other offenders, not every chronic offender will be violent, and even those who are will be more likely to commit a nonviolent offense. It is possible to predict, with approximately 40 percent accuracy, that a chronic offender who has committed two or more violent offenses will commit another. The small class of such individuals will differ markedly from the general population or from a population of offenders. How far the law should take this difference into account turns an ambiguous finding into an issue for ethical debate. It is apparent that to act on a prediction that any particular offender belongs to a class 40 percent of whom will commit a violent offense at some future time will require the decision maker to be indifferent to the restraint of the 60 percent who will abstain from further violence. The usefulness of this kind of prediction for judges and others who must make decisions about the imprisonment of offenders must constitute at best a marginal blessing.

In a study that has become a classic reference on the prediction of behavior, Meehl showed that statistical predictions are significantly more accurate than those that are made on a clinical basis.[17] Despite Meehl's scathing exposure of the inaccuracy of their predictions, forensic psychiatrists persist in making predictions concerning future criminality with unabated frequency, and judges and juries accept them as appropriate information in sentencing. It is difficult to see why psychiatrists should enter this field of prediction at all. Neither their training nor their experience provides grounds for predicting anything but the probable success of the treatment they administer. Neither psychiatric theory nor its practice leads to a conceptual basis for predicting anyone's future behavior. Except for the psychotic, the brain damaged, and the mentally retarded, and only where these conditions incapacitate the individual from any functioning in social life, psychiatrists can only guess how patients under study will respond to likely events and situations when the patients are at liberty. As to criminals without grave mental conditions, few psychiatrists have had continuing treatment relationships and even fewer have had occasion to observe them even briefly in the community.

[17]Paul Meehl, *Clinical versus Statistical Prediction* (Minneapolis: University of Minnesota Press, 1954).

MAJOR BASIC RESEARCH TO BE DONE

Although the distinction between basic and applied research is never sharp in the study of human behavior, I shall organize this section by making it anyway. For the purpose of this section, "basic research" refers to the explanation of the phenomenon of violence, and "applied research" consists of the study of measures to prevent violence and to "treat" the violent offender.

There seem to me to be four areas of research, each calling for a large number of investigations. I think it will suffice to define these areas as the components of the program needed if progress is to be made. An enumeration of the projects indicated in each area would be a cumbersome undertaking even if it were practical. The definition of the projects that might be advantageous would require a polymathic command of numerous scientific disciplines. I do not claim such versatility, but it is likely that an assemblage of scientists undertaking such a research agenda might put into better perspective than we now have the volume of the work to be done and the value of doing it.

Limiting myself to the four major areas for basic research, I shall discuss in order the nosology of violence, the biomedical substrates of aggression, the subculture of violence, and the career of violence. Each presents both ethical and political problems as well as the need to apply difficult research methods to the unstable phenomena of human behavior.

Problem 1: Psychopathy

I begin with one of the most hoary problems in psychiatry: the diagnostic classification of psychopathy. Psychopathy is also known by other designations, as if a shift in nomenclature might be expected to clarify it. We now hear of sociopathy, antisocial personality, character disorder, defective delinquency, moral defect, as well as older variants such as constitutional psychopathic inferiority and psychopathic personality. What has always been true of the original term is equally true of the newer alternatives: the definition is circular and it does not describe a process so much as a state. Clinical descriptions of psychopathy are collections of symptoms found in criminals that do not account for their appearance in noncriminals and in other persons who are not diagnosed as psychopathic.

Despite the conceptual inadequacies of the term and its lack of rigor, exposure to a population of criminals always inclines the clinically experienced observer to conclude that there is something different about them. The proper term for them may not be one that refers to a special pathology. Whether their characteristics are best understood as a disease process that might be cured by treatment or as the consequence of a career of criminal behavior in which experience creates an occupational outlook on life, a more confident understanding of the process is essential to the prevention of delinquency and the treatment of offenders.

Problem 2. The Biomedical Substrates of Aggression

In the studies undertaken by the Behavioral Studies Research Group, an appropriate emphasis has been given to research directed at the biochemical and genetic substrates of aggressive behavior. Certainly the studies attempted in this area have evoked the greatest amount of concern in the community, partly because of a history of poorly designed and executed research, partly because of a disturbing insensitivity to the rights and anxieties of the subjects, and partly because of misunderstandings.

In spite of the opposition that has arisen to research already done, I believe it is important to undertake more investigations in this area. Although it seems obvious to most workers in this field that nurture accounts for crime more frequently than nature, the possibility that some aggressive behavior can be attributed to a physical condition or abnormality is certainly evident in some violent offenders and may be an unperceived part of the problem of others.

The attempt to link the XYY abnormality to violent crime was a wild surmise gone amok. There may be genetic anomalies that are significantly related to violent behavior, but it is absurd to rush to the formulation of a hypothesis based on a sample of negligible size and without preliminary taxonomic explorations to establish physical and psychological attributes of persons affected by the syndrome. Although there may well be genetic sources of abnormal behavior, their study will have to be much more deliberate.

The central nervous system as a predisposing factor holds more promise than the genetic paradigm. Studies of this possible factor trouble some observers because of the formidable kinds of treatment that they imply. Ever since the post–World War I studies of Kurt Goldstein[18] there has been reason to connect some kinds of brain damage with violent conduct. The contemporary work of José Delgado with various primates indicates that violent behavior can be induced and controlled by applying or withholding various electric stimuli to various parts of the brain.[19] The evidence of biomedical sources of some violent behavior does not indicate to what degree behavior is a matter of physiology, but it does show that some serious kinds of violent crime may originate in nature rather than in nurture. Some research of this kind is being pursued now, but we seem to be far from conclusions that would justify new and presumably radical forms of intervention.

The technical and esoteric quality of this kind of research presents the criminologist with his most formidable interdisciplinary difficulties. It is perplexing enough to keep current with one's own discipline or those that are adjacent—as psychology is to sociology. To maintain currency with developments in neurological and intracranial research calls for a long

---

[18]Kurt Goldstein, "The Effect of Brain Damage on the Personality," *Psychiatry* 15 (1952): 245–260.

[19]José Delgado, "Control of Behavior by Electronic Stimulation of the Brain," *Naval Research Review*, May 1–7, 1959.

bridge indeed, one that few criminologists will be able to build and keep in repair.

Problem 3. The Subculture of Violence

The literature of criminology is replete with obvious conclusions about the cultural influences that produce criminal behavior. Bad associations turned normal youths into criminals; the only cure for them was removal from these associations and exposure to good influences. Some elaboration of this simple notion was achieved by Sutherland[20] with his theory of differential association. It was left to Cohen[21] to complete the transformation of common-sense observation into a theory of some elegance from which he derived the idea of a subculture. This notion postulates a section of society that accepts the norms of the dominant culture but, because of disadvantage and conflict, cannot comply with them. Instead those who live in such subcultures react with forms of behavior at variance with prevailing norms. This idea was adopted by Wolfgang and Ferracuti, who proposed that violence is one of the adaptations to disadvantage and that there exist subcultures in which all male participants are expected to act on values that call for violence in response to betrayals, insults, and other actions hostile to themselves or to the group to which they are in allegiance. These authors did not propose a remedy for subcultural violence. They were content with a survey of the anthropological and sociological literature describing violent population groups.

Not much has been done with the subculture of violence since the publication of their book.[22] The concentration of violent crime, much of it callously brutal, in the disadvantaged

[20]See Edwin H. Sutherland and Donald R. Cerssey, *Principles of Criminology*, 6th ed. (Philadelphia: J. B. Lippincott, 1960), pp. 74–80.
[21]Albert K. Cohen, *Delinquent Boys: The Culture of the Gang* (Glencoe, Ill.: Free Press, 1953).
[22]Wolfgang, Marvin E. and Ferracuti, Franco. *The Subculture of Violence*. (London: Tavistock Publications, 1967).

sections of metropolitan centers indicated the power of sub-cultural determinants. It is also evident that however com-pelling these influences may be on some, nearly all women and most men living in such communities are able to resist their call for violence. The meaning of this resistance for the hypothesis of a subculture is far from clear. In some such communities it may mean that although violence is a neces-sary element in a man's social repertory, it is proscribed for women and, perhaps, for men occupying social positions in which violence is inappropriate. It may also mean that the idea of a subculture is not as useful for understanding violent crime as it may seem to be on the surface..

The basic theory of the subculture needs further refine-ment. Although there are a few suggestive contributions of anthropological observation, notably the work of Liebow[23] and of "James Patrick"[24] we still lack an integration of em-pirical research and theory that might enable us to confirm the heuristic utility of the idea of the subculture. If it is indeed a useful path to the understanding of violence, the test will be in experiments aimed at prevention and control.

Problem 4. The Career of Violence

Studies of the careers of violent criminals are currently fashionable, and I have recently participated in two myself. The value of this kind of research in the formulation of a theory of criminal violence is critical. It is now clear that there are several different kinds of criminal careers, each with its own characteristics. Some criminals commit violence with a frequency that far exceeds the number shown on their arrest records, whereas others commit violence occasionally and out of some apparent need or in reaction to some provocation. The onset of violent delinquency in the early years of ado-

---

[23]Eliot Liebow, *Tally's Corner* (Boston: Little, Brown, 1967).
[24]James Patrick [pseud.] *A Glasgow Gang Observed* (London: Eyre, Methuen, 1973).

lescence usually presages a long and increasingly vicious series of crimes. Career studies also have practical or applied significance; they are the most authoritative sources of data about the impact of various kinds of interventions on individuals. Properly controlled, as were the formidable studies conducted in England by West and Farrington,[25] much will be learned about the taxonomy of violent criminals and the ways in which they come to differ from a "normal population."

MAJOR APPLIED RESEARCH TO BE DONE

I do not intend to present an exhaustive catalog of the possibilities of applied research. What is needed is a listing of the more important topics for study. Nearly all of those to be discussed here entail weighty ethical and political problems, some of which have received little or no general attention. Four topics are selected, but it cannot be argued that they are necessarily representative of the gamut.

Problem 5. Early Intervention and Control of Juvenile Violent Offenders

Early identification and control of violent juveniles has been urged by many authorities as a promising means of reducing criminal violence. It is argued that too many violent offenders receive too much leniency after their first offense, thereby encouraging them to continue with their destructive behavior. A natural experiment with severe intervention with youthful offenders exists in New York, where recently enacted legislation provides for mandatory trial in adult courts for juveniles charged with certain crimes against the person.

[25]D. J. West and D. P. Farrington, *The Delinquent Way of Life* (London: Heinemann, 1977). See also West and Farrington's *Who Becomes Delinquent?* (London: Heinemann, 1973).

A significant sample of these young people should be followed to assess the effectiveness and consequences of legislation of this kind.

An analogous kind of study is possible in Illinois, where intensive community supervision is provided for chronic juvenile offenders in an experiment designated as the Unified Delinquency Intervention Service.[26] Youths assigned to this program should be followed for a sufficient period of time to facilitate an assessment of the outcome.

Problem 6. Behavior Modification Techniques

The abuses that are possible in behavior modification programs have received considerable attention at The Hastings Center.[27] Several ethical issues have been explored and vigorously debated. The purpose of this chapter is not to review the various positions taken, but we can perform a modest service by discussing the concept as it relates to the correction of offenders. I will leave to my colleagues the much more onerous task of summarizing the ethical problems that the practice of behavior modification entails.

The theory of behavior modification is loose and simple. It depends on the readily verifiable proposition that animals and human beings will perform as required to obtain rewards in the form of approval, food, cash, or other benefits. They will also avoid acts that result in punishment, that is, pain, deprivation, disapproval, or shame. In a sense the criminal justice system functions as a vast and inefficient organ for behavior

---

[26]A considerable literature is accumulating on the Uniform Delinquency Intervention Service (UDIS), but the best description is to be found in Charles A. Murray, Doug Thompson, and Cindy B. Israel, *UDIS Deinstitutionalization of the Chronic Juvenile Offender* (Washington: American Institute of Research, 1978).

[27]David J. Rothman, "Behavior Modification in Total Institutions," *The Hastings Center Report* 5 (February 1975): 17–24. See also, in the same publication, Robert A. Burt, "Why We Should Keep Prisoners from the Doctors," 25–34; Leslie T. Wilkins, "Putting 'Treatment' on Trial," 35–36, 39–48.

modification. One object of criminal justice is considered to be "extinction" of criminal behavior by the imposition of aversive treatment. In earlier sections I have considered the probability that the system's effectiveness in carrying out this aim is less than generally believed. Although it can intimidate many offenders at the time of their first encounter, the deterrent effect after a second or third incarceration declines precipitiously.

Within the correctional system both positive and negative reinforcements are regularly used. For the prisoner the prospect of as speedy a release as possible from incarceration assumes a function of positive reinforcement. Almost always compliance with institutional rules will bear on determination of the time of release from incarceration, whether the determination is made by a parole board in fixing a term and granting parole or by an administrative officer awarding "good time" for good behavior. In recent years there has been a trend toward the change of criminal codes to provide for sentences fixed by law rather than to be decided by parole boards in adjustment of indeterminate sentences. All parties to this change have agreed that where it is made, there must be the incentive to compliance that is implied by early release; hence the "good time" provisions allowing the remission of substantial portions of a sentence in return for law- and rule-abiding behavior while confined.

Aversive controls are also used, usually in the form of "solitary" confinement (actually only rarely solitary in the sense of true isolation from others) for a specified number of days. Court decisions in some states have required that persons so punished must be allowed reading materials, access to visitors, and most other amenities permitted to other prisoners, thus arousing the complaint the punitive isolation is not sufficiently aversive to deter prisoners from resumption of their undesirable behavior.

Most prisons have found it necessary to maintain units for the indefinite segregation of persistent rule violators. This form of control is referred to as "administrative segregation," and is both aversive and an administrative determination that a prisoner is too dangerous or too much of a nuisance to be allowed to circulate freely in the prison.

Rewards and punishments of this magnitude are undeniably influential in inducing compliance with immediate requirements. They have no pertinence to postrelease behavior, nor are they intended to. But both administrators and correctional psychologists have been alert to the possibility that a more structured form of behavior modification might produce results with significance for behavior change after release.

Probably the first experiment in the use of designed behavior modification in a correctional setting was conducted by Harold S. Cohen at the National Training School for Boys, an institution for the youngest federal juvenile offenders, closed since the late sixties. Working with a small group of educationally disadvantaged boys, Cohen was able to use positive reinforcements with considerable success in the development of elementary reading and arithmetic skills. The achievement was impressive, but the subsequent careers of the boys were not. Experiments using token economies to reward desired behavior have since been conducted in many locales, most notably at the Robert F. Kennedy Youth Center in Morgantown, West Virginia, another federal youth facility. Although the immediate results were satisfactory enough, their impact on postrelease behavior has been disappointing.

Some positive results have been reported for aversive therapy with sex offenders, but behavior modification schemes using negative reinforcements have incurred the opposition of civil rights organizations, and there is little prospect of such treatments being put to systematic use in the climate of present federal case law relating to this form of treatment.

There is not much in the conventional prison that offers a prisoner hope for the future or an incentive to change his ways. I doubt that the methods used by B. F. Skinner to teach his pigeons to play table tennis will be enough to teach violent men to choose other ways of influencing their antagonists. More imaginative experiments with the use of incentives for adopting nonviolent responses to hostility and frustration seem possible; it would be refreshing to see them undertaken. However valid the complaint that this form of treatment amounts to "brainwashing" or "mind control," it is difficult to regard it as a more intrusive control than the squalid varieties of punishment that now prevail in nearly every prison in the land.

Problem 7. Psychopharmacology

An even more emotional issue than behavior modification in the treatment of offenders is the prospective use of drugs to control or change behavior. There is no question of the feasibility of "managing" difficult prisoners in this way; psychoactive drugs have been used as a matter of course for this purpose in maximum security prisons for many years. The sight of a once manic convict sitting quietly in his cell when formerly he was trying to tear it apart will impress any observer and inspire the lasting gratitude of his keepers.

Nevertheless the consequences of this kind of treatment are far from clear. The grave objections to the use of drugs that have deleterious side effects are obvious, and these objections are insuperable when there is danger of irreversible harm. However, there are some relatively mild drugs that seem to be beneficial without risk of damage. Recent biochemical research has indicated that the neuropolypeptides may be particularly useful for changing behavior.

The ethical problems inherent in interventions of this kind are serious and are often dismissed by prison administrators who are concerned with reducing the incidence of violent behavior in the immediate environment. So little is known about the social and psychological consequences of this kind of control, especially for the time after the treatment ends, that simple prudence should require some longitudinal and controlled studies.

Studies of this kind call for more understanding of the technical aspects of pharmacology than criminologists ordinarily possess, whereas for biochemists or psychopharmacologists the prison and the parole populations are too unfamiliar to carry out unaided experiments. The use of prisoners as human subjects is fraught with both reasoned and emotional objections. The controversies that arise are not to be readily reconciled, if they can be reconciled at all. But the heavy use of psychoactive drugs in most maximum security prisons is now common enough to permit a systematic study of a sample of prisoners exposed to differing medications. Without information about the consequences, ethical debate about the use of drugs is speculative and fruitless.

Problem 8. Sentencing

The criminal justice system is undergoing convulsive changes with the demonstration of the feasibility of "deinstitutionalization." It is agreed in principle that most persons who limit themselves to crimes against property should be sentenced to surveillance and supervision in the community, leaving the increasingly costly option of incarceration for those who commit violent crimes. Traditionally the violent have always served longer sentences than the burglars and thieves who commit the largest volume of offenses. What is not at all clear from what we know about present-day sentencing practices are the differential effects of varying lengths of sentence or different requirements for serving sentences. So far as we now know there is little reason to suppose that any individual who serves more or less time than the average will be more or less likely to recidivate. Indeed, the few experiments that have been conducted suggest that varying the length of time served in prison has no consistent effect on future conduct. Without sufficient evidence to support the contention, many criminologists assert that the United States imposes the longest sentences of any Western nation. Whether this proposition is true or not, it is probable that our sentencing policy could be liberalized without significant danger to the public. The issue could be settled with a careful statistical study, which cannot be said of any of the other problems discussed in this chapter.

THE APPARATUS FOR STUDY

Over the last fifteen years social research has been bureaucratized and placed under a battery of controls intended to assure the protection of all interests that might be affected by unintended consequences of study. It is beyond the scope of this chapter to outline the numerous kinds of reviews that govern research from the time that a proposal is submitted to the time when the final report is due. Severe obstacles though these requirements are, I cannot argue against continuing them. Where human subjects must be used in research there is an absolute responsibility on the part of the funding agency and the research group conducting the study to assure that nobody's interests are adversely affected. Because the researcher's priorities are so urgent it is easy for them to overlook the urgencies of the subjects they wish to study. No matter how obvious their responsibility may be, it is not to be expected that they alone will always be sensitive to the interests of their subjects, especially when the latter are convicts with no apparent claim on their respect or concern.

The bureaucratization of criminal justice research has gone far. Nearly all of it is conducted under government auspices with federal funding. Because the research is so carefully monitored to assure compliance with fiscal and administrative guidelines, professional and ethical issues receive much less attention. The studies completed by the Behavioral Studies Research Group have found that some of these issues have received insensitive reviews by internal committees of research institutes and also by officials of the funding agencies. A case in point is the well-designed study by Dr. Stanley Walzer of male infants with the XYY chromosomal anomaly. There was much disagreement among our informants and within our group about the propriety and even usefulness of that study, but all seemed to agree that in retrospect the Harvard committees reviewing the protocols and the NIMH review boards did not clearly identify serious defects in the procedures for obtaining informed consent from the mothers in the sample. Even more serious was the lack of planning for the protection of the interests of the children to be studied. Neither of these faults was found until scientists working with a protest group vigorously brought them to the attention of everyone concerned.

Because these issues are so sensitive and because the potential damage from ethical and professional errors is so serious, I submit that the principal federal funding agencies should limit violence research to certain qualified centers. Such centers should be designated for establishment at a few universities or research institutes strategically situated for convenient access to human subjects and a sufficient variety of consultant resources to assure scientific versatility. It should be required that each center provide for a scientific advisory committee to assure the maintenance of acceptable standards of research. There should also be an ethical council composed of persons with varied interests and experience with ethical issues in decision making. All projects to be undertaken by a violence research center would receive thorough scrutiny by both advisory committees before submission of a proposal for funding.

To assure that scientific personnel not attached to the center would enjoy opportunities to engage in violence research, it would be provided that proposals for studies from such persons would be considered without prejudice. If approved, these persons would be invited to join the center for the period of time required for the completion of their projects.

Without doubt these centers would receive a great deal of watchful attention. Such public scrutiny would be mostly beneficial. The researcher has an obligation to the taxpayer who supports his work to explain what he is doing and why; when such an explanation cannot be made, it is reasonable to infer that its value is not clear to the researcher either. In an imperfect world, the personnel of such a center will be subjected to unfair, *ad hominem*, and abusive attacks. It must be supposed that as experience is gained with successful centers such attacks will become less troublesome, but whatever the case may be this special burden of the researcher cannot be entirely lifted.

Our review of the episodes of unpleasant hostility evoked in the course of efforts to establish a Center for the Study and Reduction of Violence at UCLA may seem to demonstrate the impracticality of my proposal. It may be argued that such a center must sooner or later arouse the implacable opposition of a group looking for a cause, even if the course of its research is sound, beneficial, and apparently harmless. With all the advantages of perfect hindsight, it is possible to identify some avoidable errors in planning that may have doomed the UCLA center from the beginning. The designation of the center and its special identity with the institute called attention to what it was proposed to do. There is no necessity for a center for the study of violence; projects having to do with the control of criminal violence can be assigned to groups working within a neutrally designated institute, such as the Neuropsychiatric Institute at UCLA. The advertisement of general plans to do research on violence will create uneasiness among taxpayers, if only because public money is to be spent by people who apparently are not sure what they will be doing with it. Finally, especially as the program begins, projects should be chosen with care so that the benefits from prospective success are apparent and threats to anyone at all are minimal. Successful projects will assure that a constituency can be built for support of further research, and may even discourage those who would be inclined to campaign against the support of research.

An obvious precedent exists for such concentration of sensitive research. Just as research on atomic energy is permitted by the federal government only at specially authorized locations, research in this sensitive field should be restricted to places where it can be performed efficiently, responsibly, and under conditions that assure public confidence.

THE ETHICAL ISSUES

In criminal justice the empirically determined facts cannot determine what law and policy should be, but they should be available to legislators and opinion leaders for an understanding of their choices and the consequences. Most issues on public policy require the collection of the facts before an ethical judgment can be made. The following examples of such issues are suggestive rather than exhaustive.

The False-Positive Issue

Although the prediction of violent behavior can never approach total accuracy, it is possible to identify a class of offenders, a high percentage of whom will commit new crimes when released from restraint. These new crimes will not necessarily be violent, but the risk will be much more significant than from any random sample of the general population. Suppose, for example, that a prediction can be made as to some class of offenders that about 40 percent will commit new crimes. That will establish that this group differs markedly from the rest of the people in the community in which they live. There is, however, no way of predicting which members of this group will actually recidivate. Some 60 percent will be non-recidivists and will be statistically designated as "false-positives," persons for whom a prediction is made which will not be borne out by events.

A second ethical problem presented by this group of offenders is the instability of the predictions over time. We may suppose that we are considering a cohort of offenders who are all twenty years old at the time they are identified and that the probability of a new offense stands at 40 percent. As they age, that probability will decline, perhaps to 35 percent at age thirty, and to about 5 percent at age forty.

Can an equitable control policy be based on this set of probabilities? If so, how can we justify the retention of the entire group in custody when it is known that most will not recidivate? What would be the lowest percentage of predicted recidivism that would be consistent with the ethical principle adopted? How can a fair allowance be made for the aging offender whose probability of future criminal activity is low?

Note that a retributivist will have little difficulty with these questions. Regardless of the circumstances, the offender should be punished no more and no less than his just desert. But utilitarian expectations survive. It is never easy and it may not be practical to mix fair play for the individual with a plan to achieve wider social goals.

Just Desert for the Recidivist

A related issue is the policy of increasing the severity of sentences for recidivist offenders. The reason for such legislation is explicit: to protect the public. It is argued that a sentence appropriate for a first offender must be augmented on the expectation that a second offender has an increased likelihood of offending again. Many writers dismiss this argument as irrelevant, pointing out that to "enhance" a sentence on account of recidivism is only justifiable if an accurate prediction of a new offense can be made—and that is not now possible. How can the enhancement of sentences for recidivists be reconciled with fairness to the individual?

Waiver of Juvenile Status for Minors Committing Violent Offenses

From its beginnings in the early years of this century, the administration of juvenile justice has been grounded on the principle that the court must act in the best interest of the child, regardless of the nature of the offense he may have committed. Because of certain atrocious crimes committed by younger juveniles, (not a new phenomenon in the history of crime), there is a movement that has already had considerable legislative effect to try such children in adult criminal courts and to sentence them accordingly. If this movement gathers further acceptance, ethical safeguards must be designed and incorporated in the law to assure that children tried as adults will be protected as persons of diminished capacity when answering to the law as defendants. Both prosecutors and defense counsel, as well as judges, must take account of the inexperience and the limits of understanding in the child offender. In matters of this kind, the law cannot be relied on to assure the necessary protection. We must hope that professional ethics on the bench and at the bar will supplement the requirements of the statutes.

Informed Consent

Many writers postulate that once an offender is in custody it is impossible for him to give a valid informed consent to medical or surgical treatment that presents any risks of physical or psychological harm. This position rules out any form of psychosurgery and many kinds of psychopharmacological treatment. The history of opposition to such intervention is studded with incidents in which attempts to administer treatment have been proscribed after protest by groups professing to act on ethical grounds. Some of these cases involved prisoners whose desire for treatment was credibly documented.

Can rules be devised that will provide for the administration of psychosurgical or psychopharmacological treatment to offenders under conditions of informed consent and yet ensure the continued proscription of methods that entail undesirable and irreversible side effects?

These samples of the ethical problems confronted by judges, administrators, and researchers will not become easier to resolve over time. The conflicts between the rights of prisoners—the most completely disadvantaged citizens in the land—and the right of society to be protected against predatory and violent crime are formidable. They can be resolved under conditions of goodwill and scrupulous thought. Due regard for the opinions of the various publics concerned, even when these opinions are ignorant, can bring most conflicts to a decent resolution. Where public opposition is motivated by political objectives the settlement cannot be based on ethics or facts; the political process must decide.

CONCLUSION

It is apparent that research for the reduction and control of violence deals with an important popular concern and can, given concerted and responsible direction, produce results of value to the criminal justice system and to agencies whose mission it is to prevent crime and assist offenders. However, it is also apparent that the fundamental causes of violence are beyond the reach of criminal justice. Some of these causes are to be found in the nature of human beings; some in their nurture in a troubled society. But if violence is the puzzle to be solved, whatever questions are answered will only lead to more fundamental questions that should have been asked in the first place. An optimal research program for the study of violence should be conducted as a phase of much more profound investigations of the human condition. The really important questions about violent crime all arise within the context of intrapsychic dysfunction and social disorganization.

There is nevertheless a considerable benefit to be expected from the research program I have suggested, as limited as it is. But there is far more benefit to be expected from social action that will require no research at all. Social research is not required to justify full employment for disadvantaged youth, reconstruction of the decayed and devastated sections of our cities, and a reorganization of our economy to assure that it serves the traditional social aims of the American people—life, liberty, and the pursuit of happiness. Until we are serious about these constitutional purposes we cannot seriously expect that the necessary improvement of the criminal justice system will bring about any significant change in our experience of violent crime.

CHAPTER 7

Ethics and the Control of Research

T. M. SCANLON

The particular bitterness felt by the men whose interrupted projects were the subject of our inquiry can be understood in part simply as the annoyance and frustration of people prevented from carrying on their work. However, it is clear that they also felt a deep resentment at the charge that what they were doing was harmful and irresponsible, and that they were frustrated by their inability to convince others that their work was, as they believed, useful and proper. These are reactions that anyone might have to being interfered with and accused, but the men we interviewed seemed to feel indignation of a further, special sort. They seemed to feel that because they were doing research they had a special claim to protection from interference and criticism of the kinds they

T. M. SCANLON • Department of Philosophy, Princeton University, Princeton, New Jersey 08544.

had experienced. This feeling showed itself from time to time in claims that in their cases it was academic freedom or freedom of thought itself that was at stake.

It is these claims that I want to consider in this chapter. I do not think that they are completely groundless; questions of academic freedom are related to the control of research. On the other hand, I think that such considerations have at most a limited and indirect relevance to the cases we have studied. To explain this view, I will need to distinguish various ways in which research can have harmful consequences. I will then be able to consider whether our central interests in research are threatened when consequences of these kinds are taken to justify regulation or interference. I will begin, however, with some general remarks about the nature of research and our relation to it.

SPONSORSHIP AND PROTECTION OF RESEARCH

To do research is to set out to discover the truth about something. The word "research" has a scientific connotation, but I intend to use it in a very general sense according to which any investigation into the truth about some matter constitutes research. Research in this sense might be engaged in for many different reasons. It might be done, for example, purely for the researcher's own benefit or enjoyment, with no intention of communicating the results to anyone else. (One might want to discover more about the facts in order to do a better job of concealing them from others.) On the other hand, research might be done purely in the service of another agent, with the aim of communicating the results solely to this sponsor. I will call such undertakings "private research." At various points in this chapter I will use imaginary examples of private research as the basis for analogies. I assume, however, that an actual instance of private research would have no more claim to noninterference than any other "private" activity with similar consequences. Whether that is true of all research is the further question that is to be discussed.

Research in the full sense, which is my principal concern, differs from private research in that it is done with the aim of making the results known to a wider community, normally taken to include all those with an interest in the subject at hand. It is research in this sense that can be considered a calling: it aims to provide us, "the public," with something of general value, an increase in our collective knowledge. A person who commits himself to this calling undertakes to be guided by the goals of uncovering and reporting the truth. This commits one to choose among lines of inquiry on the basis of the returns in insight that they offer, and to report the results in a way that makes them available to others.

A person who has thus committed himself to this public good, perhaps at some personal sacrifice, may reasonably feel entitled, not to unlimited public support, but at least to a degree of understanding and appreciation of his task on the part of the public, its intended beneficiaries. This expectation includes, a researcher is likely to say, recognizing that the person who does research is not responsible for what the facts are but only for finding and reporting them, and understanding that if the researcher's decisions in carrying out an inquiry are guided by considerations other than the acquisition of knowledge, the results of the inquiry are likely to suffer. Knowledge is valuable, the researcher might say, but to get the benefit of research one must put up with the risk that the truths it yields will be unpleasant or that their being known will have unwanted effects.

This element of risk gives researchers reason to be wary of giving control over research to laymen. Those not involved in research are likely, as researchers see it, to be too concerned with its immediate consequences for good or ill, and to give insufficient weight to the benefits of unrestricted inquiry. These benefits are cumulative, and the effect on them of a given experiment or a given restriction cannot be reliably foreseen.

That, somewhat broadly put, is the perspective of the researcher, and something like it was expressed several times in our sessions.[1] To what extent is this outlook one that the public, as the intended beneficiaries of research, should also adopt? Their relation to research is something like that of a sponsor to the private research he supports. From the sponsor's point of view it is evident that increases in knowledge are not the only good. Assuming for the moment that the sponsor bears all the costs of research, it is up to him to decide how much the general goal of increasing his knowledge or learning the answer to a particular question is worth to him. Some knowledge may be fairly worthless to a sponsor, or even a burden. It is often irrational to reject new information, but not always. Some knowledge may only serve to make one unhappy—to fuel regret, for example—while not aiding one in any way.

Once the sponsor has decided what costs he is willing to bear for the sake of a general or specific increase in his knowledge, however, the question how best to expend this budget of costs on particular lines of inquiry is one that he might well leave to his researchers themselves. For the answer may well depend on the relative promise of these inquiries, and thus may require specialized knowledge that he does not possess. In deciding how to proceed within the cost limits he has set, the sponsor should want his researchers to be guided only by the goal of finding the truth. He therefore has good reason to shield them from other influences that are likely to affect the conduct of their research or to induce them to report to him anything other than their true findings. He might do this, for example, by making them financially secure or by having them work in competing teams who report separately and are required to defend any differences in their methods or results.

---

[1]Most clearly by Robert Michels. See, for example, his remarks in "Researching Violence: Science, Politics and Public Controversy" Special Supplement, *The Hastings Center Report* 9 (April 1979): 19.

The loosely defined principles we refer to as academic freedom are, like these measures, a strategy for protecting the independence of researchers. But the content of these principles is determined by features of our relation to research and scholarship that are different from the relation of a sponsor to private research as I have described it. The public[2] collectively benefits from research, or suffers the consequences of its misapplication. And it is they who bear its immediate costs: they suffer from the side effects of the research process; they pay for public support of research, or contribute privately. The public thus stands in something like the relation of sponsor, if not to individual research projects then to the process of research as a whole. It would seem to be up to them (i.e., us), as collective sponsors, to decide what they want to learn about and how much they are willing to sacrifice to increase their knowledge. But there are problems about the way in which the public, collectively, can perform these functions of setting the goals of research and delimiting its costs.

Neither the harms occasioned by research nor its beneficial results are shared equally by all members of the public. One consequence of this obvious fact is that research policy is open to criticism on moral grounds—on the ground, for example, that it impermissibly inflicts harm on some in order to benefit others, or on the ground that the knowledge it produces is in fact harmful rather than beneficial, or that it is wasteful, or that it does not address the most urgent problems but instead serves the interests of a few at the expense of others. These lines of attack are not, of course, peculiarly relevant to research. Exactly the same criticisms might be made against any other public-supported programs—highway construction or flood control.

A second consequence of the selective character of the benefits of research is that members of the public may sharply

---

[2]As things are, it is most commonly the present taxpayers of a single country who foot the bill for large-scale research projects. But "the public" that is in the long run benefited or harmed by research is apt to be much wider.

disagree over what they want to see investigated—both over what they want to know and over what they want others to know. Thus there is good reason to expect that those who are in a position to influence what gets investigated and how it is reported will use this power to protect their own interests, thereby depriving others of information they would like to have. Here again research is not unique; such conflicts arise over other public programs as well. One special feature of research is the strategic importance of knowledge: control over sources of information enables one to influence other political decisions. But there is a further important feature. Unlike the usefulness of highways, the value of the information that research provides depends in part on what one knows about the way in which its goals were set—on what questions were asked (and not asked), and how these questions were chosen. The information one does receive may be of little value if one has reason to doubt its completeness and to suspect the grounds on which it was selected.

A partial solution to this problem is to hand the selection of topics for research over to the researchers themselves, and try to insulate them from the most obvious forms of partisan control. We can then hope that with a large number of such researchers working independently and in competition we will be likely to receive a more balanced flow of information. This is one rationale for the support of "academic" institutions, that is, institutions whose goals for research and scholarship are defined by the canons of academic subjects, canons that are set through a kind of consensus among the researchers themselves. "Academic freedom" is invoked as one way of protecting these institutions from outside influence and of protecting those working within them from arbitrary or partisan control.

Of course academic institutions are not the only means for supporting research. Individuals are free to sponsor research and publication, but those who carry out this research are not protected by academic freedom. That is, their sponsors are free, leaving aside contractual bonds, to cut off support if the results displease them in any way, and free to make whatever demands they like on the conduct of the research and the way its results are reported. It may be irrational for them to interfere in these ways if their sole aim is spreading the truth, but that may not be their sole aim. The sponsors may, of course, wish to shield their investigators from influence by interested third parties, but here they can claim only the general right to noninterference that any unharmful activity enjoys, not some special right to academic freedom or "freedom of research."

A third possibility, intermediate between academic institutions and private sponsorship, is public support of particular research projects addressed to questions of theoretical or purely practical concern. This case in large part resembles that of private sponsorship in that as sponsor the public (collectively, through its political institutions) is free to support whatever research it chooses, to refuse any, and to cut off funds when research seems fruitless or its results displeasing. But for reasons already mentioned direct political control of particular research decisions is not a very effective means to the common end of increasing knowledge. It opens the door to partisan influence when research touches controversial questions, and it places decisions in the hands of nonspecialists who may not be equipped to assess the merits of different lines of research. So again it makes sense to separate decisions about the support of particular projects from the general political process through which the overall goals of sponsored research are set.

This separation can be achieved by creating semiautonomous public bodies such as the National Science Foundation (NSF), the National Institute of Health (NIH), and the National Endowment for the Humanities (NEH) to dispense research funds in pursuit of specified purposes. Once the goals of such an agency are set—usually some mixture of theoretical and practical concerns—an idea akin to academic freedom naturally applies to it. The public has a common interest in seeing to it that the agency's decisions are made on grounds rationally related to its assigned goals. They therefore have reason to be on guard against the possibility that administrators will disfavor politically unpopular lines of research or favor projects to which they have an institutional or personal commitment. Similarly, the public has reason to protect the agency against outside pressures of these kinds. These notions of institutional neutrality and independence, and the institution of peer review are like academic freedom in that they represent safeguards that are necessary if institutions are to serve their intended purposes. Moreover, the interests at stake are of the same kind—the interests of members of the public as consumers of research—and the threats are similar. The notions differ, however, insofar as the goals of these agencies differ from those of academic institutions: they are more specific, more dependent on immediate practical concerns, and hence more open to year-by-year political redefinition.

Some of the controversies we have been concerned with can be seen as examples of this political process. In the case of the UCLA Violence Center, for example, the question was whether public funds should be used to establish a research institution devoted to a particular set of (largely practical) aims. It seems clear that this question is an entirely proper subject for the normal range of legitimate political activity—publicizing, lobbying, and debate. Academic freedom is not threatened by making this decision political, nor is doing so contrary to any of the analogous notions applicable to institutions for specialized research. For these notions are all relative to some prior determination of the goals of the institution in question, and in the present case it was just the definition of those goals that was in question.

Academic freedom may seem to be an issue in a case like this one if it seems that those who oppose the research do so because they wish to prevent certain things from becoming known. This aim seems to threaten, if not academic freedom strictly speaking, then at least the interest that academic freedom is supposed to protect, namely, the public's interest in keeping its sources of information free from partisan control. This concern, I think, is what made defenders of the Boston XYY study feel that their opponents represented a threat to academic freedom.[3] But it is not clear that their opponents had this threatening aim. They were, it is true, concerned about the political significance of research on violence at that particular time (I will return to this problem later on), but their primary reason for trying to halt the Boston study was the protection of the research subjects and their families.[4] Similarly, the focus of opponents of the UCLA Violence Center was the protection of experimental subjects and others who they feared might be subjected to psychosurgery as part of the clinical programs of the center.[5] In both cases opponents saw themselves as preventing the direct infliction of harm. But in general, going beyond the bounds of this particular case, there are many ways in which research may lead to harmful consequences, and it is not always easy to separate the aim of preventing these harms from that of stopping the spread of information that others may desire to have. The following sections will be concerned with the problems of drawing this distinction.

DIRECT HARMS

In this section I will be concerned with harms that are direct consequences of the process of research itself, as opposed to those that result from the dissemination of its findings. I have in mind such things as physical injury or psy-

---

[3]See Dr. Stanley Walzer's remarks in "The XYY Controversy: Researching Violence and Genetics," Special Supplement, *The Hastings Center Report* 10 (August 1980): 8.

[4]On the priority of this aim over the concern with political consequences, see Jonathan Beckwith's remarks on p. 24 of "The XYY Controversy," and also those of Jonathan King on p. 18.

[5]See "Researching Violence," p. 9 (statements by Fred Hiestand and by Isidore Ziferstein).

chological harm to research participants, and harms to bystanders caused by side effects of the research process (e.g., radiation leakage, or, perhaps, the justified fear that such leakage will occur). Among the psychological harms to participants or bystanders I include what was referred to in the discussion of the Boston XYY study as "stigmatization." In that case this term meant the unpleasant consequences of being associated with the popular stereotype of the XYY male. I take it, however, that harms of this general type—harms to reputation or to one's self-conception—can occur as consequences of many kinds of research in history or social science, though in most cases the effects are less severe.

I take it to be clear that an ethical researcher should take direct harms of all these kinds into account in deciding what research to perform. But the matter cannot be left to the researcher's conscience alone. Where serious harms are in question some independent constraints are needed. Institutions that support or sponsor research must have reliable procedures for ensuring that this research is within moral bounds, and the law also sets standards for research institutions and sets limits to the harms that can be imposed.

These wider forms of regulation seem more reliable because they are not administered solely by researchers themselves. But, as was clear in our sessions, researchers are reluctant to see laymen given the power to veto research on the ground that it is too harmful or not worth the risks involved. This power is not formally incompatible with academic freedom or its analogs since as "sponsor" the public is quite free to decide that some ways of acquiring knowledge are not worth their costs, and free to express this judgment in legal or institutional regulation. The problems that researchers see here are more indirect. First there is the fear that the power to veto research on the ground of its immediate harmful effects will be used to stop research that is disapproved on purely partisan grounds. A second worry, voiced more often in our sessions, is what can broadly be called the fear of overregulation. This fear took two more specific forms. The first was doubt about the layman's competence to judge the merits of particular research projects. The second was the fear that when laymen balance the benefits of particular projects against the risks involved they will tend to undervalue research. For whereas the possible harms are concrete and identifiable, the most important benefits of research are cumulative and generally cannot be predicted as the result of particular projects or experiments considered in isolation.

The seriousness of these worries depends to a great extent on the form of regulation that is at issue. One way they can arise is as concerns about the authority of citizen representatives on institutional review boards. Here the dangers of partisan misuse and of overregulation seem greatest if it is assumed that what citizen representatives are supposed to do is to estimate the benefits of each research proposal and to weigh these against the costs or risks involved. The estimation of benefits is an uncertain matter at best, and requires real knowledge of the subject at hand. In addition, a process of wholesale balancing on a case-by-case basis, to the degree that it is bounded by no clear guidelines, gives great scope for bias against unpopular or controversial projects.

It is the responsibility of institutional review boards to determine whether human subjects of research will be "placed at risk" and, if so, to ascertain whether (a) the benefits of the research to its subjects or others outweigh these risks, (b) "the rights and welfare of any such subjects will be adequately protected," and (c) their legally informed consent will be obtained.[6]

To begin with the first of these questions, which benefits are they that are to be weighed against the possible harms resulting from a piece of research? It would seem that these are not, in general, the estimated benefits of the particular piece of research in question since these benefits are, as has been said, often impossible to predict with any clarity. I suggest

[6]Code of Federal Regulations 45 CFR 46, revised as of January 11, 1978, §46.102(b).

that the value in question is instead the value attached to the general objective of increasing knowledge of the area under study. Given an idea of what this value is we can arrive at an upper limit to the risks and harms that must be borne in order to allow significant research in this area to proceed. The breadth of the relevant "area" will of course vary. In some cases, where the research simply consists in the collection of data needed to answer one specific question that is of interest for its own sake and not because of some wider theoretical significance, the "area" will be defined simply by this question itself. But more often the significance of research lies in its contribution to some larger theoretical or practical objective. In this case it is the importance of these larger objectives that is taken into account in balancing. The question that is to be asked about a particular experiment or a subsidiary investigation is whether it is in fact well conceived and worth doing as a part of this larger program.

This approach suggests a division of the work of institutional review boards into two stages. The first stage is the process of defining the ethical limits to permissible research. To carry out their legal mandate under §46.102, they need to answer such questions as these: What "rights" of subjects are at stake in research of this kind and how is their "welfare" affected? What are the benefits at which such research aims, and what risks are "warranted" by these benefits? This process of defining the limits of permissible research in a given area will involve the weighing and comparing of different interests, but it need not involve evaluating the scientific merits of particular experiments. The question addressed in this stage is a hypothetical one: Assuming that a given experiment is a sound proposal for research in this area, and that informed consent is obtained, what are the limits to the risks it may involve? The second stage of the institutional review board's task is the application of these guidelines to particular pieces of research. This stage involves ascertaining that the proposal is scientifically sound, that the requirement of informed consent is satisfied, and that the risks are within the limits previously arrived at. These determinations will not be a matter of balancing interests.

It would of course be unrealistic to think that these two stages could in practice be kept entirely separate. The application of guidelines to particular cases will always involve an element of judgment and of weighing conflicting considerations. Nonetheless the distinction between the two stages is a useful analytic device, helpful as a way of making clear the function and authority of lay participants on institutional review boards.[7] In what I have called the first stage of the review process the interests being balanced are the public's interests in the acquisition of various kinds of knowledge and its interests in avoiding risk and harm. The point of having lay participants in this process is to represent the public as sponsors and beneficiaries of research by arriving at judgments about the relative weight of the public's various interests. Here the expertise of researchers themselves gives them no special authority. Since, like others, they benefit from research, their interests are included among the public's interests, but whatever special interests they may have, as researchers, in having research go forward are more likely to count as a form of bias.

In the second stage of the review process expert judgment is called for to determine whether particular pieces of research are worth performing as contributions to larger programs of research. Here, at the level of application of guidelines to particular cases, the function of lay participants is not to serve as spokesmen for certain interests but rather to ensure that the guidelines are evenly and conscientiously applied.

Let me turn now to the requirement of informed consent. Why should this requirement apply only to those who are the subjects of experiment? What about those who may be af-

---

[7]Helpful, in particular, in making clear the function they can reasonably have even though they may lack specialized scientific training. The need for clarification on this point was stressed by Robert Michels in "Researching Violence" (p. 18) and was also mentioned by Robin Williams (p. 16).

fected in equally serious ways by research even though they are not themselves subjects of study? What is special about those who are subjects of experiments is not the severity of the effects that research has on them but rather the fact that it involves them in ways that normally require consent: their active cooperation is required, for example, or their bodies are manipulated, or their immediate environment is altered in significant ways. Given this initial need for consent, if there are further effects or risks not immediately apparent to the subject it would be deceptive not to reveal them. That is, the consent must be informed, even where the further effects that are revealed are no more severe than effects that may legitimately be imposed on nonparticipants whose consent is in no way required. What makes informed consent necessary is not the particular severity of the possible harms that are revealed but the fact that failure to disclose them to the subject who is in any case asked to give consent would be deceptive. In cases of medical research where the experimental subject is also a patient of the experimenter there is also a further reason. Even if there are no significant risks, the requirement of written informed consent is justified by the need to inform the patient—whose initial consent is to *treatment*—that treatment is not the doctor's only concern.

Informed consent strikes one intuitively as a natural requirement: something to which the subject is entitled and that is, at worst, a mild inconvenience to the researcher. This perception is based on several reasons. First, it is assumed that, since the experimenter deals directly with his subjects, it is easy to ask for consent. Second, it is assumed that being informed of the nature and possible effects of the research is not itself a significant burden for the subject. Third, it does not seem likely that subjects will use the power to withhold consent as a way of stifling research with which they are in partisan disagreement.

But all three of these conditions can fail in easily conceivable circumstances. The second failed to hold in the Bostom XYY study, since it is by no means costless to be told that one's child is to be included in a study with that purpose. In this case the costliness of obtaining properly informed consent led to the conclusion that the study should not be carried out. The first and third conditions fail in the case of much social science research, for example, demographic studies or studies of the behavior of politicians. In most of these cases, however, the impracticality of obtaining informed consent is no bar to the research since there is no reason why consent need be required in the first place. Although the subjects of such research may be affected by its results (or even by the general knowledge that it is being carried out), the research does not involve acting on them or intervening in their lives in ways that normally require consent.[8] That is a fortunate thing; if consent were required, say in studies of political behavior, the manifest failure of the third condition would present us with an acute conflict between this requirement and our interest in the unfettered flow of information about our political institutions.

There are cases, however, in which this conflict occurs. Consider, for example, research that requires access to records or papers held privately by the families of deceased politicians or other powerful figures. Here there is a basis for an initial requirement of consent to see the papers, analogous to the requirement of consent to touch the bodies of experimental subjects. Does this initial need for consent give rise to the further requirement that the consent be fully informed, that is, that the researchers disclose their objectives, intents, and methods? This requirement would certainly open the door to partisan use of the power to withhold consent. My inclination is to draw the opposite conclusion: where the materials have

[8]Specific consent is not required because the aspects of their lives that are observed are taken to be already "in public," or because the observation is not observation "of them" in the relevant sense because information is collected anonymously and cannot be traced back to them. Intuitions such as these seem to underly HEW's proposed categories of research exempted from the requirement of informed consent. See *IRB: A Review of Human Subjects Research*, October 1979, p. 9.

bearing on important public issues the right of the family to control access is highly qualified. Since the right to withhold consent is closely circumscribed so also is the information that may be demanded of the researcher.

FURTHER EFFECTS

I turn now to the more difficult problem of the harmful effects that research can have through the dissemination of the knowledge it yields. The most obvious harms of this kind result from the applications of this knowledge—for example, to the production of weapons. When researchers are criticized for doing research that may have harmful applications it is often urged in reply that a given piece of research can always be applied in many ways and, whatever its most obvious applications may be, it is impossible to predict whether its applications as a whole will turn out on balance to have been for good or for ill. But this uncertainty is not enough to absolve the researcher from all responsibility. We often know what at least some of the applications of a piece of research will be. Moreover, when we know who controls the resources necessary for the application of research we often have a good ground for predicting which of its possible applications will be exploited and for what ends. Knowledge of this kind sometimes requires ethical researchers (and ethical sponsors) to suspend research even though, for all they know, the research might turn out later to have beneficial consequences. Here the operative ethical notion is the wrongfulness of knowingly aiding another's immoral course of action.

The judgment that research should be suspended is easiest to make when the results of research would be used by malevolent agents to inflict harm. But suppose it would be used by well-intentioned people to inflict harm on themselves or on each other by, for example, building faster and more dangerous automobiles. In such cases, which are probably more common, research can lead to harm without any malevolent intervening agent. Cases of this kind are more difficult than cases of aiding immoral action because they involve a clash between "our" desire to be informed by research and the value of avoiding harmful outcomes. If the value of research is its value to *us*, the public, should not we be the ones to decide how to apply its results (as long as we do not use them to pursue clearly immoral courses of action, e.g., to injure or subjugate others)? Should we as "sponsors" delegate to researchers the right to decide which applications are worth making?

Here the idea of "collective sponsorship" is misleading. In most cases we have no mechanism for reaching a "collective judgment" about the applications of research. Such decisions are largely dependent on the choices of intervening individual agents (e.g., manufacturers) who act for their own reasons, with no special authority to decide "for all of us" which applications are worth their risks. Second, researchers are under no obligation to us as "sponsors" to make their research decisions and report their findings without regard for the consequences of "our" application of their results. The idea that there is such an obligation, or that it is always objectionably "paternalistic" for researchers to refuse to pursue certain lines of research because of what they foresee as the likely consequences of their application seems to me mistaken—an inviting way of denying responsibility.[9]

Bad consequences of this kind are sometimes a sufficient reason for a researcher or a funding agency to avoid a certain line of research. They are, however, only one consideration among many, and one that has less force than the requirement not to aid immoral courses of action. It might be quite right to pursue a theoretically promising line of inquiry despite the great likelihood of foolish and harmful, though innocent misapplication. There would be more reason to think that the

[9]I have argued for this claim in "Individual Responsibility and Political Obligation," *Proceedings of the Working Group on Philosophy, Science and Technology* (Cambridge, Mass.: The Hunsaker Endowment, MIT, 1971).

same research should be suspended if the harm flowed from the use of the results by an evil dictator. Perhaps part of the difference here lies in the greater certainty of harm in the latter case. In addition to this consideration, however, I think that there is a more important difference in the force of the underlying moral requirements. It is worse knowingly to aid an immoral course of action than to have contributed to a mistaken, though harmful policy.

I turn now from harmful applications of research to what might be called its persuasive effects. Research could aid an evil dictator not only by increasing his capacity to inflict harm, but also by contributing to the general belief in his legitimacy or the illegitimacy of his opponents. Doing research that one knows will have such consequences can constitute aiding an immoral course of action.

Some politically important beliefs flow from the publication of research findings. Others, however, can result simply from the general knowledge that research is being done. The fact that responsible scientists are engaged in research that could have a certain application may give many people reason to believe, correctly or not, that this application is a likely possibility in the not too distant future. This situation can give rise, for example, to fear that a new technique of control is in the offing, or support confidence that a technical solution to a pressing social problem is near at hand. Critics of the Boston XYY study were concerned, in general, about effects of this kind. In addition to their primary concern to protect research subjects, they were suspicious of any research on genetic bases of violent behavior. One reason was that they believed that research of this kind was unlikely to have a good scientific basis.[10] Beyond this reason, however, they feared that even if its results were scientifically worthless, the research would be so reported in the public press as to support a climate of opinion in which repressive measures against the

[10]See, for example, remarks by Jonathan Beckwith on p. 24 of "The XYY Controversy."

groups concerned would be politically acceptable.[11] Furthermore, they thought that research on a genetic basis of crime and violent behavior would distract attention from the social causes of these phenomena by suggesting that they were inevitable or attributable simply to individual aberrations.[12]

There are two distinguishable elements in this attack: the alleged political consequences of the research, and the likelihood of misrepresentation in the way that such consequences are thought to be produced. In the cases at hand, I find it hard to believe that the actual political consequences of the research projects would have been at all significant. But the issue of misrepresentation is more troubling. It would be generally agreed, I take it, that researchers ought not to misrepresent the results of their research. In addition to whatever bad consequences doing so may have, and to the wrongness of the misrepresentation itself, inaccurate reporting undermines the positive case for the research since at least many of its supposed beneficiaries are misled rather than informed by it. The same objection holds against doing research when one knows that its results will be effectively misrepresented by others in a way that one cannot prevent or counter.

In the cases we studied, this issue arose most clearly in the form of what I will call the problem of fair labeling. Researchers in the Boston XYY study, for example, accepted funding under programs aimed at the control of violence and juvenile delinquency despite the fact that they appear not to have believed that there was any connection between the XYY genotype and these types of violent behavior. Ironically, it is the researchers themselves who seem to have suffered most from this misrepresentation, which clearly helped make their research the subject of controversy and criticism.

I have spoken critically of the researchers here although in this case it seems that their role was in fact largely passive.[13]

[11]Ibid., pp. 22–23 (statement by Jonathan Beckwith).
[12]Ibid., p. 21 (statement by Jonathan King) and p. 22 (by Jonathan Beckwith).
[13]It is less clear that that was so in the case of the UCLA Violence Center. See "Researching Violence," pp. 7, 10, 14.

They merely accepted the description of their work applied by federal funding agencies. The administrators who made this categorization of the work took a more active role.[14] If they thought, as presumably they did, that the work was worth doing, they might have funded it under some other program in order to avoid misleading labeling. Moreover, since their function is more clearly that of serving as "our" agents, they have an even clearer responsibility than individual researchers for seeing to it that research is reported in a way that guards against public misunderstanding of its significance, or at least not in a way that panders to popular misconceptions.

Whatever undesirable political effects the Boston XYY study may be thought to have had could have been largely avoided by proper description of the research (though that would not have alleviated other problems concerning the design of the study and its effect on its subjects). A more difficult choice is presented when undesirable political consequences are not easily avoidable and are likely to result even without any misrepresentation on the part of researchers or funding agencies. Such an example is provided by a case described by Robin Williams. Suppose that in the late 1950s social scientists proposed to study the psychological effects of desegregation on the first black children introduced into white schools in the South. Would it have been permissible for federal research agencies to refuse to support such research on the ground that if, as seems likely, the effects were in many cases traumatic, publication of these findings would have a disruptive effect on an already explosive political situation? My judgment is that this decision would certainly be permissible and probably the right one to make; but I admit that there is something troubling about it.

What is troubling, I suggest, is the idea of a government agency having the power to decide that certain things are better not known. Now certain things are in fact better not

[14]See "The XYY Controversy," p. 15.

known; as I remarked earlier, a sponsor of private research might be quite rational in declining to acquire new information that would be disturbing to him yet be of no value since it was not relevant to any question he wanted to answer or any decision he needed to make. My tendency to support the decision not to fund in the case just mentioned rests on the belief that it fits just this pattern. The knowledge in question might produce great unease, but it has no theoretical importance and it is not relevant to the important question of policy that it might affect: the correctness of desegregation is not affected by the distress it may cause for the first few children to whom it applies. But the NSF is not a sponsor of private research. Its relation to us is more like that of an investigator to a sponsor. When it decides that certain things are better not known it is deciding not that *it* would rather not know them but that *we* would be better off not knowing them. This decision is one we are reluctant to have someone else make for us, particularly an arm of the government.

The risks of granting such authority are well illustrated by another example, of a kind suggested to me by Robert A. Burt. Suppose that HEW has committed itself to a particular policy regarding the treatment of mental patients and that federal research agencies thereafter refuse to support research by outsiders that would determine the effects of this form of treatment and form the basis for evaluation of the policy. This kind of institutional self-protection is clearly something to be guarded against, but it does not seem advisable to do so by requiring that funding agencies pay no attention at all to the relevance that research may have to political issues.

It is a special feature of both of these examples as I have described them that the research in question has no real theoretical motivation but is of interest purely because of its relation to a particular question of policy. The desegregation example would be a more difficult one if we supposed that the research in question had clear theoretical importance and the question was whether it should be funded despite its likely political consequences. One might deny that studies aimed at specific practical questions and lacking any more general theoretical motivation constituted "research" of the kind that agencies such as the NSF and the NIH are supposed to support. But unless practical objectives are excluded altogether from the aims of such agencies (which would be a very significant change from present policy as I understand it), it will sometimes happen that in order to assess the relative merits of proposals with theoretical merit an agency will need to take account as well of the relevance that these inquiries have to important questions of policy on which decisions need to be made. And the most obvious difference between the two cases I described appears to be of this kind: the information at stake in the mental health example is clearly relevant to the policy in question, whereas in the desegregation example that is not the case and, consequently, if the proposed study lacks theoretical merit it lacks merit altogether. Undoubtedly, if government agencies have the authority to make such judgments of relevance they will sometimes, through partiality or for other reasons, make them wrongly. But this possibility does not seem to justify denying them that authority altogether. The question "knowledge for what?" cannot be set aside even though there is no mechanism to ensure that it will always be answered correctly.

Index

Violence and the politics of
research